NO BETTER
PLACE TO DIE

THE BATTLE OF STONES RIVER

NO BETTER
PLACE TO DIE

Peter Cozzens

UNIVERSITY OF ILLINOIS PRESS
Urbana and Chicago

For
Dee Ann

© 1990 by the Board of Trustees of the University of Illinois
Manufactured in the United States of America

This book is printed on acid-free paper.

Library of Congress Cataloging-in-Publication Data

Cozzens, Peter, 1957–
    No better place to die : the Battle of Stones River / Peter
Cozzens.
        p.   cm.
    Bibliography: p.
    Includes index.
    ISBN 0-252-01652-1 (alk. paper)
    1. Murfreesboro, Battle of, 1862–1863.   I. Title.
E474.77.C69   1990
973.7'33—dc19   89-30577
                                                          CIP

CONTENTS

MAPS

PREFACE

HISTORIANS have devoted more attention to the Civil War than to any other struggle in our nation's history. Gettysburg alone has been the subject of hundreds of books and articles; scores have been devoted to such lesser battles as Shiloh and Chancellorsville. By contrast, Stones River has been the subject of only three book-length studies, two of which were written by Northern eyewitnesses so decidedly partisan as to make their works of little value.

No account has fully told the story of this important campaign. From a tactical perspective, none has traced troop movements below the division and occasionally brigade level. The five-day Federal advance from Nashville and Bragg's response to it similarly have been neglected. And such critical moments of the battle itself as Phil Sheridan's defense of the Wilkinson Pike line, judged by many to be among the most determined stands against overwhelming numbers of the war, or Breckinridge's attack on the Federal left, a doomed assault with the poignancy of Pickett's charge, have remained shrouded in uncertainty.

I wrote *No Better Place to Die* to fill this gap in our understanding of the war. I have traced the campaign in its entirety, from its beginnings in Bragg's disastrous invasion of Kentucky to the dissension that rent the Army of Tennessee in the months following Stones River. The movement and combat of individual regiments, the character and generalship of commanders, the choices and constraints confronting leaders as the battle developed, and the larger impact of Stones River on the outcome of the war—I have tried to address each of these elements of the campaign in detail.

In general, I have treated the campaign chronologically. Although not formally divided into parts, this book may be considered segmentally. Chapters 1 through 4 provide background: they describe the state of both armies following the battle of Perryville, introduce the primary actors, and explain the planning and preparation that preceded the campaign. In chapters 5 and 6, the campaign unfolds as the Army of the Cumberland advances on Murfreesboro. Chapters 7 through 15 are devoted to the battle itself. The final chapter presents an evaluation of the impact of Stones River and its effects on the contending armies. An appendix following the main text lists the opposing forces in the Stones River campaign.

Although Stones River was a tactical draw, it had far-reaching consequences. The impact of Stones River on the Confederacy was decidedly negative. Not only were some ten thousand irreplaceable veterans killed, wounded, or captured, but Tennessee was effectively lost and the high command of the South's principal Western army hopelessly divided.

For the Union the results were felt less on the battlefield, where over thirteen thousand were lost, or in the army high command than on the home front and abroad. Bragg's retreat after the battle gave the North a victory at a time when defeat would have made the Emancipation Proclamation look like the last gasp of a dying war effort and perhaps brought England and France into the war on the side of the Confederacy.

Stones River is worthy of study on another, more personal level as well. In few other battles were the characters of the commanding generals so completely eccentric. And in fewer still did the level of support offered each commander differ so greatly. Although a scarcity of resources plagued Southern field commanders throughout the war, during Stones River this normal state of want was heightened by the policies of an administration that acted as though Tennessee were a strategic backwater, rather than the key to the Confederate heartland. As Thomas Connelly ably demonstrated in his seminal study of the Army of Tennessee, *Autumn of Glory*, Richmond routinely accorded the army "second-class treatment" and acted without a sound appreciation of Western problems. Compounding Bragg's difficulties was an administrative system that divided the West into highly legalistic departments that the Army of Tennessee was expected to defend but from which it could draw neither food, nor recruits, nor equipment. Even within his own geographical department, Bragg faced competition for resources. While he was driving north through Kentucky in the fall of 1862, Confederate Commissary General Lucius Northrop's agents were combing Middle Tennessee for corn, wheat, cattle, and hogs. Able to offer more than Bragg's agents, they diverted much of the region's foodstuffs to the commissary depot in Atlanta for use by Lee's army.

If those in Richmond were indifferent to the fate of Bragg and his army, a majority of the senior officers of the Army of Tennessee behaved in a manner openly destructive of both it and the authority of the commanding general. In the weeks following Perryville, Bragg faced a cabal that grew increasingly militant. Led by Leonidas Polk, the group worked through informal channels and a myriad of subgroupings to engineer Bragg's removal. Polk maintained a regular correspondence with sympathizers in Richmond, while Tennessean Ben Cheatham, Kentuckian John C. Breckinridge, and others appealed to the support they enjoyed at home and from home-state regiments that constituted personal armies within the army.

Bragg, then, faced both dissension from inside the army and the cavalier support of an often indifferent administration in Richmond. Rosecrans, on the other hand, labored under no such handicaps. Although some—most notably Grant—doubted his fitness for high command, most were willing to give him a chance to prove himself. From the day he assumed command of the Army of the Cumberland, Rosecrans never wanted for the essential material of war. Washington filled his interminable requests—for pontoon bridges, repeating rifles, more pontoons, more rifles—as rapidly as the War Department was able, asking only that he use the equipment in battle. And although Rosecrans had his share of incompetent subordinates, of whom Thomas Crittenden and Alexander McCook as wing commanders were shining examples, he did not have to worry that personal enmity or the ambitions of factious lieutenants would stand in the way of the rapid execution of his orders.

As you follow the two armies to the banks of Stones River, bear in mind these considerations. Perhaps then you will agree with me that it is not surprising that Rosecrans won or that Bragg lost, but that Rosecrans came so close to defeat, and Bragg so near victory.

ACKNOWLEDGMENTS

THE staffs of a number of institutions have been most helpful in the conduct of my research for this book. I especially wish to thank Bonnie Demick and Rose Hane of the Seymour Library, Knox College, for their assistance during my numerous visits to the Ray D. Smith Civil War Collection, held by the college. I would also like to thank the staff of the U.S. Military History Institute at Carlisle Barracks, Pennsylvania, not only for manuscript materials cited in the bibliography, but also for generously providing photocopies of passages from regimental histories and personal narratives not otherwise available. Similarly, I am grateful to the staff of the War Library and Museum of the Military Order of the Loyal Legion of the United States, Philadelphia, for copies of articles carried in MOLLUS publications. I also wish to thank Mrs. T. D. Winstead of the Hardin County Historical Society, Elizabethtown, Kentucky, for making available materials pertaining to the Orphan Brigade's participation in the battle. I also wish to thank Mike Mullins for his many thoughtful suggestions as he read the manuscript.

Finally, I wish to express my deepest gratitude to Dan Weinberg, proprietor of the Abraham Lincoln Book Shop in Chicago, for his interest and assistance in seeing this manuscript brought to publication.

CHAPTER ONE

SUMMER OF HOPE,
AUTUMN OF DESPAIR

GENERAL Braxton Bragg needed a scapegoat. Defeat in Kentucky had cast a pall over his army and the nation; retreat into Tennessee transformed the loss into a clamor for the general's dismissal. For much of this, Bragg had only himself to blame. His buoyant predictions of victory and subsequent rapid advance into Kentucky had excited the imagination and hopes of the Confederate people who, reading the exuberant dispatches emanating from the Army of the Mississippi as it pushed northward, came to expect nothing less than the total restoration of Confederate authority over the border region. The sudden collapse of the autumn campaign, coming in the wake of Lee's withdrawal from Maryland, left them profoundly shaken, and their shattered expectations erupted into a wave of censure that none were more anxious to ride than Bragg's own most-senior lieutenants. As the army filed through the Cumberland Gap and out of Kentucky, lieutenant generals William J. Hardee and Leonidas Polk urged President Davis to recognize that only a change of commanders could save the army and salvage Confederate fortunes in the West. Their allegations echoed throughout the South. In Richmond, "earnest and angry" debate shook the floor of the Confederate Congress as members endorsed a resolution reflecting the demands of Hardee and Polk. The Southern press, never known for its self-restraint, quickly added its voice to the clamor.

As much as he might wish to protect his longtime friend, Davis could not ignore the demands of the general's defamers, who were legion and powerful. On the other hand, the president had no intention of relieving Bragg without a hearing, and so he summoned the general to Richmond to present his version of the campaign. Bragg lost no time. Perhaps sensing an opportunity to shift blame for the Kentucky debacle to his subordinates, he boarded an eastbound train out of Knoxville the morning after Davis's message was delivered to him.[1]

Although many were only too anxious to heap responsibility for the sorry state of affairs in the West on the North Carolinian's shoulders, his abandonment of Kentucky was merely the culmination of a chain of events predating Bragg that had left the Confederate heartland vulnerable, its people fearful and discouraged. In fact, many thoughtful Southerners believed that the nadir actually had been reached four months earlier, in June 1862, when Pierre G. T. Beauregard's Army of the Mississippi, principal defender of the heartland, relinquished Corinth to three converging Union armies without firing a shot, thereby conceding the northern tip of Mississippi, and with it the vital Memphis and Charleston Railroad. Not only did Beauregard's withdrawal result in the cutting of a rail artery that had pumped supplies critical to the survival of the Confederacy eastward to the Atlantic, but it opened the way to a Federal advance on Chattanooga, gateway to the Deep South.

It was at this moment, under the shadow of impending doom, that Braxton Bragg replaced Beauregard as commander of the Army of the Mississippi, then lying idle at Tupelo. Several weeks later, he was elevated to command of all Confederate forces between Mississippi and Virginia.

Bragg faced three immediate challenges: he must protect Chattanooga, reopen the Memphis and Charleston Railroad, and recover at least a portion of Tennessee.

As the defense of Chattanooga was most urgent, Bragg rushed the division of Major General John P. McCown to the threatened city. After several weeks of correspondence with the commander of the Department of East Tennessee, Major General Edmund Kirby Smith, Bragg elected to transfer his entire army to Chattanooga. In doing so, he countered an advance against the city by Major General Don Carlos Buell's Army of the Ohio, which, despite a head start of over a month, had moved at a snail's pace.

With Chattanooga secure, Bragg met Kirby Smith on 31 July, ostensibly to discuss future operations. But if Kirby Smith had expected to have a voice in what was about to transpire, he was disappointed—the North Carolinian had already decided on his next move. Since assuming command of the Army of the Mississippi, Bragg had entertained a number of Kentucky's leading citizens, all of whom offered assurance of their state's fidelity and of the willingness of her men to join the Confederate service, should Bragg's army but appear on bluegrass soil. Bragg was convinced. A successful thrust into the state, he believed, not only would relieve pressure on the Deep South, but would return much of Tennessee to the Confederacy. And, if his Kentucky guests were correct, his army would be augmented by thousands of desperately needed volunteers. For the moment Bragg's enthusiasm was contagious, and Kirby Smith returned to his Knoxville headquarters committed to a joint advance. Before leaving, he told Bragg: "I will not only cooperate with you, but will cheerfully place my command under you subject to your orders."[2]

Despite the apparent agreement between Bragg and Kirby Smith, their subordinates doubted the prospects of a campaign in which neither general commanded the other, and in which neither was willing to relinquish his autonomy, Kirby Smith's pledge to the contrary notwithstanding. As Bragg's chief of cavalry, Brigadier General Joseph Wheeler, later wrote, mere agreement as to intent was a poor substitute for unified command, particularly in an operation calling for the synchronized movement of two armies.[3]

But could Bragg have exercised such authority effectively had it been his? Contemporaries were skeptical. The dyspeptic martinet was having trouble enough with his own subordinates. Witness the experience of Major General Richard Taylor, son of former president Zachary Taylor and a shrewd observer, who visited army headquarters in Chattanooga just prior to the invasion of Kentucky. At dinner one evening, Taylor inquired casually about a widely esteemed division commander. In the presence of his staff, Bragg retorted that the officer in question was "an old woman, utterly worthless." Taylor was shocked. "Such a declaration privately made would have been serious," he noted, "but publicly, and certain to be repeated, it was astonishing." Retiring with Bragg to a private room, Taylor asked with whom he intended to replace the general. With no one, Bragg answered. "I have but one or two fitted for high command, and have in vain asked the War Department for capable people." From that moment Taylor doubted that the Kentucky campaign would succeed.[4]

Taylor's encounter was painfully typical of dealings people had with the commanding general. Bragg seemed to repel men with disarming ease. To the visiting Englishman Arthur Freemantle, he was "the least prepossessing of the Confederate generals." Photographs of Bragg confirm this. Bushy black eyebrows and a stubby, iron-grey beard were the only distinguishing features of an otherwise plain, almost cadaverous countenance, the work of years of dyspepsia, dysentery, and chronic headaches, afflictions that also conspired to sour his temper and enfeeble him, so much so, according to an intimate, that he was unable to endure long periods of stress or responsibility. Richard Taylor agreed. He suggested simply that Bragg "furnished a striking illustration of the necessity of a healthy body for a sound intellect." Even Bragg's staunchest supporters admonished him for his quick temper, general irritability, and tendency to wound innocent men with barbs thrown during his frequent fits of anger. His reluctance to praise or flatter was exceeded, we are told, only by the tenacity with which, once formed, he clung to an adverse impression of a subordinate. For such officers—and they were many in the Army of the Mississippi—Bragg's removal or their transfer were the only alternatives to an unbearable existence.

As their leaders endured Bragg's indignities, so the men in ranks suffered the more palpable sting of the general's rigid and unyielding brand of discipline. The "martinet of the old army" had a reputation, not entirely gratuitous, for shooting liberally for insubordination, as the following story, then circulating throughout the army and the country, demonstrates. During the retreat from Shiloh, when absolute stealth was imperative, Bragg directed that no gun be discharged, death being the penalty for disobedience. A drunk young Rebel chose to flout the order with a few random shots at a chicken along the roadside. The chicken escaped unscathed, but not so the soldier, who was summarily shot for having betrayed the route of march. Not surprisingly, given the army's antipathy to Bragg, the incident became exaggerated in the telling. The unlucky soldier was said to have been condemned by Bragg for having killed a chicken. Similar tales followed. Some whispered that the commanding general had had a man shot for stealing apples, others insisted that he had hanged sixteen more from a single tree for an unspecified offense. It is pointless to demonstrate the absurdity of these accusations. What is significant is that many men within the Army of the Mississippi believed them, and that is more damning to Bragg's reputation than a score of battlefield reverses.[5]

Such was the state of the army as it marched out of Chattanooga on 28 August, crossing the Tennessee River the same day. Two weeks earlier, Kirby Smith had struck out for Lexington, Kentucky, and, after skirting around the Federal garrison at Cumberland Gap, soundly defeated a Union column at Richmond that had been dispatched to oppose him. Kirby Smith's Army of Kentucky entered Lexington without further incident, where it remained until October.

Bragg also was doing well. He had driven as far north as Carthage, Tennessee, just below the Cumberland River, before Buell decided that the Confederates did not have designs against Nashville. Moving out of that city on 12 September, he engaged Bragg in a race for the real Confederate objective: Louisville, Kentucky.

It was a fair contest. Although Bragg was twenty-five miles nearer the river city, Buell had at his disposal the Louisville and Nashville Railroad, which Bragg moved at once to eliminate as a factor in the campaign. While Joe Wheeler and his troopers tore up the line at selected points above Nashville, Bragg pushed his infantry on to Bowling Green, reaching the southern Kentucky town ahead of Buell on 14 September. He then turned his column toward the Federal fort at Munfordville, where the railroad crossed the Green River. Earlier that day, Brigadier General James Chalmers had attacked the garrison with the Rebel vanguard, only to meet with a sharp repulse. Learning of his subordinate's check, Bragg ordered the remainder of the army to Munfordville on 15 September. Buell followed, but he was too late. Bragg reached Munfordville first and, after "boldly displaying" his army, accepted the surrender of the garrison.

A new spirit of elation infused the Army of the Mississippi as many believed the campaign to be all but won. And well they could. With his infantry entrenched on commanding ground south of the Green River, squarely across the path of the advancing Federals, Bragg held the key to Louisville. And with the fort at Munfordville incorporated into their defenses, the Confederates occupied a position of "great natural strength" that Buell could not circumvent. Accordingly, he prepared to attack.[6]

But the battle everyone expected never came. For reasons that remain unclear, Bragg chose not to fight. His generals were baffled. Visiting headquarters on the morning of 18 September, Joe Wheeler had found Bragg determined to do battle and confident of success. The entire army was in high spirits. Even the aporetic Polk expected victory. But just two days later, Bragg ordered a withdrawal to Bardstown, muttering that the campaign must be won by marching, not fighting. In stepping aside, he opened the road to Louisville. Buell was surprised, Kirby Smith "astonished and disappointed." Bragg's generals deplored the movement.[7]

To a handful of trusted subordinates, Bragg explained the reasons for his action. His staff, it seems, had received information that Buell was being reinforced heavily. In reality, only George Thomas's lone division had joined the Federal army below Munfordville; nevertheless, Bragg was determined not to "expose his army to disaster, nor take any chances."

While Federal prospects brightened, thanks largely to Confederate vacillating, Bragg grew morose. Self-doubt and exasperation plagued him as he began to question the wisdom of the entire operation. Kentuckians were not flocking to the Stars and Bars as promised; instead, they turned a contemptuous cold shoulder to the tattered infantry as it passed. "The people here have too many fat cattle and are too well off to fight," Bragg complained to Colonel David Urquhart, a trusted member of his staff. On 25 September, as the Army of the Ohio marched unmolested into Louisville, Bragg echoed the same feeling in a note to President Davis: "I regret to say that we are sadly disappointed in the want of action by our friends in Kentucky. We have so far received no accession to this army. General Smith has secured about a brigade—not half our losses by casualties of different kinds. Unless a change occurs soon we must abandon the garden spot of Kentucky."[8]

Bragg did not abandon Kentucky, but he might as well have. In abandoning Munfordville, he had relinquished the initiative to the Federals. As the Army of the Mississippi fell back on Bardstown to await the inevitable Union advance, the campaign lost its purpose and direction. Kirby Smith understood this and begged Bragg to turn and fight. Only a decisive victory, he argued, would draw Kentuckians to the Confederate armies. But the fight had gone out of Bragg. While Buell prepared to move on Bardstown, Bragg left his army to confer with Kirby Smith at Lexington, returning by way of Frankfort, where he attended the empty inauguration of Kentucky's provisional Confederate governor.[9]

The expected Federal advance came while Bragg was away. On 2 October, Buell marched against Bardstown over three routes, while a fourth column under Brigadier General Joshua Sill demonstrated against Kirby Smith at Frankfort. Incorrectly assuming that the main thrust was against Kirby Smith, Bragg ordered Polk to concentrate at Harrodsburg so as to be in a position to slash at Sill's flank as it passed. Hardee, meanwhile, was already being pressed by the Union center, led by Major General Charles Gilbert. Turning to fight, Hardee deployed his corps along Doctor's Creek, west of Perryville. Hardee notified Bragg that he was facing a portion of Buell's army of undetermined size, and the North Carolinian responded by ordering Polk to Perryville with one division. Momentarily energized, Bragg told Polk to "give the enemy battle immediately." His instructions reached Polk and Hardee after sundown on 7 October. Hardee, who had held his ground against a Federal push toward Doctor's Creek, was horrified. He considered it a fundamental error of tactics to give battle with only a portion of the army present, and wrote Bragg a pedantic letter admonishing the commanding general in textbook language to delay an attack until his army could be united with Kirby Smith's. Polk, who assumed command of the forces before Perryville by virtue of seniority, agreed.

Daylight of 8 October found only Gilbert's isolated corps opposite the Confederates, but Polk and Hardee, awaiting an answer to the latter's note to Bragg, did nothing. Instead, the Federals attacked. Brigadier General Philip Sheridan seized a stretch of Doctor's Creek with one brigade in the early morning twilight and, finding little opposition, brought up his remaining brigades and held. A lull followed. Morning came and went. By noon, the remainder of Buell's army was up, and the advantage shifted to the Federals. Bragg arrived two hours later. Angered that his emphatic instructions had been ignored, he directed that an attack be made immediately. Despite the presence of the entire Union army on the field, the attack went well. Major General Alexander McCook's corps was shattered, and the Confederates gained a mile of ground before darkness put an end to the bloodshed. The Army of the Ohio passed a fitful night preparing to renew the contest at dawn.

But Bragg had had enough. Unwilling to sacrifice his army in what he now believed was a bankrupt campaign, he fell back to Harrodsburg under cover of darkness to organize a retreat from Kentucky. Bragg really had been looking over his shoulder for some time. In late September he had dispatched Nathan Bedford Forrest to secure the Middle Tennessee town of Murfreesboro and the surrounding country from the depredations of Union foragers. And on 14 October, just two days after choosing to abandon Kentucky, Bragg ordered Major General John C. Breckinridge's division there as well.[10]

With these dispositions, Bragg decided to occupy Middle Tennessee. Although he never fully explained them, Bragg's reasons for choosing this course of action are apparent. As the initial objective of the Kentucky campaign was simply the restoration to the Confederacy of a portion of Tennessee, Bragg could argue that, by securing its central counties, his campaign had succeeded. As to the choice of Murfreesboro in particular, lying as it did astride the Nashville and Chattanooga Railroad, it was the key to the rich Stones River Valley and, in Bragg's mind, to the equally fertile Duck and Elk river valleys. And although the area had been heavily foraged by Buell that summer and by the Nashville garrison that fall, it nevertheless offered more to a hungry army than any other part of the state.

With the objective decided upon, the question now was whether the army could reach it. Battle losses, straggling, and desertion had devastated the Confederate infantry. It was near collapse. Food gave out, corn brought forage-wagon teamsters a dollar an ear, and driving rains slashed at the men, clad only in tattered homespun. Stony roads, swollen mountain streams, and impassable fords slowed the march to five miles a day, forcing Joe Wheeler's rearguard to fight twenty-six actions in two weeks.

But then, as McClellan's caution saved Lee after Antietam, so did Buell's unwillingness to risk another major battle save Bragg. Buell was content simply to see Bragg go. He broke off pursuit below Rock Castle, allowing his prey to descend the Cumberland Gap into East Tennessee unmolested. After a brief halt at Morristown, the Confederate army pressed on to Knoxville. There, on 31 October, Bragg boarded the Richmond train, intent on winning presidential approval for a movement into Middle Tennessee and on clearing himself of blame for the recently concluded fiasco in Kentucky.[11]

There is no record of precisely what transpired during Bragg's conversations with Davis. It is documented that he presented a written memorandum requesting permission to occupy Middle Tennessee, and that the request was approved. It also may be inferred from Bragg's unusually good spirits upon returning from the capital that Davis had approved of his conduct in Kentucky. But he was far less successful in presenting Polk as the scapegoat for the ill-fated campaign, perhaps because Polk too was a favorite of the president. Finding Bragg's testimony in this regard to be suspect, Davis called Polk to Richmond on 3 November.[12]

Davis and Polk had developed an enduring friendship while at West Point. After graduation, Davis went to serve at remote military posts in the West, while Polk resigned his commission to enter the Episcopal ministry, eventually becoming Missionary Bishop of the Southwest. Unlike the saturnine Bragg, Polk was well received by the Army of the Mississippi. His good looks and affabil-

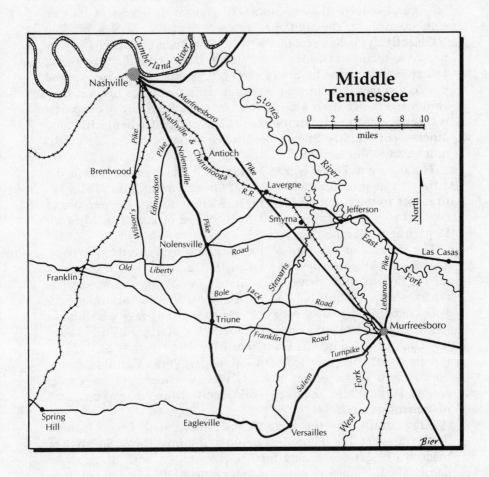

Middle
Tennessee

0 2 4 6 8 10
miles

North

Cumberland River

Stones River

Nashville

Murfreesboro Pike

Nashville & Chattanooga R.R.

Antioch

Lavergne

Edmondson Pike

Nolensville Pike

Brentwood

Wilson's Pike

Jefferson

Smyrna

East Fork

Las Casas

Nolensville

Pike

Road

Lebanon Pike

Franklin

Old

Liberty

Bole

Jack

Stewarts

Road

Murfreesboro

Triune

Franklin

Road

Turnpike

Spring
Hill

Salem

West Fork

Eagleville

Versailles

Bier

ity won over distinguished visitors like Arthur Freemantle; his courage and gentlemanly manners earned him the unwavering devotion of his troops. Private Sam Watkins of the First Tennessee, whose charming recollections are generally critical of the army high command, held the death of Polk at Pine Mountain in 1864 to be second only to that of Stonewall Jackson in terms of its dire consequences for the Southern cause.

Objectively, Polk's record was less than spectacular. His performance as a corps commander at Shiloh had been undistinguished, and at Perryville his failure to obey orders was censurable. Yet the Bishop escaped censure, once again demonstrating his uncanny ability to emerge from a disaster unscathed. Partly by his popularity, partly by the sanctimonious air he affected when criticizing others—particularly Bragg—he always managed to deflect culpability away from himself.[13]

The nature of Polk's trip to Richmond was no secret within the army. It was promulgated in Special Order Twenty-nine: Polk was to report to the Adjutant General in Richmond for "the purpose of conferring personally in regard to the state of affairs in Military Department Number Two."

The state of affairs was deplorable, Polk told Davis on arrival. The Kentucky campaign had failed; Bragg alone was responsible for the failure; and, above all, a change in command was imperative. On every count, Polk added, Hardee and Kirby Smith agreed. Polk concluded by suggesting that Davis replace Bragg with Joseph Johnston, who had commanded the Army of Northern Virginia until being wounded at Fair Oaks that May. His business in the capital finished, Polk traveled to his Raleigh, North Carolina, home on a leave of absence that probably was as welcome to Bragg as it was to Polk. While at home, Polk received his commission as a lieutenant general.

Kirby Smith was the next to visit Richmond. Davis had no doubt of what the Floridian would tell him—Kirby Smith had made his objections to any further cooperation with Bragg abundantly clear. He had rejected Bragg's request for troops to join him in a move into Middle Tennessee, refusing even to return John McCown's division, which had been temporarily assigned him during the Kentucky campaign. Kirby Smith's contempt for Bragg was complete. "You are astonished at our exodus from Kentucky no doubt," he wrote his wife. "No one could have anticipated it— Bragg's movements since taking command in Kentucky have been most singular and unfortunate."

Before coming to Richmond, Kirby Smith wrote Davis in terms equally critical of Bragg, intimating he would undertake no future operations with the North Carolinian. Davis tried to cool Kirby Smith's anger while at the same time implying that Bragg was in command to stay and that Kirby Smith had better learn to live with him. The president agreed that the Kentucky campaign had been a "bitter disappointment," but reaffirmed his confidence in Bragg. Others might "excite more enthusiasm," but given Bragg's administrative and organizational talents, they would not be "equally useful." Davis continued: "When you wrote your wounds were fresh, your lame and exhausted troops were before you, I hope time may have mollified your pain and that future operations may restore the confidence essential to cheerfulness and security in campaign."[14]

Both Davis and Kirby Smith, then, knew what to expect from one another before their Richmond meeting. When they met, Kirby Smith made one final appeal for Bragg's removal and replacement by Johnston. Davis restated his decision to retain Bragg, and Kirby Smith returned to East Tennessee. During his return trip he met Bragg on the train. "Every one prognosticated a stormy meeting—I told him what I had written to Mr. Davis but he spoke kindly to me and in the highest terms of praise and admiration of my personal character and soldierly qualities—I was astonished but believe he is honest and means well," Kirby Smith recalled to his wife. Once again, Bragg had demonstrated he could be magnanimous with factious subordinates and colleagues for the good of the service, a quality his detractors seldom acknowledge.

Meanwhile, Davis neither replaced Bragg nor transferred Polk or Kirby Smith. The army was fated to enter Middle Tennessee with a high command torn by dissension. By his inaction, Davis helped sow the seeds of defeat at Stones River.

CHAPTER TWO

THE ROSECRANS TOUCH

JUDGING by the reaction North and South, the invasion of Kentucky was a campaign without a victor. Although that state had been saved for the Union, many Northerners considered the campaign a defeat, suggesting that the Confederacy, by regaining control of northern Alabama and Middle Tennessee, had ended with more than it had begun. The press was more direct. It labeled Bragg's retreat from Kentucky an escape and laid the blame squarely upon the shoulders of Major General Don Carlos Buell.

When the press took aim at Buell, it set its sights on an easy mark. Unlike Bragg, Buell could not claim the protection of the nation's chief executive, nor of any other influential civilian leader, for that matter. And even more than Bragg, he had lost whatever confidence his army may have had in his generalship.

The roots of the Army of the Ohio's estrangement from its commanding general predated Perryville and the lackluster pursuit of Bragg. They lay in Buell's contempt for the volunteer soldier and in his insistence that Regular Army standards of discipline be forced upon him. This, of course, was a fundamental error, reflecting Buell's inability to understand the western volunteer and how he might best be led. Like his counterpart in the Army of the Mississippi, he had joined up out of patriotism and a sense of duty. Although ready to give his life for what he believed, the young Illinoisan, Indianian, or Ohioan had no intention of abandoning his western distaste for authority or his spirit of self-reliance—it was to escape an overbearing government that many had moved west in the first place. Such a man would obey an order if sensible, otherwise not. And to be treated as a "mere machine," as most felt

Buell regarded them, was absolutely intolerable. As one veteran later wrote: "It was the universal experience in our late war, that the volunteer soldier could be led by justice, kindness and sympathy up to any point of excellence, but was made sullen and disobedient by what was thought to be injustice or tyranny."[1] This point was lost to Buell, but not to his army. During the hard and tedious marches about Kentucky, hundreds expressed their disaffection through desertion; the thousands who remained wrote home of Buell's severity.

Their complaints found many a receptive ear on the home front. Especially receptive to these allegations was Indiana's war governor, Republican Oliver P. Morton, as imperious a politician as the war produced. It had been Buell's singular misfortune to run afoul of the powerful governor, though the conflict probably was unavoidable. Morton had long been reluctant to relinquish his hold on Hoosier volunteers, going so far as to send his own staff to attend to their welfare after they had been mustered into United States service. On one occasion, he exchanged the arms of an Indiana regiment without the knowledge of its brigade commander. Buell did what any commander worthy of his charge must do and halted Morton's meddling within the army; but in so doing, he incurred the Indianian's enduring wrath.

Morton was joined in his opposition to Buell by the military governor of Tennessee, Andrew Johnson. Like Morton's, Johnson's enmity stemmed from considerations largely personal and selfish. Without victories, Federal authority in Tennessee was limited. And without an expansion of Federal authority, Johnson's office was an empty one—his personal authority could extend only as far as the reach of the Army of the Ohio. Eager to enlarge his bailiwick, Johnson naturally regarded Buell's June 1862 advance on Chattanooga as dilatory and his subsequent failure to pursue Bragg into East Tennessee as nothing less than treasonous—treasonous, that is, with respect to Johnson's ambitions. Buell's refusal to violate the sanctity of private property in territory conquered by his army also infuriated Johnson, who maintained that all Southerners—combatants and civilians alike—must be punished for their role in the rebellion. When Buell summarily dismissed a brigade commander who had sacked the Alabama town of Athens, Johnson, with the support of Morton, lashed out at the general's "kid-glove policy."

Buell might have survived the vendetta of Morton and Johnson, had it not been for Perryville. But that indecisive bloodbath, followed by the army's sluggish pursuit of Bragg, allowed the two governors to deliver the fatal blow. On 21 October, Morton sent Lincoln what was in effect an ultimatum: Replace Buell or lose the Northwest. It read: "An officer, just arrived from Louisville, announced that Bragg has escaped with his army into east Tennessee, and that Buell's army is countermarching to Lebanon. The butchery of our troops at Perryville was terrible. Nothing but success speedy and decided, will save our cause from utter destruction. In the Northwest distrust and dispair are seizing upon the hearts of the people."

To Lincoln the solution was obvious, the more so as he himself had lost patience with Buell. Like Morton and Johnson, he was angry that Bragg had been allowed to withdraw without a decisive battle having been fought. To prevent further damage to Union morale, Lincoln issued peremptory orders instructing Buell to give chase over the mountains and into eastern Tennessee. He reminded the general of the importance of securing an area in which the largely loyal population already had suffered considerably at the hands of Confederate guerrillas, adding that the Army of the Ohio certainly could march anywhere Bragg's army did.

But Lincoln's admonitions went unheeded. Insisting that any advance be made from Nashville, Buell turned his army westward as soon as the last Rebel disappeared into the Cumberland Mountains. Lincoln had had enough. Motivated also by a desire to remove as many McClellan supporters as possible from the Union high command, he relieved Buell on 24 October, naming in his place Major General William Starke Rosecrans. Speaking for Governor Richard Yates of Illinois as well as for himself, Morton sent Lincoln the following telegram the next day: "We were to start tonight to Washington to confer with you about Kentucky affairs. The removal of General Buell and appointment of Rosecrans came not a moment too soon. . . . The action you have taken renders our visit unnecessary."[2]

Rosecrans joined the army at Bowling Green on 30 October. The same general order that brought Rosecrans to the army also changed its name. The Army of the Ohio was now the Fourteenth Army Corps, composed of a left wing, right wing, and center. It was to be the principal Union force in the new Department of the Cumberland, embracing all of Tennessee east of the Tennessee River and such parts of northern Alabama and Georgia as might be taken by Federal arms. Long since lost to history, the title Fourteenth Army Corps proved to be a temporary designation. On 9

January 1863—a week after Stones River—the army was renamed the Army of the Cumberland, the name it was to carry to the war's end, and its wings became corps.[3] (In keeping with tradition, the Union army at Stones River hereafter will be referred to as the Army of the Cumberland, despite its official designation as the Fourteenth Army Corps at the time of the battle.)

The change of names probably left the men unmoved, but they heartily applauded the change of commanders. "We were glad to be delivered of Buell," wrote the sergeant major of the Fifty-first Indiana. "However good a military man General Buell may have been . . . he never won the love, and entirely lost the confidence, of the army he commanded," noted Robert Stewart of the Fifteenth Ohio. "There was silent rejoicing everywhere when Rosecrans took his place." The officers agreed. "I have just been up to Rosecrans's headquarters and had a shake of the old fellow's hand," Colonel Hans C. Heg of the Fifteenth Wisconsin wrote just after the general's arrival. "You don't know how pleased everybody is at the change of Buell for him." Colonel John Beatty of the Third Ohio was also favorably impressed. He characterized the army's new commander as "an educated officer, who has rubbed much against the world."[4]

As much as the army delighted in the change, it was not entirely sure what to make of its eccentric new commander. At first glance, Rosecrans seemed typical of the generals who had come before him. There was little in his background to suggest eccentricity. Like most Union officers of comparable rank, Rosecrans had attended the United States Military Academy, where he graduated fifth in a class of fifty-six in 1842. Routine assignments followed. The Ohioan spent one year at Fortress Monroe and seven years along the eastern seaboard supervising the construction of various wharf, harbor, and coastal fortifications, with a three-year stint as an instructor at West Point sandwiched in between. In November 1853 his health broke down, and Rosecrans resigned his commission the following April.

"The next seven years," Ohio journalist Whitelaw Reid wrote, "were to Lieutenant Rosecrans years of more varied than profitable activity." He enjoyed modest success, first as president of the Canal Coal Company of Cincinnati, then at the head of the Cincinnati Coal Oil Company. While with the coal company he invented a round lamp wick and a new method of manufacturing soap; at the coal oil company he labored after-hours in his laboratory trying to perfect a pure, odorless oil. During one such experiment a safety lamp exploded, and Rosecrans was so badly burned that he was bedridden for eighteen months.

Rosecrans's recovery coincided with the outbreak of the war. Major General George B. McClellan, commander of the Ohio militia, immediately requested his appointment as staff engineer officer, but Governor William Dennison had other ideas. He assigned to Rosecrans the task of procuring arms for the state's newly recruited volunteer regiments. On 21 June 1861 Rosecrans received a much-desired field commission as colonel of the Twenty-third Ohio; four days later he was elevated to the rank of brigadier general in the Regular Army. McClellan again requested his services. This time Little Mac was successful, and Rosecrans performed admirably under him at Rich Mountain in western Virginia, where his discovery of an obscure mountain path around the Confederate flank resulted in a spectacular Union victory. When McClellan was called to Washington after Bull Run, Rosecrans assumed command of the Department of West Virginia. There he remained until April 1862, when he too was summoned to Washington. After only three short weeks in the office of the secretary of war, Rosecrans was back in the field commanding a portion of Grant's army at Corinth. There on 4 October he defeated a Confederate attempt to take the city and cut Grant's line of communications in Mississippi. For this timely victory he was given command of the Department of the Cumberland.[5]

Despite Rosecrans's conventional background, the army learned quickly that its new commanding general was anything but moderate in temperament. Erudite, animated, indefatigable, Rosecrans possessed many of the qualities of genius. But he could also be indiscreet, intolerant, and mercurial, with an impulsiveness that suggested instability under pressure. The Ohioan's idiosyncratic personality elicited strong reactions from those with whom he came in contact, and a person's opinion of the general depended largely on which side of himself Rosecrans chose to reveal most often in the observer's presence. To Right Wing commander Thomas Crittenden, Rosecrans was "of the first order of military mind . . . both brave and generous." The normally critical J. Warren Keifer thought him a "great soldier," a "man of many attainments." But even his staunchest supporters acknowledged the general's shortcomings. Attributing Rosecrans's gallantry under fire to his impulsiveness, Crittenden believed it at the same time a serious liability, as it led him to issue too many orders during combat.

Critics took Crittenden's observation one step further. Contemporary accounts suggest that Rosecrans was hampered by stuttering—that he stammered and faltered even while routinely addressing a line of soldiers during a review. In combat, if his defamers may be believed, his stuttering rendered him incoherent. Said New York *Herald* correspondent William Shanks: "I have known him, when merely directing an orderly to carry a dispatch from one point to another, grow so excited, vehement, and incoherent as to utterly confound the messenger. In great danger as in small things, this nervousness incapacitated him from the intelligible direction of his officers or effective execution of his plans."[6]

Although Shanks seldom had anything good to say about anyone, there was more than a little truth in his allegation, as shown by the following unfortunate incident involving Colonel John Beatty, a victim of the general's rage in a situation that scarcely merited such vehemence. Lying in his tent one night after Stones River, Beatty was awakened by an unexpected caller who introduced himself as an officer from Stokes's Chicago Board of Trade Battery. The officer claimed to have been ordered to report to Beatty for a reconnaissance mission. Having no knowledge of any such mission, Beatty dismissed the matter as a case of mistaken identity and suggested to the officer that he report instead to Brigadier General Sam Beatty of Van Cleve's division. The officer followed Beatty's advice. The Ohioan had just fallen back to sleep when there came another knock at his tent door. Assuming it to be the same importunate young officer, Beatty again told him to see Sam Beatty. The tired colonel thought no more of the incident until the following morning, when he was handed a note directing him to conduct a reconnaissance toward Nashville with a regiment of infantry and Stokes's battery, a reconnaissance that was to have begun nine hours earlier. Realizing his error, Beatty rode at once to army headquarters to explain to the commanding general the reasons for his failure to undertake the reconnaissance. Rosecrans flew into a rage. In the presence of fellow officers and civilians he chastised Beatty in language "most ungentlemanly, abusive, and insulting." Beatty's first impulse was to strike his commanding general. Thinking the better of it, he instead turned and left the room as quickly as possible. "Death would have had few terrors for me just then," he recalled later. "I had never felt such bitter mortification before, and it seemed to me that I was utterly and irreparably disgraced." Beatty was a scrupulous officer whose recollections are forthright and honest. We therefore may assume the incident to have occurred as presented.[7]

But there was another side to Rosecrans's character. The same nervous energy that rendered him "incomprehensible" under the stress of combat and produced outbursts of rage made him a voracious worker under routine conditions. "Labor was a constitutional necessity with him," wrote W. D. Bickham of the Cincinnati *Commercial*. Rosecrans began the duty day at 10:00 A.M.— rising earlier on Sundays and Wednesdays to attend mass—and worked well into the night, seldom retiring before 2:00 A.M. and often laboring until dawn. In the field, to the chagrin of his staff, the commanding general was apt to be the first out of his blankets in the morning and the last to dismount at night. Nor did the completion of the day's work, in garrison or in the field, necessarily promise a respite for Rosecrans's weary staff. As Bickham observed while a guest at army headquarters throughout the Stones River campaign: "When lectures were concluded, orders executed, correspondence all disposed of, somewhere about midnight—an hour earlier or later was altogether immaterial—dull care was dismissed and pleasure assumed supremacy."

Unfortunately for his staff, the general's idea of pleasure was to keep his young aides, with whom he was affable and affectionate, awake all night while he ruminated aloud on religion in general and Catholicism in particular. To Rosecrans, the Catholic church was supreme and infallible; all other theological systems were mere corruptions of the church. The general brooked no dispute on this point. Having embraced Catholicism over the objections of his staunchly Methodist parents while a cadet at West Point, Rosecrans displayed the sort of dogmatism common in adult converts to any faith. He attended mass faithfully and took his friend and confidant, the Reverend Father Patrick Treacy, to the field so as not to be separated from the rituals of the church.[8]

Rosecrans, in short, was unique. Perhaps, for all his eccentricities, he was the only true genius to command a Union army in the field; certainly he was among the most colorful.

Whatever the Ohioan's shortcomings, the Army of the Cumberland needed a commander with Rosecrans's energy and enthusiasm in the weeks following Perryville. The Kentucky campaign had shattered morale. Rosecrans found himself faced with regiments that had not been paid in six months, officers without any means of subsisting, and troops deserting by the thousands. Fully one-fourth of the army was absent; some 26,482 were elsewhere by authority, but a startling 6,484 had left without authority, in effect, deserted. Other problems equally serious beset the army. To begin with, the cavalry was useless. By Rosecrans's own estimation, fully half lacked weapons of any kind. As long as the mounted arm of the Army of the Cumberland remained impotent, the security of Confederate lines of communication and supply was guaranteed. Union communication and supply lines were in a shambles by contrast. The railroad between Louisville and Nashville, upon which the Federals were dependent both for supplies from Louisville and communication with Nashville, had been ruined by marauding bands of Rebel cavalry. From the Green River, where Rosecrans's army was concentrated, to Nashville the track was almost entirely wrecked.[9]

Not only had communications with Nashville been severed, but it appeared that the city itself might fall. Reports received at army headquarters in the early days of November warned that elements of the Army of the Mississippi of unknown strength were threatening the Tennessee capital. Although the force menacing Nashville proved to be nothing more than a small cavalry outfit led by the intrepid John Hunt Morgan, Rosecrans, not knowing this, had to act. Marching orders went out, and the Army of the Cumberland filed onto the road to Nashville. McCook's Right Wing led the way. Breaking camp on 4 November, it entered Nashville three days later, just as the pickets of Brigadier General James Negley's garrison command drove away the last of Morgan's troopers. McCook wired Rosecrans that the city was safe and that the latest intelligence placed the Confederate army at Murfreesboro. A much-relieved Rosecrans rode into the capital six days later.[10]

Having successfully met the most immediate threat to his command, the Ohioan turned his attention to the army's remaining problems. Rosecrans had provided a glimpse of things to come with the promulgation of General Order Number Four on 3 November, in which he appealed to his officers and men to help him bring the army to "a state of discipline at least equal to that of the Rebels." That same day the War Department granted him the authority to dismiss officers for "satisfactory military reasons."

Now, with the army settled into camp around Nashville, Rosecrans applied his authority. Incompetent or otherwise unfit officers were stripped of their rank and marched from camp in the presence of their troops; officers' leave was slashed drastically and all soldiers, officers and enlisted men alike, were required to present written passes on demand when outside their camps. Within camp, discipline was tightened. Five roll calls now sounded during the duty day; those failing to muster for any were subject to harsh and summary punishment. Camp life also became more regulated, so that the day passed much the same, regardless of the unit to which a soldier was assigned. Every morning between 4:00 and 5:30 A.M. the fife and drum roused the camps with the familiar sound of reveille. The orderly sergeant called roll, and those failing to respond were placed on extra duty. Breakfast followed. After a thorough police of the unit area, sick call was sounded. The orderly sergeant presented the company sick to the regimental surgeon, whose responsibility it was to distinguish the legitimately ill from the malingerers. At 8:00 came guard mount. A part of the detail was assigned to picket duty, the remainder to camp guard. As the guards walked their two-hour shift, stopping all who attempted to leave camp to insure that they had passes signed by the colonel, the extra-duty personnel swept the company area and adjacent grounds. The remainder of the company busied itself with drill until noon, when dinner was served. Battalion drill followed dinner and continued until 4:00 P.M., when the men broke for supper. Additional drill or perhaps a dress parade ended the duty day, and tatoo sounded at 9:00 P.M.[11]

All of these actions had the effect Rosecrans desired. Morale improved. Being more evenly distributed through the ranks, his brand of discipline succeeded where Buell's had failed. Sensing the change, the men rapidly developed respect for their new commander.

Their respect turned to affection as Rosecrans made his presence felt in the camps. Despite his aversion to public speaking, the Ohioan seemed to enjoy reviewing and inspecting the troops. He would examine their equipment with the exactitude of a drill sergeant. The private without a canteen was asked when it was lost and why another had not been obtained. If he replied that he was unable to get one, Rosecrans enjoined him to go to his captain and demand the item: "Bore him for it! Bore him in his quarters! Bore him at meal time! Bore him in bed! Bore him; bore him; bore him." The captain was to bore his colonel, the colonel his brigade commander, the brigadier his division commander, the division commander his wing commander, until it reached the commanding general himself. "I'll see then," Rosecrans said, "if you don't get what you want." Whether done for "theatrical effect," as Shanks suggested, or sincere, the men appreciated the attention that Rosecrans gave them.[12]

Rosecrans followed his own advice in seeking to improve his cavalry. As his troops were to bore their superiors for needed equipment, so Rosecrans doggedly appealed to the War Department in the early days of November. To properly arm his troopers he demanded from Stanton five thousand repeating rifles, of which he eventually received three thousand. And with only half of his assigned cavalry present for muster—a portion of these being "chiefly valuable for their capacity to evade danger and good service"—Rosecrans pleaded for a chief of cavalry capable of restoring order and discipline. His object was the talented David Stanley, then commanding a division under Grant. Rosecrans applied for Stanley's services with an annoying persistence, alternately writing Henry Halleck and Edwin Stanton, until in late November his request was granted.[13]

With Stanley present to rejuvenate the cavalry, Rosecrans concentrated on the reorganization of the army as a whole. Its three wings were structured so as to approximate corps: the Left and Right Wing each contained three divisions of infantry and nine batteries of artillery; the Center contained four divisions and fourteen batteries, three of which were unattached as a reserve. Numbers varied. The Right Wing mustered 15,832 present in early December, the Left Wing 14,308, and the Center 29,337. A fifth division under Brigadier General Robert Mitchell, numbering 5,346, was detached for extended garrison duty in Nashville.[14]

It was no accident that the Center was the largest command in the army, or that it went to Thomas. In fact, it was the price of his continued service in the department. Thomas too had been offered command of the army now entrusted to Rosecrans. As Buell hesitated in the weeks following Bragg's occupation of Chattanooga and confidence in him fell, Andrew Johnson, who made no secret of his disdain for Buell and for his "dilatory steps" at unseating the enemy, had expressed to Thomas directly his hope that the Virginian might be placed in command. Thomas answered Johnson at once, hoping to stop any groundswell on his behalf before it could begin: "I most earnestly hope I may not be placed in the position, for several reasons. One particular reason is that we have never yet had a commander of any expedition who has been allowed to work out his own policy, and it is utterly impossible for the most able General in the World to conduct a campaign with success when his hands are tied. . . . I can confidently assure you that Genl. Buell's dispositions will eventually free all of Tennessee and go very far to crush the rebellion entirely."[15]

But as the summer deepened it became increasingly evident Buell would meet neither Thomas's nor the War Department's expectations, and the calls for his removal grew. Finally, on 29 Sep-

7777777

777

777777

777777777

tember, the blow fell. Washington ordered Buell to hand over command to Thomas. No sooner did Thomas catch wind of the order then he was on Buell's doorstep, declining the command. To his credit, Buell told Thomas he was willing to accede and went so far as to encourage him to take command. But Thomas was immovable. The War Department, caught off balance, suspended the order.

Thomas's refusal to assume command in September, as laudably disinterested as were his motives, cost him advocates, so that when Buell was dumped after Perryville, there were few to speak on behalf of the Virginian. His only significant support in cabinet came from Stanton, while the secretary of the treasury, Ohioan Salmon Chase, urged Rosecrans's appointment. Thomas's earlier refusal seems to have weighed heavily with Lincoln. Then there was his Southern heritage, while Rosecrans was a Northern Catholic whose selection would be popular during upcoming gubernatorial and congressional elections with voters of the same faith who saw the conflict as a "Yankee war, originating with Puritans." "Let the Virginian wait, we will try Rosecrans," Lincoln said, and the matter was closed. Only the question of seniority remained, and Lincoln answered that with the stroke of a pen, changing the date of Rosecrans's commission from 21 August to 31 March.

News of the appointment of Rosecrans shocked Thomas. Perhaps the Virginian felt that, with Buell's removal a fait accompli, there now were no obstacles to his assuming command if asked. In any case, the normally taciturn Thomas lost no time in making known his feelings. On 30 October, he protested to Halleck:

> On the 29th of last September I received an order . . . placing me in command of the Department of the Ohio and directing General Buell to turn over his troops to me. This order reached me just as General Buell had by most extraordinary exertions prepared his army to pursue and drive the rebels from Kentucky. Feeling convinced that great injustice would be done him if not permitted to carry out his plans, I requested that he might be retained in command. The order relieving him was suspended, but today I am officially informed that he is relieved by General Rosecrans, my junior. Although I do not claim for myself any superior ability, yet feeling conscious that no just cause exists for overslaughing me by placing me under my junior, I feel deeply mortified and aggrieved at the action taken in this matter.[16]

Thomas confronted Rosecrans with his feelings as well. Although he thought Rosecrans capable and a good choice to command on his own merits, Thomas asked to be transferred out of the department. But Rosecrans knew a good soldier when he saw one. He appealed to Thomas to stay, reminding him that "you and I have been friends for many years and I shall especially need your support and advice." Thomas agreed, but on the condition he be assigned command of the Center rather than hold the empty post of second in command of the army. Rosecrans readily agreed.

To his credit, Rosecrans employed Thomas well. Rather than shun him as a threat to his command, Rosecrans leaned on the Virginian as his "chief counselor." Rosecrans openly expressed a deep, almost reverential respect for Thomas. "Thomas is a man of extraordinary character," he told his staff. "Years ago, at the Military Academy, I conceived that there were points of strong resemblance between his character and that of Washington. I was in the habit of calling him General Washington."

Veteran soldiers of the army shared their commanding general's opinion of Thomas, whom they affectionately called "Pap" or "Old Slow Trot," the latter sobriquet stemming from the general's steady and sedate temper, a quality much admired by the troops. Thomas impressed even the most critical observers. "Most men diminish as you approach them, General Thomas grows upon you," wrote W. D. Bickham. William Shanks agreed. He likened Thomas's fighting style to that of a "heavy, ponderous pugilist, whose every blow is deadly." Colonel Beatty thought him a "gentlemanly, modest, reliable soldier."

Thomas was all these things. Although a Virginian by birth, his sentiments were firmly with the Union. Thomas was a good though not brilliant student at West Point, where he graduated twelfth in a class of forty-two that included Confederate brigade commander Bushrod Johnson. He owed his success in the army to patience and steadfastness. Seldom would he make a decision without "long and mature reflection." Not surprisingly, Thomas's greatest triumphs came in defensive actions, where his imperturbability steadied officers and men under his command.

Thomas's appearance mirrored his character. Thick-set and robust, his heaviness made him look shorter than his five feet ten inches. Grave of countenance, the sandy-haired, square-jawed Virginian seldom smiled. He appears to have taken life quite seriously, so much so that many contemporaries wondered if he had any sense of humor at all. None, however, questioned his ability.[17]

The same could not be said for Rosecrans's remaining wing commanders. Major General Alexander McCook, commander of the Right Wing, was to prove singularly disappointing as a troop commander, although much was expected of him. The former West

Point tactics instructor had enjoyed success early in the war, winning promotions for gallantry at Bull Run and Shiloh. But it was not his courage that was questioned; rather, many doubted his ability to handle large bodies of troops. At Perryville, his first opportunity to refute the skeptics, McCook saw his corps shattered after he deployed it prematurely. Buell left him in command, perhaps feeling that his own eroded reputation left him without the authority necessary to replace McCook.

Not only was McCook widely regarded as incompetent, but he was unpopular as well. Although good-natured and jovial, he came across in a way that many considered undignified. John Beatty thought him a "chucklehead," with a grin that excited "the suspicion that he is either still very green or deficient in the upper story." A veteran of the Fifty-ninth Illinois recalled a chance meeting with the general: "While the column was passing, General McCook and staff came dashing by in magnificent style. They came, they were seen, and they were gone. Like most his rank, he prides himself on being General McCook."

McCook's reputation suffered equally outside the army. His political views offended Northern abolitionists, who thought him Southern and Democrat in his sympathies. A slave-catcher allegedly visited McCook's camp during the Kentucky campaign. It was said that McCook accorded him the most courteous treatment possible, promising to return any fugitive slaves unfortunate enough to wander into his lines.[18]

Major General Thomas Crittenden of the Left Wing was no better. Like McCook, he was notorious for his profanity; in the same manner, noted Beatty, he was capable of blowing his own horn exceedingly well. A lawyer by profession, Crittenden's sole military experience prior to the war had been as an aide on the staff of Zachary Taylor during the War with Mexico. But he had other credentials. As a member of the powerful Crittenden family of Kentucky, he exercised great influence within the state. His commissioning as a brigadier general in 1861 was an acknowledgment of the state's critical role during the early days of the war.[19]

Rosecrans had inherited McCook and Crittenden, and he was stuck with them. But when left to appoint subordinates as he saw fit, Rosecrans chose reasonably well. His new chief of cavalry, Brigadier General David Stanley, had commanded a division of infantry under Rosecrans at Corinth. Although his last cavalry service had been on the frontier before the war, Stanley knew enough of the mounted arm to recognize that it had been "badly neglected" in the Army of the Cumberland. "It was weak, undisciplined, and scattered around, a regiment to a division of infantry," Stanley wrote. "To break up this foolish dispersal of cavalry, and to form brigades and eventually divisions, was my first and difficult work." Stanley's initial attempts to pry the cavalry loose from the infantry met with resistance from division commanders, but Rosecrans intervened on his cavalry chief's behalf, and soon Stanley had two mounted brigades and a three-regiment reserve at his disposal to begin training in the fundamentals of security and reconnaissance operations.

Stanley was a good organizer, but he had some odd ideas about how the cavalry should fight. He attributed the cavalry's previous failures not so much to their dispersal as to their dependence on carbines rather than sabres. "I insisted on the latter," wrote Stanley. "I sent for grindstones and had all sabres sharpened, each squadron being provided with the means for this work. This soon gave confidence to our men, and the opportunity was only lacking to show their superiority over the enemy."

Rosecrans could forgive Stanley his eccentricities; after all, the two were much alike. Moreover, Stanley was loyal; long after the war, he continued to defend Rosecrans publicly against Grant's censure of him for failing to pursue Van Dorn after Corinth.

Rosecrans's choice of a chief engineer officer also proved a wise one. The youthful James St. Clair Morton, a Regular Army captain with flowing blond hair, not only occupied a place on the general's staff but was given an independent command as well. Rosecrans had hit upon the novel idea of creating a brigade of combat engineers responsible for the construction of field fortifications, corduroying of roads, and building and repair of bridges. Detachments were drawn from each regiment of infantry within the army; the detachments drawn from the regiments of a single brigade were consolidated into a company of pioneers; these companies were in turn brigaded under Morton and numbered 1,938 troops present for duty in December. Some criticized Rosecrans for having appointed one so young to a post so important, but the commanding general had a reply ready: "Young men without experience are better than experienced old men. Young men will learn; old men fixed in their habits will not learn."

This philosophy guided Rosecrans in his choice of a chief of staff as well. To this post he appointed the eccentric but capable Lieutenant Colonel Julius Garesche, a close friend known throughout the army for his quick mind and refined manners. Like Rosecrans, the native of Cuba was a tireless worker. Unpretentious, thoroughly dedicated to his commander, Garesche was the ideal chief of staff.[20]

Washington appreciated Rosecrans's efforts in reorganizing and rejuvenating the Army of the Cumberland, but they were not enough. As November drew to a close, pressure mounted for an advance before winter put an end to active campaigning. Patience with field commanders was not a virtue of the War Department. As early as 18 November, in response to Rosecrans's repeated requests for revolving rifles for his cavalry, Secretary of War Stanton warned the general that, although the arms would be provided, "something is expected from you."

Rosecrans parried this and similar demands for action by ascribing his inactivity to the lack of rail communications between Nashville and the North. This excuse kept Washington at bay until 26 November, when repairs were completed and rail communications reopened. From that date forward, threats replaced admonitions, culminating in Halleck's ultimatum of 4 December: "The President is very impatient at your long stay in Nashville. The favorable season for your campaign will soon be over. You give Bragg time to supply himself by plundering the very country your army should have occupied. . . . Twice have I been asked to designate someone else to command your army. If you remain one more week at Nashville, I cannot prevent your removal. As I wrote you when you took the command, the Government demands action, and if you cannot respond to that demand someone else will be tried."

"I have lost no time," replied Rosecrans. The railroad may have been repaired, but supplies were still hazardously low. Only five days' rations were on hand at Nashville, meaning that any advance would have to be halted after just three days to allow the army to replenish its stock. And because the cavalry remained questionable, infantry units had been scattered to protect forage trains from depredations by Confederate horsemen. "To threats of removal or the like I may be permitted to say that I am insensible," the Ohioan concluded.

Rosecrans was on thin ice. The War Department read the Ohioan's dispatches, then Grant's, whose only concern was "to do something before the roads get bad and the enemy can entrench and re-enforce," and Rosecrans's reservations appeared petty.

Halleck and Grant understood the importance of Union offensives before winter put an end to active campaigning, even if Rosecrans did not. The fortunes of the Union, at least on the diplomatic front, were at their nadir. Failure to conquer substantial amounts of Confederate territory, or at the very least recapture lost ground, raised the specter of foreign intervention on behalf of the South. Parliament would convene in January of the new year. It was widely feared in Northern circles that Confederate sympathizers within that body would compel the British government to recognize the Confederacy; should this come to pass, France gave every indication that it would follow suit.

So now, in November, as the last of the Confederate summer offensives flickered and died, Washington prepared for a concerted drive by all the major Union armies in the field. Grant asked for and was given permission to undertake a water-borne turning movement against Jackson, Mississippi, supported by a demonstration against Grenada by General Samuel Curtis, operating out of eastern Arkansas. Grant believed that the capture of Jackson would ensure the fall of Vicksburg.

In Virginia, Major General Ambrose Burnside, having superseded McClellan as commander of the Army of the Potomac, moved his headquarters on 16 November from Warrenton to Catlett's Station and his army toward Fredericksburg. Burnside's move forced a countermove by Lee, whose communications with Richmond were now in jeopardy. He sent Longstreet's corps at once to occupy the heights above Fredericksburg. For a time Lee sought to maintain a presence in the Shenandoah Valley, both to snap at Burnside's flank and rear and to protect the valley's abundant supplies for the Army of Northern Virginia. But Stonewall Jackson's presence there failed to deter Burnside, who continued with his designs on Fredericksburg, and Jackson was called in to meet the main threat. President Davis called four brigades from western Virginia to assist Lee, meanwhile scouring the coast for other reinforcements.

Lee hoped to draw reinforcements from the West. As Herman Hattaway and Archer Jones have pointed out in their *How the North Won*:

> Lee was thus applying what had been the Confederacy's consistent policy since the fall of Fort Donelson. Faced with a major Union offensive, Lee hoped that he might secure reinforcements from the West and the South. In early September, not knowing that Bragg was advancing northward through Tennessee, Lee wrote: I hope that Bragg's army can "be advantageously employed in opposing the overwhelming numbers which it seems to be the intention of the enemy now to concentrate in Virginia." In December, faced with Burnside's

advance, he applied the general principle to suppose that "should there be a lull of war," in the South and West, "it might be advantageous to leave a sufficient covering force to conceal the movements, and draw an active force, when the exigency arrives, to the vicinity of Richmond. Provisions and forage in the meantime could be collected in Richmond. When the crisis shall have passed, these troops could be returned to their departments with reinforcements."

Lee's plan for inter-departmental transfers of large bodies of troops was not far-fetched; nine months later, Lee himself would send Longstreet's corps into northern Georgia to help Bragg defeat Rosecrans at Chickamauga.

Stanton and Halleck understood the willingness of the Confederates to shift forces across departments, although they assumed Bragg would move into Mississippi against Grant, rather than into western Virginia to relieve pressure on Lee. In any event, the need for Rosecrans to keep him occupied was obvious. And, as Halleck again reminded Rosecrans in early December, even if Bragg were to stay where he was, should "the enemy be left in possession of Middle Tennessee, it will be said that they have gained on us."[21]

All these arguments and admonitions were lost on Rosecrans, who thought only in terms of his theater of operations and his needs. Grant on his right and Burnside on his left advanced; but, for the moment, Rosecrans was standing behind his fortifications at Nashville.

CHAPTER THREE

A HASTY ADVANCE

"GENERAL Bragg returned from Richmond in good spirits," Lieutenant Colonel George Brent of the general staff wrote on 2 November. "He brought the gratifying fact that his conduct in Kentucky had been approved by the President."

Sustained by Davis, Bragg set the army in motion for Middle Tennessee. Time was at a premium. The North Carolinian faced the same problems on returning to East Tennessee that he had left behind two weeks before, and every day the army lingered about Knoxville things grew worse. Desertion was rampant, particularly among the Kentuckians. Field returns of 3 November showed only 30,801 present; in other words, nearly 50 percent of the army was absent, either lying in hospitals or gone home. An autumn drought had ruined crops, and an early winter blanketed the mountains with six inches of snow before November. Unable to shelter themselves properly and short of clothing, blankets, shoes, and food, troops by the hundreds succumbed from exposure to the elements. Many more, weakened by hunger, fell victim to pneumonia, typhoid, scurvy, and dysentery.[1]

The necessary orders were issued, and the army began to move during the first week of November. Breckinridge's division had been in the Stones River Valley, encamped at Murfreesboro, since 28 October. Major General Ben Franklin Cheatham, meanwhile, was on the east bank of the Tennessee River, opposite Bridgeport, Alabama, ready to advance on order. As the remainder of the army left Knoxville, Bragg wired Breckinridge to fall back, if necessary, on Tullahoma, where he would be met by Cheatham's advancing division.

The army moved slowly, their progress impaired by the poor condition of the railroads and the indirectness of the route. Boarding the cars at Knoxville, Bragg's infantry rattled along the dilapidated East Tennessee and Georgia Railroad to Stevenson, Alabama. There they changed trains, completing the journey to Murfreesboro without incident on the Nashville and Chattanooga Railroad. On 14 November army headquarters were advanced to Tullahoma. Twelve days later, the commanding general and his escort rode into Murfreesboro.[2]

As Bragg had no objective beyond the occupation of Middle Tennessee, he now was content merely to await an advance by Rosecrans. He entertained no thoughts of attacking the Federals in their Nashville fortifications; but, if they ventured from their entrenchments, as he believed they would, Bragg was confident of success in a defensive battle at Murfreesboro.

Bragg's confidence was misplaced. His choice of Murfreesboro as the anchor to a defense of Middle Tennessee was a poor one, reflecting his ignorance of the state's topography. Bragg had concentrated his forces at Murfreesboro so as to gather foodstuffs in the rich Stones River Valley, while forestalling a Federal advance on the gateway city of Chattanooga. But the same could have been accomplished elsewhere, and at a lesser risk. To the south, at the base of the plateau of the Cumberland Mountains, were the Duck and Elk river valleys, equally fertile and far more easily defended. The former river was especially well suited to a defending army, as it snaked through numerous defiles and impassable woods. It also flowed beneath the Nashville and Chattanooga Railroad east of Shelbyville, blocking that avenue just as effectively as could a defensive line at Murfreesboro. Adopting the Duck River line admittedly might mean surrendering a portion of Middle Tennessee, assuming that Rosecrans chose to leave his Nashville bastion. But even within the Stones River Valley there was a position far better than Murfreesboro. Just twelve miles to the southeast, at the edge of Rutherford County, a chain of rolling, forested foothills ranging in altitude from 570 to 1,352 feet rose from the valley, providing a spectacular view of the countryside and of any approaching enemy force.

The main problem with Murfreesboro was the ease with which it could be bypassed, leaving a defending army outflanked. To the west, the well-maintained Columbia Pike and parallel Nashville and Decatur Railroad offered swift passage to Columbia, some fifteen miles below Murfreesboro. And nearer Murfreesboro, a country road led to Shelbyville, twenty-five miles below the town, by way of Nolensville, Triune, and Eagleville. To the northeast, Murfreesboro could be flanked by way of the turnpike between Lebanon and McMinnville, again, placing an advancing Federal army below the defending Confederates. In fact, only two routes south were blocked from Murfreesboro. One was the Nashville and Chattanooga Railroad, of doubtful use to an invader as it twisted tortuously for miles through the Cumberland Mountains before debouching at Stevenson, Alabama; the other was the Nashville Pike (or Nashville Turnpike), a macadamized road that forked below Murfreesboro, the principal branch becoming a mere dirt lane as it left Millersburg.[3]

All these considerations left Bragg unmoved. As November drew to a close and winter approached, he grew less concerned about a Federal offensive and ordered Breckinridge's division and Polk's corps to build winter quarters outside Murfreesboro. At the same time, Bragg reorganized his depleted forces. Orders were issued consolidating the Army of the Mississippi and Kirby Smith's Army of Kentucky into the Army of Tennessee, the name it was to carry for the remainder of the war. Three corps of infantry were created, led by Polk, Hardee, and Kirby Smith. Polk's corps contained three divisions. Major General Benjamin Franklin Cheatham commanded the first. A hard drinker and a hard fighter, Cheatham was immensely popular with his troops, most of whom were fellow Tennesseans. The Nashville native, a major general in the state militia before the war, was influential in Tennessee politics and therefore not to be taken lightly. In the service of the Confederacy, the stout, rough soldier had distinguished himself in all of the Western campaigns, first as a brigade, then as a division commander.

Major General Jones Withers, a member of the West Point Class of 1835 who resigned his commission after graduation to study law, commanded Polk's second division. Withers practiced law in Alabama until the War with Mexico, at which time he was appointed lieutenant colonel of the Thirteenth United States Infantry. Withers resigned at the end of the conflict and returned to Mobile, where he served as mayor from 1858 until the outbreak of hostilities. He began the war with Bragg at Pensacola, Florida; now, a year and a half later, he was a close friend and loyal subordinate of the commanding general, one of the few division commanders on whom Bragg could rely for support.

Major General John Cabell Breckinridge led the third division. He was by far the most influential, and potentially the most dangerous, division commander in the Army of Tennessee. A lawyer by profession, he had risen rapidly to prominence in his native Kentucky and was elected to Congress in 1851. From 1856 to 1860 he was vice president in the ill-starred Buchanan administration. A candidate for the presidency in 1860, he finished behind Lincoln and Stephen Douglas, ahead of John Bell in popular votes. That winter he was elected to the Senate, but resigned his seat to cast his lot with the Confederacy. Assuming command of the famous "Orphan Brigade" of Kentuckians in November 1861, he rose quickly to the rank of major general, largely a result of political considerations, as Bragg was quick to point out after relations between the two had deteriorated.

Bragg had not always been this quick to criticize Breckinridge. For a time they got along well. Bragg had been impressed with Breckinridge's performance at Shiloh, and much of his hope for success in Kentucky rested on his belief that the mere presence of Breckinridge in his home state would bring new recruits to the army in droves.

But Breckinridge was then in Louisiana, chafing under the command of the mercurial Earl Van Dorn. Bragg begged the Kentuckian to join him. "I should be much better satisfied were you with me on the impending campaign," he wrote. "Your influence in Kentucky would be equal to an extra division in my army. . . . A command is ready for you, and I hope to see your eyes beam again at the command 'Forward,' as they did at Shiloh, in the midst of our great success." When Van Dorn would not consent to Breckinridge's transfer, Bragg went over his head to Secretary of War Randolph, who ordered his release. Breckinridge prepared at once to join Bragg. On 19 September, he put twenty-five hundred men of his division—all that Van Dorn would allow him to take—onto trains in Louisiana. Two weeks later, he and his men arrived at Knoxville, Tennessee, ready to join Bragg—a remarkable feat given the dilapidated state of Southern railroads.

Breckinridge wired Bragg of his movements. "I hope you are satisfied with my energy since I was allowed to leave. I have encountered every difficulty a man could meet." But Bragg was not satisfied. Breckinridge could not have known, since the causes lay deep in the recesses of Bragg's troubled mind, but Bragg already blamed him for a campaign that was on the verge of defeat. Bragg had convinced himself that Breckinridge was responsible for the failed recruiting effort in Kentucky. That more Kentuckians would have joined the Army of the Mississippi had Breckinridge been present is undeniable. Breckinridge, however, had done everything in his power to reach Bragg, overcoming an uncooperative Van Dorn and an unreliable railroad system. Bragg, in the bitterness of his disappointment, forgot all this. "The failure of General Breckinridge to carry out his part of my program has seriously embarrassed me, and moreover the whole campaign," he complained to President Davis. From this point Bragg's relationship with Breckinridge declined rapidly, a process that was to have dire consequences two months later on the bank of Stones River.

Lieutenant General William J. Hardee commanded Bragg's second corps. A member of the West Point Class of 1838, the Georgia native was an able lieutenant. Labeled "Old Reliable," Hardee was a professional soldier who had seen action in the Seminole War and the War with Mexico. As a major he had authored the two-volume *Rifle and Light Infantry Tactics* that later came to be known simply as Hardee's *Tactics*. Endorsed by the War Department in 1855, his *Tactics* was a response to the replacement by the rifle of the musket as the standard infantry weapon. As the rifle both extended the range and increased the accuracy of infantry fire, new tactics were imperative. Jefferson Davis, then Secretary of War, directed that a manual be prepared addressing these advances in weapons technology, and Hardee's *Tactics* was the result. In working together on the manual, Hardee and Davis formed a relationship that was later to assist Hardee in undermining Bragg's authority as commander of the Army of Tennessee.

Hardee's most significant contribution was in changing the rate of advance, as the "double quick time" and the "run" supplanted the "quick time" as the standard pace during an attack. Hardee's double quick time called for 165 steps per minute, as opposed to the old quick-time rate of 110 steps per minute; each step was lengthened to thirty-three inches. The longer stride and faster rate enabled troops to deploy from column more rapidly. In addition, it was no longer necessary for units to halt while passing from one formation to another.

For these and other innovations, Hardee was acknowledged to be one of the leading military scholars, North or South. He apparently regarded himself in much the same light, as his official reports during the Civil War are sprinkled with pedantic references to generalship and tactics. But the forty-seven-year-old widower had other interests as well. Tall, broad-shouldered, looking "rather like a French officer," Hardee enjoyed a wide reputation as a ladies' man. During the Kentucky campaign, it is said, he availed himself of the "privilege of his rank and years, and insisted upon kissing the wives and daughters of all the Kentucky farmers." What effect this had on the outcome of the campaign is unknown.

Hardee profited from the services of two able division commanders. Major General Simon Buckner commanded the first division at the time of the November reorganization, but was transferred to garrison duty at Mobile in early December. His replacement proved to be one of the finest combat leaders that the war produced: Patrick Ronayne Cleburne. Cleburne was a fascinating character with an even more fascinating background. At seventeen he ran away from his home in County Cork, Ireland, to join Her Majesty's Forty-first Regiment of Foot, serving three years before purchasing his discharge and emigrating to Arkansas. Here he studied law and later established a successful practice with T. C. Hindman, also a future Confederate general. At the outbreak of the Civil War, Cleburne enlisted as a private in the first regiment raised in Arkansas; by the year's end he was a brigadier general. A courageous leader, always at the forefront of battle, he was wounded twice during the invasion of Kentucky. At Richmond, while shouting a command to his troops, a minie ball passed through his mouth, carrying with it five lower teeth. Cleburne was back in action at Perryville, where he was wounded a second time. Fiery in combat, Cleburne was under normal circumstances distant and reserved, almost shy. He may have been modest and unpretentious, but as a division commander he drove himself and his men relentlessly, working to improve an already fine command. The strain left its mark: although only thirty-five, the combative Irishman was already graying. But his efforts were appreciated. Hardee held him in high regard, and he was among the few not criticized by Bragg.

Hardee's other division commander was forty-year-old Brigadier General Patton Anderson of Florida. Anderson had seen action in the War with Mexico, during which he was elected lieutenant colonel of a Mississippi battalion at the age of twenty-one. As was the case with most of the general officers in the Army of Tennessee, Anderson had connections in Richmond. After the War with Mexico, President Franklin Pierce introduced Anderson to Jefferson Davis, who subsequently secured Anderson an appointment as a marshal in the Washington Territory. But unlike his fellow general officers, Anderson would not use his relationship with Davis to undermine Bragg; he had served with Bragg at Pensacola and Mobile in the early days of the war and, with Withers, was a firm supporter of the commanding general.

The remaining corps of the Army of Tennessee was composed of the two divisions that Kirby Smith had furnished Bragg. Neither Carter Stevenson nor John McCown, Kirby Smith's division commanders, relished the prospect of serving under Bragg; McCown already was estranged of the commanding general. Kirby Smith shared their distaste for service in the Army of Tennessee, and he did not join his command until early December.

The cavalry also was reshuffled. Brigadier General Joseph Wheeler, a twenty-five-year-old favorite of Bragg, was appointed chief of cavalry. His selection won for Bragg yet another enemy, the more experienced but less flamboyant Nathan Bedford Forrest. Forrest's anger at having been passed over is understandable. There was little in Wheeler's record to date to merit such a promotion, except perhaps loyalty to Bragg. He had failed repeatedly to provide effective reconnaissance during the invasion of Kentucky, although he did conduct an admirable delay as commander of the rear guard during the retreat. In any event, the youthful general was now in command of Bragg's three regular brigades of cavalry, one of which was assigned to each corps of infantry. Bragg prudently allowed Forrest and John Morgan to retain independent commands.[4]

Bragg firmly believed that the move into Middle Tennessee and the reorganization of the army was having a salutary effect on his troops. On 24 November, two days before establishing his headquarters in Murfreesboro, Bragg wrote Davis that deficiencies in clothing, shoes, and blankets were being overcome; that supplies were abundant; that, in short, "the health and tone of my old Army of the Mississippi were never better."

Davis was skeptical. Although he wanted to believe his old friend, too many disquieting reports of continued unrest within the army's officer corps were reaching his office, mostly from the headquarters of Polk and Hardee. Affairs outside of Tennessee were disturbing him as well. Cooperation was at a minimum in the West, and coordinated action was nonexistent. While Bragg prepared for his advance into Middle Tennessee, Lieutenant General John C. Pemberton was in peril of losing much of Mississippi, including Vicksburg, to Grant's late-autumn offensive. Pemberton turned to Bragg (who, theoretically at least, was his commander) for reinforcements, but instead got only advice and the suggestion from Bragg that his move into Middle Tennessee might relieve pressure on the Confederates in Mississippi, to the extent that it created a diversion in Grant's rear. Bragg did, however, take advantage of his position by having the commands of Earl Van Dorn and Mansfield Lovell, both operating in northern Mississippi, placed under his authority. Everyone concerned—everyone but Bragg, that is—was upset. Pemberton wrote Davis for special instructions, and Van Dorn asked to be relieved. When his request was denied, he countered by wiring Richmond that Union transports were threatening Vicksburg and his rear and that Bragg should be ordered to attack these forces. Replying for Secretary of War Randolph, Samuel Cooper, the Adjutant and Inspector General of the Confederacy, merely told Bragg to take whatever action he deemed necessary to save Vicksburg without really ordering him to do anything. Consequently, Bragg did nothing. In a wire to Cooper on 21 November, he argued that the dispatching of troops to Mississippi would be tantamount to abandoning Middle Tennessee. From the tone of his correspondence, Bragg appeared surprised that he was responsible for Pemberton's army; it was a burden he neither wanted nor then felt himself capable of assuming.

Bragg's reluctance to accept this authority probably stemmed from his experience as department commander during the invasion of Kentucky. Then he honestly tried to act the part, only to be undermined from below and circumvented from above. While planning the occupation of Chattanooga, Bragg actually turned command of the Army of the Mississippi over to Hardee in order to better orchestrate movements within the department. Taking a broader strategic view of the situation around him than Rosecrans ever contemplated (although still insisting that the needs of the Army of the Mississippi came first), he assigned Van Dorn to command of the District of the Mississippi, along the east bank, with orders to defend Vicksburg, keep open communications with the trans-Mississippi, and deny the Federals northeastern Mississippi. Sterling Price was placed in command of the District of the Tennessee. Bragg instructed him to hold the Mobile and Ohio Railroad and, of paramount importance, prevent Grant from reinforcing Buell in Middle Tennessee. Kirby Smith was told to move from Knoxville, and Humphrey Marshall from western Virginia into Kentucky. Bragg made Polk "second in command of the forces" and, as mentioned, gave Hardee the Army of the Mississippi, with which Bragg traveled.

Problems arose almost at once. On 29 July, as Hardee left Tupelo for Chattanooga, Price wrote Van Dorn seeking his cooperation in a joint movement against Corinth to keep Grant occupied. Van Dorn declined and instead asked Price for troops to support an expedition against Baton Rouge. Price referred the matter to Bragg, who approved Price's conduct and ordered Van Dorn to cooperate with him. But Van Dorn refused to quit. This time he wrote the president, insisting not only that Price send him arms, wagons, and men, but that he, Van Dorn, be given command of any joint operation.

Van Dorn's audacity paid off. Without consulting Bragg, Davis granted both of Van Dorn's requests. Meanwhile Bragg, unaware of this latest development, was urging Price to hasten to Nashville as Rosecrans, protecting Corinth on behalf of Grant, had sent Buell three divisions of reinforcements. Price hesitated. Despite Bragg's orders to the contrary, he felt his duty lay in northern Mississippi and in northern Mississippi alone. Any thought he may have entertained of joining Bragg left him on 18 September, when a courier from Van Dorn brought word of Davis's decision and directed Price to join Van Dorn at Baldwyn.

Bragg's squabble with Van Dorn ended on 24 November, when Davis intervened to unite the commands of Pemberton and Van Dorn in Mississippi and Bragg in Tennessee under General Joseph E. Johnston, idle since his wounding at Fair Oaks in May.

Johnston's responsibilities were enormous. Davis expected him to coordinate the efforts of Bragg and Pemberton so as to maintain control of the Mississippi River Valley. As Tennessee was of secondary importance to Davis, he assumed that Johnston would take from the Army of Tennessee such troops as might be needed to save Vicksburg. But this Johnston declined to do. He held that the trans-Mississippi command of Major General Theophilus Holmes could reinforce Pemberton rapidly and at lesser risk. Untold dangers awaited should Bragg be compelled to move to Pemberton's relief, Johnston wrote Richmond from his headquarters at Chattanooga. He doubted the ability of the country between the Tennessee River and Vicksburg to sustain Bragg's forces and, of more immediate concern, feared that Rosecrans might avail himself of the departure of all or part of the Army of Tennessee to march unimpeded against Lee's flank in Virginia or to Grant's assistance in Mississippi, thereby negating any advantage that might be gained from a reinforcement of Pemberton by Bragg. At any rate, Johnston argued, Tennessee would be lost.[5]

Johnston's arguments convinced Davis only that the time had come for a presidential trip to the West. He would visit Murfreesboro and Chattanooga, inspect the troops and interview their generals, and then decide what to do with the commands of Pemberton and Bragg. Leaving Richmond by train, Davis arrived in Murfreesboro on Friday, 12 December, to find the army enjoying a spell of unseasonably balmy temperatures. On Saturday Davis reviewed the three divisions of Bragg's principal defamer, Bishop Polk. "It was a truly imposing scene," wrote Captain J. J. Womack of the Sixteenth Tennessee, "and a time of rejoicing throughout the army and surrounding country." A warm, brisk wind churned small clouds of dust as Davis and his staff rode along the lines. Polk's corps then passed smartly in review, after which the president addressed the assembled troops, perhaps hoping that his admonitions to loyal and dedicated service would have some effect on their contentious generals. During a dinner that night at army headquarters, Davis queried the senior officers as to morale within their units and Union intentions.

The president left Murfreesboro for Chattanooga the next morning in high spirits. The troops, he wrote Secretary of War James Seddon, were in good condition and ready to fight, their officers anxious to lead them. Bragg was as downcast as Davis was uplifted. For him, the presidential visit had been a major setback. Not only had Davis failed to find any visible evidence of the discontent and disloyalty within the senior officer corps of which Bragg had been so loudly complaining, but conversations with his lieutenants had convinced Davis that Rosecrans's intentions were strictly defensive and that a winter campaign was therefore unlikely. That was all that Davis needed to hear. With any doubts as to the wisdom of his Mississippi River-first strategy removed for at least the remainder of the winter, he ordered the immediate reinforcement of Pemberton with a division from the Army of Tennessee. On 16 December, Carter Stevenson and his seventy-five hundred infantrymen boarded railcars at Murfreesboro, bound for Mississippi.[6]

Stevenson's detachment prompted another reorganization of the army. Kirby Smith's command, now reduced to the division of John P. McCown, was abolished. McCown was attached to Hardee's corps, and Kirby Smith returned to East Tennessee. As Breckinridge's division had been transferred to Hardee's corps several days earlier as well, the division of Patton Anderson was disbanded, its regiments divided equally between the two corps to achieve greater numerical balance. The army was to retain this two-corps structure throughout the Stones River campaign.[7]

But the detachment of Stevenson did more than necessitate a structural reshuffling. It seriously weakened the army, depriving it of nearly one-sixth of its infantry—infantry that would be sorely missed on the battlefield of Stones River.

CHAPTER FOUR

WE LIVED LIKE LORDS

"I do not feel quite at ease at the disposition of our troops at Murfreesboro, Manchester, and Shelbyville," wrote Colonel Brent on 22 November. "It is a triangular position, with the apex at Murfreesboro. Polk's corps is exposed." Bragg apparently agreed. On 4 December he brought McCown's division forward to Readyville, twelve miles east of Murfreesboro, and Hardee's corps to Eagleville, astride the Shelbyville Pike. Hardee in turn advanced one brigade up the road to Triune, and Wharton detached a battalion to protect the army's extreme left at Franklin.

In positioning his forces so as to cover the primary avenues leading to Murfreesboro, Bragg had scattered the Army of Tennessee across a fifty-mile front, making rapid concentration difficult at best. But this latest vulnerability did not seem to trouble the commanding general or his lieutenants who, as autumn gave way to winter, with its driving rain and biting cold, came to believe that Rosecrans would make camp at Nashville until spring. For a time, Bragg even entertained the notion that the Ohioan would abandon the city and retire across the Cumberland River. So certain was Bragg that his opposite would not venture south of Nashville that he dispatched Nathan Bedford Forrest with twenty-five hundred troopers into western Tennessee to harass Grant.[1]

Sharing Bragg's conviction, the men of the Army of Tennessee raised winter quarters around Murfreesboro. Typically, their shelters took the form of a simple log cabin with a square hole dug in the center as a fireplace. Crude as they may have been, the cabins were a blessing after the retreat through East Tennessee, the memory of which was still painfully acute within the army. Captain

James Womack of the Sixteenth Tennessee was particularly proud of his winter home. "Spent the day building a chimney to my tent," he noted in his diary, "which, after I finished, was a complete success. It drew finely, and made my tent as comfortable as a stove."

Being near to their Kentucky home, the soldiers of the Orphan Brigade fared especially well. Volunteers, dubbed "blockade runners," were elected to run the gauntlet of Federal patrols between Kentucky and Murfreesboro at regular intervals. They brought back so many parcels of clothing and provisions that Gervis Grainger of the Sixth Kentucky later recalled that "we lived like lords." The Orphan Brigade found the countryside pleasant too, not unlike its native Kentucky. Grainger's company made camp in a "beautiful grove" south of town, and Lot D. Young's regiment set up camp on a "beautiful little plain."

The beauty of their surroundings could not erase a deeper ugliness that festered among the Kentuckians. Their resentment of Bragg was growing. Unable to attract recruits in large numbers in Kentucky, Bragg had resorted to conscription to fill his ranks. Breckinridge in particular objected to the drafting of Kentuckians when the state was not a part of the Confederacy, and the rumor spread that he had threatened to resign. Bragg, for his part, grew increasingly contemptuous of the Kentuckians. The men of Kentucky were cowards, he wrote. They had not been worth liberating.

The smoldering feud between Bragg and Breckinridge turned red hot in December over the fate of a young deserter. Private Asa Lewis of the Sixth Kentucky had declined to reenlist when his term had expired and his regiment reorganized several months earlier. Nevertheless, he stayed on until December, when word reached him that Union soldiers had burned the home of his widowed mother, leaving her alone and without means of support. Lewis apparently appealed without success to his regimental and brigade commanders for a thirty-day furlough. He may also have had his appeal denied by Breckinridge, which, if true, certainly dilutes the purity of the general's outrage over Lewis's ultimate fate.

In any event, Lewis deserted. Some asserted later in his defense that he had intended to return before the start of the next campaign. But Lewis was captured before he had a chance to prove his good intentions, court-martialed, and condemned to death. Bragg approved the sentence. He ignored repeated requests by Breckinridge and his officers—presumably the same who denied Lewis's request for leave in the first place—and directed that the Orphan

Brigade be assembled to witness the execution on 26 December. Bragg evidently felt no remorse over his decision. Kentucky blood was too feverish for the health of his army, he was quoted as telling Breckinridge. He would stop the corn-crackers' grumbling if he had to shoot every man. Breckinridge was furious. He retorted that Kentuckians would never be treated like slaves and that the execution of Lewis would be tantamount to murder.

On the morning of 26 December, the Orphan Brigade marched sullenly to an open field outside Murfreesboro amidst a cold, numbing rainstorm to witness the end of Private Lewis. At precisely 12:00 noon the lieutenant in command of the detail barked the orders "Ready-Aim-Fire." Rifles cracked, and the prisoner fell dead, pierced by eleven balls. At that moment, recalled veterans of the brigade, "General Breckinridge was seized with a deathly sickness, dropped forward on the neck of his horse, and had to be caught by some of his staff."

The volley that struck down Private Lewis also killed any chance of a reconciliation between Bragg and Breckinridge. From that day on, Breckinridge was implacable in his opposition to Bragg and unwavering in his suspicion that any order from Bragg committing his Kentuckians to battle was given with a view toward their destruction.[2]

Although a dark cloud had settled over the Kentuckians, most of the army continued to find Murfreesboro a charming place in which to pass an idle winter. Twenty-nine of Bragg's eighty-eight regiments of infantry had been recruited in Tennessee, and many of the soldiers had family in Murfreesboro. But everybody in the army, regardless of the state from which they hailed, enjoyed the hospitality of the staunchly Confederate townspeople. Homes were opened to the troops, and kitchen hearths turned out bread and cakes for the army.

The citizens of Murfreesboro were proud of their town and took pains to maintain it. Since 1811 Murfreesboro had been the county seat of Rutherford County, and from 1819 to 1826 it played host to the state general assembly. Murfreesboro also hosted visits by three presidents in the years before the war: Andrew Jackson and Martin Van Buren were given receptions by the community, and James Polk, married to a local girl, was a frequent visitor. Thus far, Murfreesboro had escaped the ravages of war. It still boasted many fine brick residences, clean white fences, and oak- and elm-shaded avenues. The macadamized Nashville Turnpike connected the town with the state capital, and two institutions of higher education—Soule Female College and Union University—continued to graduate students, although in lesser numbers than before the war.

As the Yuletide approached and Rosecrans showed no intention of moving beyond his fortifications, Murfreesboro played host to a number of gatherings that reinvigorated its languishing social life. The premier event was the 14 December wedding of seventeen-year-old Murfreesboro debutante Mattie Ready to John Hunt Morgan, fresh from a stunning victory at Hartsville, where he had captured the two-thousand-man garrison in a lightning raid the week before. All the high command was present, and Bishop Polk donned his sacerdotal garb to perform a ceremony that started a parade of celebrations lasting until Christmas.[3]

Unusually clear skies and mild temperatures helped promote the festive spirit that pervaded the normally strife-ridden Army of Tennessee. "Nothing can surpass the beauty and pleasantness of the weather," Colonel Brent jotted in his diary on 17 December; four days later it was the same: "I feel quite cheerful and contented this morning under the balmy and delightful influence of the weather," he confessed. By Christmas Eve the skies had become overcast, but the temperature still hovered above normal. That night, the officers of the First and Second Louisiana entertained the single women of Murfreesboro with a lavish ball at the courthouse. "It was a magnificent affair," remembered Kentuckian Charles Robert of Bragg's escort. Four large "Bs" of cedar and evergreen—signifying Bragg, Beauregard, Buckner, and Breckinridge—adorned the walls, and the names of the victories of the two regiments hung draped in cedar over the windows. Union flags, captured at Hartsville and donated by Mrs. Mattie Ready Morgan, provided the finishing touch.

While their officers danced and drank, the men in ranks passed the holiday simply, but not necessarily more quietly. Gambling and chicken fights were common, recalled Mississippian John Magee, who went into town on Christmas Day to have his watch repaired. Yankee whiskey netted during the Hartsville raid flowed freely in the camp of the Ninth Kentucky, remembered Johnny Green. The teetotaling Green left camp and struck out into the countryside in search of a Christmas turkey. Neighboring farms provided Green and his messmate with eggs, onions, and biscuits, but the area had been swept clean of turkeys. Undaunted, Green bought a goose and, after baking a poundcake, enjoyed a quiet dinner. Sergeant Major James Maxwell of the Thirty-fourth Alabama, on the other hand, believed that Christmas was a time for drink, and so sacrificed a bottle of fine French brandy to share a holiday toddy with his colonel.

Those officers not invited to formal celebrations generally spent the day in much the same manner as their soldiers. Bishop Polk composed a long letter to his family in which he lamented the absence of worship services within the army. Captain Womack stayed indoors to enjoy his new fireplace and write in his diary. Reflecting on the Confederacy's prospects, he wrote: "May the coming Christmas in sixty-three find our now distracted and unhappy country reposing in the lap of an infantile and glorious peace."[4]

At Nashville, John Beatty also hoped for peace—the peace of a reunited nation. In the meantime, the Ohioan tried to make the best of a Christmas away from home: "At an expense of one dollar and seventy-five cents, I procured a small turkey and had a Christmas dinner; but it lacked the collaterals, and was a failure." Colonel Hans Heg, the jovial commander of the Fifteenth Wisconsin, spent a more boisterous evening. Invited to a Christmas party in an appropriate schoolhouse near camp, Heg and the brigade surgeon dressed two of the soldiers as women, and the colonel made an entrance "just as if I had a lady on my arm. . . . We kept the house roaring for a good long time." Heg thought his men jolly that night despite rumors of an impending advance; perhaps his merry disposition, made merrier by the free-flowing liquor, prevented him from seeing things as they really were. Colonel Charles Manderson's description of his camp that evening is far more plausible. Homesickness crept into all efforts by the men of his Nineteenth Ohio at merrymaking, until it became the "all-pervading complaint." As Manderson observed from his tent: "The men gathered about the camp fires during the evening hours with abortive attempts at merriment, soon to be given up, and then to talk in whispers of friends and family and home. The bugle calls, holding out the promise that balmy sleep might bring forgetfulness, were welcomed; although tatoo seemed a wail, and lights-out a sob."[5]

At departmental headquarters the candles burned deep into the night, but not to light a party. After weeks of threats from Washington, Rosecrans at last had agreed to move. No longer could he justify delay on the basis of insufficient rations, as by Christmas enough food had been gathered in Nashville to feed the army until February; nor could he attribute his inaction to fears that the Confederates outnumbered his army, as recent intelligence confirmed the detachment of Stevenson's infantry division and Forrest's cavalry. In fact, dispatches to Halleck reveal that Rosecrans knew of Morgan's intent to cross the Cumberland River as early as 15 December and that he learned of Forrest's departure before 19 December. The consensus at headquarters now was that Bragg, not expecting a Federal advance before spring, had gone into winter quarters around Murfreesboro after sending the majority of his cavalry into western Tennessee and Kentucky. As Rosecrans later explained: "In the absence of these forces, and with adequate supplies in Nashville, the moment was judged opportune for an advance on the rebels."

The moment was not only opportune, it was imperative. Burnside already had met with a bloody repulse at Fredericksburg, and Sherman, floundering about in Chickasaw Bayou above Vicksburg, was about to meet the same fate on the moss-choked bluffs of the same name. With one army routed and the progress of the other checked, the administration now focused all its dwindling hopes for a victory before the new year on the Army of the Cumberland. The defeat of Burnside and the frustration of Grant and Sherman had so raised the stakes that any failure in Tennessee would almost certainly result in Rosecrans's immediate removal and disgrace.

With the hopes of the nation (or at least of those loyal to the administration) riding on his offensive, Rosecrans needed sound tactics and good intelligence. His scouts and spies failed him the latter, and the general formed his plans on the incorrect assumption that Bragg would organize his defense behind Stewart's Creek, a narrow stream with steep banks that flowed under both the Murfreesboro Pike (Nashville Turnpike) and the Nashville and Chattanooga Railroad before joining Stones River at a point some fifteen miles northwest of Murfreesboro.

The consultation at headquarters wore on. Shortly after midnight, Rosecrans announced to his gathered lieutenants the plan that he and Thomas had developed. The army was to move at first light along three routes toward three separate objectives, that of the Right Wing being most distant. McCook would advance rapidly along the Nolensville Pike to Triune, twenty-eight miles away, where Rosecrans erroneously placed the majority of Hardee's corps. Thomas, meanwhile, would march within supporting distance of McCook's right along the Franklin and Wilson pikes, threatening Hardee's left as he moved. At the intersection of the Wilson Pike with the Old Liberty road he was to turn east and continue on the latter road until he reached Nolensville, thirteen miles north of Triune. Rosecrans assigned Crittenden the direct route to Murfreesboro, instructing him to march along the Murfreesboro Pike as far as Lavergne. Stanley, whom the commanding general directed to screen the infantry, divided his cavalry into three columns: Colonel Robert Minty's brigade (temporarily under the direction of Colonel John Kennett) was to precede Crittenden's infantry along the Murfreesboro Pike; Colonel Lewis Zahm was to ride ahead of Thomas with his brigade and dislodge the battalion of Confederate cavalry at Franklin, after which he was to move parallel to and protect the right flank of McCook; Stanley, meanwhile, would retain command of his reserve—consisting of the First and Second Tennessee and Fifteenth Pennsylvania, all feared to be unreliable—and screen the movement of the Right Wing along the Nolensville Pike.

Rosecrans's plan allowed for two contingencies. As soon as Thomas reached Nolensville, McCook was to move against Hardee at Triune. If McCook discovered Hardee to have been reinforced, Thomas would march immediately to support the Right Wing; if, on the other hand, McCook defeated Hardee or the latter withdrew without giving battle and Bragg chose instead to defend along Stewart's Creek, Crittenden would attack the enemy in front while Thomas came in on his flank and McCook—after detaching a division to observe or pursue Hardee, as the case warranted—maneuvered to get into the Confederate rear. The plan was sound. Its success depended largely on the ability of the cavalry to screen effectively and to provide accurate intelligence. Should Stanley fail, McCook and his exposed command might be faced with defeat in detail as they neared Triune in advance of Thomas and Crittenden.

Aides distributed brandy toddies as Rosecrans concluded his briefing. A few moments of levity were permitted, McCook facetiously suggesting that he "would be under the painful necessity of defeating his old friend, Hardee," before Rosecrans slammed his glass on Garesche's field table and announced to the gathering: "We move tomorrow, gentleman! We shall begin to skirmish, probably, as soon as we pass the outposts. Press them hard! Drive them out of their nests! Make them fight or run! Strike hard and fast! Give them no rest! Fight them! Fight them! Fight, I say!" With that, the generals returned to their commands.[6]

Word of the impending movement spread rapidly through the camps. Orderly sergeants moved from tent to tent, peering in and announcing "reveille in the morning at four o'clock; march at daylight, with three days' rations." Corporal Ebenezer Hannaford and his comrades of Company B, Sixth Ohio, received the news with indifference. Like the rest of the army, they had been under marching orders for several days; Rosecrans had originally scheduled the movement for 24 December, only to postpone it to allow the forage trains of the Left Wing to complete their work. One unit did move that day, however. Negley's division advanced eight miles to Brentwood, secured the town, then pushed another three miles down the Wilson and Franklin pikes. No resistance was encountered, and the men bivouacked for the night.[7]

This activity did not go unnoticed at Murfreesboro. By Christmas night it was evident that a Federal offensive was imminent. Apparently satisfied with the disposition of his army, Bragg took no action, and nightfall found the Army of Tennessee aligned essentially as it had been since the first week of December. Polk's corps and three brigades of Breckinridge's division rested in winter quarters around Murfreesboro. The small brigade of Brigadier General John Jackson was on its way by rail to Murfreesboro from Bridgeport. At his College Grove headquarters near Eagleville, Hardee had with him the division of Pat Cleburne and the brigade of Brigadier General Dan Adams, on detached service from Breckinridge's division. Brigadier General S. A. M. Wood's understrength brigade remained at Triune, providing infantry support to the cavalry operating in the area. Brigadier General George Maney and his Tennessee brigade had been detached from Polk's corps for similar duty along Stewart's Creek, as was Dea's brigade, under the command of Colonel J. Q. Loomis, near Las Casas. Each of these brigades supported a brigade of cavalry. The cavalry was spread across the entire army front; all approaches were effectively screened to within ten miles of Nashville. On the left, Brigadier General John Wharton, operating out of Nolensville, had his picket lines extended southwest across the Old Liberty road from Nolensville to Franklin. To his right, Wheeler's brigade, bivouacked along Stewart's Creek astride the Murfreesboro Pike, covered the direct approaches to Murfreesboro. John Pegram patrolled the army's right flank northeast of town, screening the approaches from Lebanon.

As Christmas drew to a close and the hour of the Federal advance neared, patrols from the three Southern cavalry brigades sat quietly among the dark cedar glades along the roads leading from Nashville, alert to any indication of movement. They would not have long to wait.[8]

CHAPTER FIVE

TO MURFREESBORO

THE clear skies and warm breezes that for two weeks had lifted the spirits of both armies ended abruptly on 26 December. The morning opened ominously. Chill gusts swept down the valleys and swirled through the camps around Nashville. Low-hanging black clouds promised a winter storm. Union soldiers awoke to see a thick curtain of mist draw across their line of march; by the time they doused their breakfast fires, a driving rain had set in, accompanied by a harsh wind that blew steadily from the west.

At his Mill Creek camp five miles south of Nashville, McCook received a telegram at 4:30 A.M. directing him to advance. Movement orders were prepared and dispatched to the division commanders. At 6:00 A.M.—an hour and a half before dawn—the men of Brigadier General Jefferson C. Davis's division filed onto the Edmondson Pike. Although they could see little in the predawn twilight, what they felt underfoot was not to their liking. Already the rain was carving rivulets along the road, and the veterans knew that after the first regiments passed, the surface would be reduced to a soft, pasty ooze that would slow the advance to a crawl.

A daylong march was difficult under the best of conditions. The Union volunteer of 1862 bore a load seemingly calculated to make each step a challenge. On his back he carried a knapsack stuffed with extra clothing, underwear, a blanket, and such personal effects as he might elect to take to the field. A canteen and tin cup hung over the knapsack. Draped over his hip was a haversack with three days' cooked rations—rations that were anything but appetizing: one pound of hard bread (known as hardtack in the Eastern armies), three-fourths of a pound of salt pork, a small bundle of coffee, a bit of sugar wrapped perhaps in paper, and a pinch of salt sufficed to keep the soldier alive during a day of active campaigning. Forty rounds of ammunition were carried in a cartridge box worn below the haversack. A rifle and bayonet with scabbard completed the load.[1]

Thus equipped, Davis's Bluecoats turned their faces away from the rain and set out. Already Rosecrans's Achilles' heel, the cavalry, was threatening to disrupt his plans. While the infantry slogged along the Edmondson Pike, Stanley's cavalry reserve was still breaking camp in the rear. By the time his troopers appeared, the infantry and their trains had effectively blocked the road, and Stanley was unable to reach his assigned positions until after they had bivouacked for the night. Deprived of his cavalry screen, Davis was compelled to use his own small escort, Company K of the Fifteenth Illinois Cavalry, to reconnoiter ahead of the division.[2]

Despite the rain and absence of the cavalry, the march went well at first. Prim's Blacksmith Shop was reached quickly and without incident. Here Davis turned east off the Edmondson Pike and onto "a rugged country road, rendered almost impassable by the incessant rain." Moments later, the advance ground to a halt as Davis's mounted escort uncovered an outpost belonging to Wharton's cavalry brigade some five miles northwest of Nolensville. A spirited exchange of rifle fire followed before the troopers of Company K, leaving the road and galloping across the sodden fields, turned the Confederates' flank and drove them through the cedar brakes toward Nolensville. The pursuit continued until the Illinoisans were within a mile of the town. Here they pulled rein. To their front, among the cedar thickets and overgrown fields on the outskirts of town, lay the remainder of Wharton's dismounted cavalry brigade and a battery of artillery. The Yankee troopers formed a hasty skirmish line and prudently awaited the arrival of the infantry.

Davis and his infantry appeared just as the rain was subsiding. A quick examination of the Rebel lines convinced the Indiana brigadier that he could take them unaided. Orders were issued, and the muddied soldiers deployed. Colonel P. Sidney Post marched his brigade to the left, Colonel William Woodruff led his to the right, and Colonel William Carlin remained astride the road. But Wharton's orders were simply to impede the Federal advance by forcing them to deploy repeatedly, and so, his mission accomplished, he retired through Nolensville before Davis sent forward his line of battle.

Wharton chose as his second delay position Knob Gap, a rocky defile that commanded the road to Triune. Under the cover of a two-battery barrage, Davis deployed again. This time he caught the Rebels napping. As Davis's men crested the surrounding hills, Wharton's troopers fell back on Triune in confusion, less one gun abandoned to the charging Federals. It was now nearly dark. Unwilling to drive his exhausted men further this early in the campaign, Davis gave the order to halt and make camp by the roadside.

McCook's other divisions had a less eventful day. Phil Sheridan's column had marched at 6:00 A.M. on the Nolensville Pike, followed closely by the division of Brigadier General Richard Johnson. Encountering only light resistance from scattered cavalry outposts, they reached Nolensville at 4:00 P.M. As Davis had already driven Wharton from Knob Gap, McCook directed Sheridan and Johnson to bivouac for the night outside town.[3]

To the west, Thomas's advance went unopposed. Striking their tents at 7:00 A.M., his infantry marched initially along the Franklin Pike to join Negley at Brentwood. Again the cavalry was nowhere to be found. By the time Zahm's troopers rode up, it was mid-morning and the pike was impossibly congested. Zahm fell in at the rear of the column, to bide his time until the infantry left the Franklin Pike at Brentwood. Meanwhile, another Federal command was without a screen.

Thomas's objective for the day was Owen's Store, just south of Brentwood on the Wilson Pike. Negley, in the lead, reached it handily. From there he caught the sound of gunfire rolling westward from Davis's engagement at Nolensville. Without orders, the impetuous brigadier pressed on to Nolensville over the same country lane traversed by Davis earlier in the day. Arriving to find Knob Gap clear and the fighting over, Negley bivouacked his division alongside those of Sheridan and Johnson. The division of Major General Lovell Rousseau, unable to follow Negley as the country lane to Nolensville had deteriorated to "the consistency of cream or very thick paste," went into camp as planned at Owen's Store. Colonel Moses Walker's brigade remained at Brentwood.[4]

Zahm's cavalrymen had a busy day once they broke free of the infantry. With some 950 troopers, Zahm rode hard down the Franklin Pike, the Third Ohio in the lead. Two miles outside Franklin, they ran headlong into Wharton's pickets. A running skirmish ensued. Galloping through the streets of Franklin and across the bridge over the Big Harpeth River, the Ohioans pursued the Confederates two miles beyond town before they called off the chase and returned to Franklin, bringing with them a prisoner who told Zahm of Wood's presence in Triune. Zahm forwarded the information to Thomas before joining his men for the night on the Wilson Pike outside town.[5]

The cavalry gave a better account of itself in support of the Left Wing, although once again they were absent at the outset. Colonel Robert Minty was fortunate. He found the Murfreesboro Pike (Nashville Turnpike) less congested than other roads taken by the Union infantry that day and was able to join the lead division of Brigadier General John Palmer after only a short delay. Minty shook out his three regiments—the Third Kentucky to the left of the pike, the Seventh Pennsylvania to the right, and the Fourth Michigan astride the pike in reserve—and rode forward to screen the advance. Moments later, at the eleven-mile marker, his troopers surprised an outpost belonging to Wheeler's brigade.

Word of the incident quickly reached Bragg's cavalry commander at his Lavergne headquarters. Wheeler was astonished. This was the first report he had received of an advance along the Murfreesboro Pike, and the Yankees were now just two miles away. Leaving brigade headquarters, the youthful brigadier galloped to the front to have his worst fears confirmed: strung out along the pike and into the horizon were the several thousand Bluecoats of Palmer's division, removing any doubt that the Federals were advancing in force. Remaining with his vedettes, Wheeler dispatched a staff officer to bring up the command from their cantonment below Lavergne. Within minutes the grayclad troopers were wheeling into position along Hurricane Creek, a narrow stream that crossed the Murfreesboro Pike two miles northwest of Lavergne. There they dismounted and, with their commander, waited for the Yankees to make the next move.

Meanwhile, Minty had deployed along the opposite bank. Observing the line of Rebels in the woods across the creek, he directed Battery D, First Ohio Artillery, to open fire while couriers were dispatched to hurry along the infantry.

Palmer arrived just as evening twilight settled over the field. A brief reconnaissance revealed the Confederate right to be exposed. Anxious to strike a decisive blow before darkness put an end to the day's operation, Palmer ordered his lead regiments into action as they came on the field. To the left of the pike, Brigadier General Charles Cruft sent a hastily formed assault force composed of the Thirty-first Indiana and First Kentucky across the creek to turn the Rebel flank; on his right, the Ninth Indiana and Sixth Kentucky applied pressure simultaneously against Wheeler's left to divert attention from the crossing downstream. As the attack began,

Wheeler's troopers became disoriented in the gathering darkness, allowing Cruft's assault force to splash across handily. After a brief but sharp struggle, Hazen's supporting units also succeeded in forcing a bridgehead on the east bank. Wheeler's cavalrymen, outnumbered and demoralized, fell back onto their mounts and into Lavergne. Palmer, no more willing than Wheeler had been to bring about a night engagement, called a halt along the east bank, his division a mere sixteen miles from Murfreesboro.[6]

It was now dark. From Hurricane Creek to Franklin, weary, muddied Bluecoats gathered around campfires to prepare their simple evening meals. On the march, cooking utensils were few: a tin cup, tin plate, and sharpened branch were all that the soldier typically took to the field. Salt pork was suspended over the fire on the tin plate or at the end of the sharpened stick; when ready, it was dispatched with hard bread and washed down with coffee.

On a clear night, the men might linger by the fire to discuss the events of the day or to speculate on what the morrow held in store. This evening, however, all attention must have been devoted to finding a dry spot on which to sleep, no easy matter as rain began to fall again at midnight—a fine, chilling drizzle that continued until morning. For many, a few cornstalks or cedar boughs and a gum blanket were all that were to be had. Few were as fortunate as the men of the Seventy-third Illinois, who had their "pup" tents with them. Consisting of two cotton or rubber "half-shelters," the tents had been derided as kennels or dog holes at issue. But on this night, with storm clouds menacing, the men had to admit that their little shelters weren't so bad after all.

Officers also had to improvise. Captain Horace Fisher of McCook's staff considered himself lucky to find an empty tool box by the road. He crawled into it, and all was well until the rain began and he discovered that his unorthodox shelter leaked badly at the hinges; by daybreak, Fisher was as wet as before he lay down.[7]

While the soldiers struck out among the thickets and fields in search of a bit of dry ground, Rosecrans and his staff made ready for the next day's operations. Orders were transmitted to Thomas, directing him to move Negley to Stewartsboro and Rousseau to Nolensville and to leave Walker on the Wilson Pike to cover the right flank of the army. Crittenden was instructed to advance on Stewart's Creek; should the enemy fall back on Murfreesboro, McCook and Thomas would join Crittenden in effecting a concentration there. Having heard nothing from the Right Wing during the day and fearing a clash with Hardee to be imminent near Triune, Rosecrans saddled up and, accompanied by a handful of staff offic-

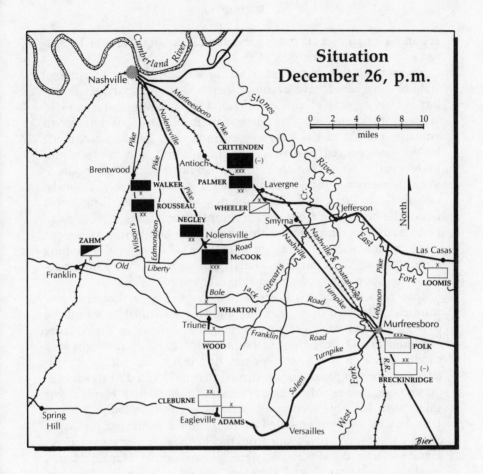

Situation
December 26, p.m.

Cumberland River

Nashville

Murfreesboro Pike

Stones

CRITTENDEN (−)

Brentwood

Nolensville Pike

Antioch

PALMER

Lavergne

WALKER

Pike

River

ROUSSEAU

WHEELER

Jefferson

Smyrna

ZAHM

NEGLEY

Nolensville

East

Las Casas

Franklin

Old

Liberty

Road

McCOOK

Nashville & Chattanooga

Fork

LOOMIS

Wilson's

Edmondson

Bole

Jack

Stewarts

Turnpike

Road

Lebanon Pike

Murfreesboro

WHARTON

Triune

Franklin

Road

POLK

WOOD

Turnpike

R.R.

(−)

Salem

BRECKINRIDGE

CLEBURNE

Eagleville   ADAMS

West Fork

Spring Hill

Versailles

Bier

0   2   4   6   8   10
miles

North

Map Symbols

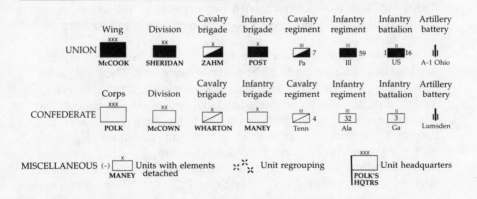

	Wing	Division	Cavalry brigade	Infantry brigade	Cavalry regiment	Infantry regiment	Infantry battalion	Artillery battery
UNION	McCOOK	SHERIDAN	ZAHM	POST	7 Pa	59 III	1 16 US	A-1 Ohio

	Corps	Division	Cavalry brigade	Infantry brigade	Cavalry regiment	Infantry regiment	Infantry battalion	Artillery battery
CONFEDERATE	POLK	McCOWN	WHARTON	MANEY	4 Tenn	32 Ala	3 Ga	Lumsden

MISCELLANEOUS (−) MANEY Units with elements detached   Unit regrouping   POLK'S HQTRS Unit headquarters

ers and a small escort, rode from his field headquarters at Hamilton's Church in search of McCook.

It was a decision as rash as it was unwarranted—an exchange of staff officers could have accomplished as much at far less risk—but it was typical of the emotional Ohioan. War correspondent William Bickham, who traveled with Rosecrans, has left us an amusing picture of the general's evening ride. Heading southeast by way of "rugged narrow lanes and gloomy forests, upon unknown paths, which but an hour ago had rattled under the hoofs of Rebel horsemen," the small party soon found themselves unmistakably lost. Rosecrans dismounted at a nearby dwelling (most likely the home of a Confederate sympathizer) to beg directions to Nolensville; he continued in this manner for some time, occasionally stopping at farmhouses for directions while generally groping blindly through the darkness. Finally, more by chance than by design, his troop emerged onto a ridge above Nolensville.

Rosecrans spurred his horse across the valley, making his way through a "tangled mass of mules and wagons" until he found the two roadmaster cars, drawn together, that served as Right Wing headquarters. On the floor of one of these cars, by the light of a candle stuck in a bayonet socket, Rosecrans and McCook conferred. Although prisoners confirmed that only Wood's brigade was present at Triune, McCook expressed concern that Hardee was there with his entire corps. Rosecrans shared McCook's conviction, but he was not troubled by it. Rather, he directed his Right Wing commander to advance on the town at daylight and press Hardee. Three contingencies were allowed for: If Hardee offered battle, were defeated, and retreated toward Shelbyville, McCook would pursue with one division, sending the remaining two on to Murfreesboro; should Hardee retreat on Shelbyville without a fight, McCook would pursue with two divisions; and, in the event Hardee fell back on Murfreesboro, McCook would follow with his entire command.

McCook acknowledged the instructions, and Rosecrans started back to headquarters. Again the party became lost. They rode aimlessly for an hour until the trail on which they were traveling ended abruptly at a fence along the edge of a wood. Rosecrans lost his temper. Jumping his horse over the fence, he galloped into the forest. A few staff officers rode after him, the remainder elected to stay on the trails. Fortune smiled on the Ohioan. After spending fourteen hours in the saddle, climaxed by his night ride, Rosecrans arrived safely at Hamilton's Church at 1:00 A.M. Those members of his staff who had stayed on the trails stumbled into camp two hours later.[8]

Hampered by incomplete intelligence, Bragg too passed an exasperating night. His cavalry had been unable to develop fully the nature of the Federal advance during the day; not until 2:00 P.M. did Wheeler report Crittenden's advance along the Murfreesboro Pike and McCook's movement on the Nolensville Pike to Bragg. Even then, he said only that Wharton and he were warmly engaging the columns. Sometime later, the Stewart's Creek telegraph operator confirmed Wheeler's dispatch, wiring that he could hear small-arms fire from the direction of Lavergne and cannonading from the direction of Nolensville. It was well after dark before Wheeler was able to gather from prisoners' statements that the Federal army was engaged in a general forward movement. This information was not received at army headquarters until 9:30 P.M.

Bragg's exasperation with his mounted arm would continue throughout the campaign. Deprived of his finest cavalry lieutenants, Forrest and Morgan, and their veteran troopers, Bragg was left with a young, inexperienced brigadier general and three understrength brigades. It is intriguing to speculate on the havoc Bragg could have wrought on the advancing Federal columns had he had his full complement of cavalry.

Bragg was surprised and troubled by the swiftness of the Federal advance. Crittenden, outside Lavergne, was eight miles nearer Murfreesboro than Hardee, twenty-four miles away via the Salem Pike. Should McCook succeed in taking Triune, his column would be only seventeen miles away. If Hardee were withdrawn to Murfreesboro by way of the Salem Pike, Federal cavalry would be able to interdict his marching columns via two high-quality country roads that ran perpendicular to the Salem Pike while McCook's infantry came up in support.

Despite the obvious need for action, Bragg was reluctant to order a concentration at Murfreesboro until the objective of the approaching Federals had been ascertained. Fairly sure, however, that the principal threat lay west of Stones River, Bragg issued orders at midnight directing McCown to march at once from Readyville to Murfreesboro. As the success of a concentration at Murfreesboro, should it appear necessary, would depend largely on the ability of the cavalry to conduct an effective delay, Bragg next summoned Wheeler to headquarters. He pointedly asked his chief of cavalry how long he could hold the enemy on the roads. Four days, replied Wheeler. His fears calmed, Bragg wired Hardee to be prepared to abandon Eagleville and march to Murfreesboro at a moment's notice.[9]

Hardee also was anxious for information regarding Rosecrans's dispositions and intentions. To obtain it, he sent Major W. D. Pickett of his staff forward to reconnoiter the Federal camp near Nolensville. Pickett rode to the outpost of the Eighth Texas Cavalry, then on picket duty, where he was joined by its commander, Colonel Tom Harrison. Together, they crept to within 150 yards of the Union camp. Perched on a ridge, Pickett and Harrison could see the brightly burning campfires of several divisions of infantry shimmering the length of the valley. It was enough to convince them that a general advance of the Army of the Cumberland had begun. Pickett briefed Hardee, who passed the information on to Bragg at 4:00 A.M., adding that—although he believed the Federal objective to be Shelbyville—he was prepared to march to Murfreesboro, should Bragg so direct.

Despite Hardee's uncertainty regarding McCook's objective, his telegram convinced Bragg that the time had come for a concentration at Murfreesboro. Movement orders were issued, and Bragg awaited the arrival of his scattered units.

McCown was already across Hickory Creek; his men would enter Murfreesboro at 9:00 A.M. after a grueling night march. It would take Hardee considerably longer. Leaving Wood at Triune with Wharton's cavalry to contest McCook's advance and protect his flank, Pat Cleburne had his division on the road before dawn; nevertheless, his men would spend the entire day slogging along the Salem Pike, turned to mire by the constant rainfall.[10]

Although Cleburne would complain later in his after-action report of the "cold, drenching rain" that slowed his rate of march to a crawl, the miserable weather in reality was a godsend to the Confederates: the same storm front that brought cooler temperatures and rain was preceded by a dense blanket of early morning fog that limited visibility to less than 150 yards and hampered the Federal advance. Observing the sky that morning, Rosecrans remarked: "Not much progress today, I fear."

McCook thought otherwise. The Right Wing commander decided to send Johnson's division forward with the expectation that the fog would soon lift. He was disappointed. After marching two miles, his infantry encountered light resistance; in the mist, confused skirmishers fired into their cavalry screen, toppling several members of the Third Indiana Cavalry before McCook called a halt.

Wood and Wharton, meanwhile, reformed their lines under the cover of the fog. Fearing that a rapid Union advance after the fog lifted would overwhelm his skirmish line, Wood called back the Forty-fifth Mississippi and Darden's battery of light artillery from their exposed position one and a half miles north of Triune to the south bank of Nelson's Creek. The remainder of the brigade he posted on a hill immediately south of town, while Wharton's troopers fanned out to protect the flanks and delay forward of the Forty-fifth Mississippi.

At 1:00 P.M. the fog lifted, and McCook resumed the advance. After firing a few rounds, Wharton's cavalry retired across the creek with the men of the Forty-fifth, who destroyed the bridge behind them. The Federals were right behind. As Battery B, First Ohio Artillery, shelled the Rebel positions across the creek with deadly accuracy, Richard Johnson shook out his lead units and prepared to attack. But Nature once again favored the Confederates: the rain that had earlier cut the fog now turned to sleet; moments later, a blistering wind came up and threw hail across the road, cutting visibility to a few feet. At McCook's command, the infantry halted to wait out the storm.

Taking stock of the strength of the Federal attackers and the feebleness of their own defenses, Wood and Wharton agreed that they stood little chance of holding on once McCook renewed his attack, and so decided to withdraw under cover of the storm. The artillery was sent to the rear, followed shortly by the infantry. Only the cavalry remained to contest the crossing.

A little before 4:00 P.M. the storm stopped as suddenly as it had begun, and the Union line of battle splashed across Nelson's Creek. Wharton's troopers delivered a parting volley, then galloped down the Eagleville Pike to join the infantry three miles north of Eagleville.

McCook chose not to pursue. It was getting dark. As night settled in and the temperature dropped, a fine sheet of ice began to form on the muddy pike, making the footing hazardous for the already exhausted Federals. Orders went out to Stanley and Johnson to bivouac a mile south of Triune. Sheridan, who had followed in support of Johnson during the day, made camp in Triune. Davis, meanwhile, stopped at the intersection of the Nolensville Pike and Bole Jack Road, a mile north of town.[11]

To the northwest, Thomas's divisions passed an uneventful day slogging over what to many must have seemed the worst roads in Tennessee. It took Negley nearly the entire afternoon to cover the five miles between Nolensville and Stewartsboro, and his men reached the latter town only at dusk, in time to bivouac for the night on Crittenden's right rear. Rousseau had an even more difficult time of it; with cannon and limbers frequently mired up to the hubs, his division did not enter Nolensville until nightfall.[12]

Out on the Murfreesboro Pike, at least, the weather proved more cooperative. Although a drenching rain fell throughout the day, the fog lifted early, allowing Crittenden to start shortly before noon. His objective for the day was the bridge over Stewart's Creek, which must be taken intact. The mission fell to Wood. Aware of the difficulty of the task, Crittenden hedged, dispatching the brigade of Colonel William Hazen down the Jefferson Pike to seize the bridge east of Smyrna as an alternate crossing site.

Marching through "densely wooded country, in a drenching rain storm," Wood's men entered Lavergne shortly after noon. They found the town in ruins, "a pitiful exhibition to the devastation of war," wrote Corporal Ebenezer Hannaford of the Sixth Ohio. "Half a dozen of the smaller houses still remained, blackened chimneys standing lone and desolate above gray beds of ashes—significant monuments of the folly and crime of rebellion—told the fate of the rest." Wood's men did not pause to reflect on the destruction, but pushed on beyond the town. They covered the five miles to Stewart's Creek so quickly that Wheeler's pickets on the north bank were thrown into confusion. Those on the right of the pike fell back hastily across the bridge, leaving it aflame behind them. Those on the left were less fortunate; trapped in the rear of Brigadier General Milo Hascall's brigade, the majority surrendered. Hascall's shirmishers, meanwhile, had come up to find the surface of the bridge ablaze. Joined by members of the Third Kentucky, they ran forward into Confederate fire. Under a hail of bullets they tossed the burning logs and debris into the water, and by their actions saved the structure. The importance of securing the bridge intact could not be overstated. As Wood later explained in his report, "it was a matter of cardinal importance to secure possession of the bridge, as its destruction would entail much difficulty and delay in crossing the stream and, perhaps, involve the necessity of constructing a new bridge."[13]

Hazen also accomplished his mission in a spectacular fashion. Before moving out, he placed ninety troopers of the Fourth Michigan Cavalry under Captain James Mix in advance of the infantry, with orders to spur their mounts at the first sight of the enemy and not to rein them until they had crossed the bridge. Mix obeyed Hazen's instructions to the letter. Three miles north of Stewart's Creek, he encountered resistance. His troopers charged, the Confederates fled, and a "steeplechase was made of the whole affair." Captain Mix drove the panicked Rebels across the bridge and held it until Hazen arrived with the infantry. There the brigade camped for the night.

This day, on the Jefferson Pike, it was clearly the Union cavalry that gave a better account of itself. Indeed, Wheeler's cavalry had been hurled into precipitate retreat all along the line. Now, as night fell, they regrouped south of Stewart's Creek with Maney's infantry, a mere ten miles from Murfreesboro.[14]

Wheeler's poor performance only added to the anxiety and uncertainty at army headquarters. Wiring Johnston that night, Bragg could say only that Rosecrans was advancing on him in great strength and that all available troops should be sped to the Army of Tennessee to oppose him. With his subordinates, however, Bragg displayed more confidence. In a letter to Cheatham and Withers, he expressed his belief that Rosecrans's objective was Murfreesboro. In truth, Bragg could ill afford to think otherwise, having by now committed his army to a defense along Stones River. As the sun set on 27 December, all Confederate units except those detailed to delay the Federal advance were at Murfreesboro, awaiting further orders. They came at 9:00 P.M., in the following memorandum for general and staff officers:

1st. The line of battle will be in front of Murfreesborough; half of the army, left wing, in front of Stone's River; right wing in rear of river.

2d. Polk's corps will form left wing; Hardee's corps, right wing.

3d. Wither's division will form first line in Polk's corps; Cheatham's, the second line. Breckinridge's division forms first line Hardee's corps; Cleburne's division, second line Hardee's corps.

4th. McCown's division to form reserve, opposite center, on high ground, in rear of Cheatham's present quarters.

5th. Jackson's brigade reserve, to the right flank, to report to Lieutenant-General Hardee.

6th. Two lines to be formed from 800 to 1,000 yards apart, according to the ground.

7th. Chiefs of artillery to pay special attention to posting of batteries, and supervise their work, seeing they do not causelessly waste their ammunition.

8th. Cavalry to fall back gradually before enemy, reporting by couriers every hour. When near our lines, Wheeler will move to the right and Wharton to the left, to cover and protect our flanks and report movements of enemy; Pegram to fall to the rear, and report to commanding general as a reserve.

9th. To-night, if the enemy has gained his position in our front ready for action, Wheeler and Wharton, with their whole commands, will make a night march to the right and left, turn the enemy's flank, gain his rear, and vigorously assail his trains and rear guard, blocking the roads and impeding his movements every way, holding themselves ready to assail his retreating forces.

10th. All quartermasters, commissaries, and ordnance officers will remain at their proper posts, discharging their appropriate duties. Supplies and baggage should be ready, packed for a move forward or backward as the results of the day may require, and the trains should be in position, out of danger, teamsters all present, and quartermasters in charge.

11th. Should we be compelled to retire, Polk's corps will move on Shelbyville and Hardee's on Manchester pike; trains in front; cavalry in rear.

Braxton Bragg,
General Commanding.[15]

Criticism of Bragg's selection of the line of defense came almost immediately. Hardee, in particular, considered the ground peculiarly unsuited to the defense: "The open fields beyond town are fringed with dense cedar brakes, offering excellent shelter for approaching infantry, and are almost impervious to artillery. The country on every side is entirely open, and . . . accessible to the enemy." Moreover, Stones River could be crossed anywhere, he argued; at the usual fords, the water was no more than ankle deep. The greatest danger, however, lay not in the then low level of the river, but rather in how quickly it might swell to an "impassable torrent" during a violent rainstorm. If that occurred, Hardee warned, Bragg's two wings would be isolated from one another on opposite banks of the river.[16]

Hardee's assertions were well founded. Bragg did not know the ground his army was committed to defend. Six hundred yards beyond Breckinridge's assigned position lay a commanding prominence known locally as Wayne's Hill. From it, artillery batteries could enfilade Polk's right on the west bank of Stones River. Its importance to the Confederate defense should have been obvious; yet, inexplicably, Bragg made no provision for its occupation. Considering that Bragg had been in Murfreesboro since November, his failure to better acquaint himself with the terrain is inexcusable.

As the troops broke camp Sunday morning, 28 December, and marched out to their designated positions, other shortcomings in the line of battle became apparent, particularly on the east side of

Stones River. There Breckinridge deployed his division between the river and the Lebanon Pike, a mile and a half northwest of Murfreesboro. On the left, Brigadier General Roger Hanson placed his Orphan Brigade astride the river, along the edge of a wood of oak. When Chalmer's brigade settled into position along the west bank a short time later, it was discovered that a gap of some two hundred yards existed between Chalmer's right and Hanson's left, making mutual support difficult. Again, no steps were taken to correct the error in alignment.

Colonel J. B. Palmer's brigade fell in on Hanson's right, along the edge of a large, cultivated tract. Next came the brigade of Brigadier General William Preston, deployed across an open field, its right resting in a narrow belt of timber. Here the line was broken by a field three hundred yards wide, east of which Brigadier General Dan Adams lined up his regiments. Brigadier General John Jackson's independent command, temporarily assigned to Breckinridge, rested on high ground to the right of the Lebanon Pike, thus completing Hardee's first line of battle. Eight hundred yards to the rear, Pat Cleburne's division paralleled that of Breckinridge.

Withers's division was generally less exposed in its front-line position on the west bank, the exception being Chalmer's brigade, which occupied the high though largely open ground southeast of the Cowan house, near the intersection of the Nashville Turnpike (the name given the Murfreesboro Pike as it passed through town) and the Nashville and Chattanooga Railroad. To compensate for the absence of natural cover, Chalmers set his men to work constructing temporary breastworks. To Chalmers's left, Anderson—recently relegated to brigade command—also had his troops fortifying their wooded line. Colonel A. M. Manigault, whose command ran alternately through cedar brakes and across cultivated tracts, elected not to entrench. On its return from outpost duty that night, Colonel J. Q. Loomis's brigade was placed on Manigault's left, extending the Confederate line of battle to the Franklin road. Cheatham's division, meanwhile, did not break camp and move up until Monday morning.[17]

Bragg's movements went unchallenged throughout the day, thanks to Rosecrans's characteristic reluctance to conduct military operations on the Sabbath. In deciding that 28 December was to be a day of rest, Rosecrans was moved by operational as well as theological considerations: as the army was exhausted from two days' marching and skirmishing through rough country and over poor roads, it was deemed wiser to do battle later with a well-rested force than to press forward with a blown one. Whatever the reason, the men in the ranks appreciated the respite and the fine weather that greeted them that Sunday morning. Of Rosecrans's decision to remain in place, David Lathrop of the Fifty-ninth Illinois wrote: "All honor and praise to him for setting such a noble example"; of the weather, Corporal Hannaford of the Sixth Ohio observed: "A beautiful, bright, quiet Sabbath morning. Following two such days of amphibious life, how delightful it seemed."[18]

But two days of marching and skirmishing had not developed the situation sufficiently for Rosecrans to feel any degree of certainty regarding Bragg's intentions. The display of force along Stewart's Creek on the one hand suggested that Bragg might choose to make a stand along the south bank and contest the Federal advance on Murfreesboro; on the other hand, it would be to Bragg's advantage to defend nearer Shelbyville, thought Rosecrans, thereby drawing the Union army farther away from its base at Nashville and rendering its lines of supply and communication vulnerable to attack.

The first step to unraveling Bragg's plans was to find out where Hardee had gone the day before: If he had retired to Shelbyville, it could be assumed that Bragg was abandoning Murfreesboro in order to draw Rosecrans farther south; if he had marched to Murfreesboro, the Confederate line of battle might be expected to lie somewhere between that town and Stewart's Creek.

Rosecrans assigned the mission to McCook. (Rosecrans apparently was not averse to a Sabbath reconnaissance.) Later that morning, McCook dispatched Captain Horace Fisher with orders to take Willich's brigade, accompanied by a small cavalry escort, and trace the route of Hardee's withdrawal. Fisher promptly gathered twelve local farmers to serve as guides—assuring them that, should they lead Willich's Bluecoats into a trap, they would be shot and left by the roadside—and moved south along the Eagleville Pike, the cavalry having ridden ahead to pick up Confederate stragglers. By noon, Fisher was able to report that Hardee had been at College Grove with six brigades, but that he had left the day before. As the haversacks of captured stragglers contained only one day's cooked rations, and Shelbyville was two days away from Triune while Murfreesboro represented a march of just fifteen miles, Fisher surmised the latter town to be Hardee's destination. McCook agreed and informed Rosecrans accordingly.

Rosecrans prepared at once for battle along Stewart's Creek. Garesche wrote Stanley at 12:30 P.M. that there was "every prospect of the enemy's fighting a battle between Stewart's Creek and Murfreesboro." Minutes later, the commanding general and his staff cantered down the Murfreesboro Pike toward the front. They arrived to a flurry of activity. A mile to the south, across the creek, a Rebel battery was taking position atop a hill. Along the creek, for several hundred yards in either direction, the picket lines exchanged a desultory fire, making a great deal of noise but doing little real damage. After inspecting the ground, Rosecrans's staff agreed that the opposite bank of the creek was so well suited to the defense that the Confederates most certainly would resist any crossing. Satisfied, Rosecrans turned and rode back to Crittenden's headquarters. After instructing Crittenden to feel his way across Stewart's Creek in line of battle at dawn, Rosecrans returned to army headquarters at Lavergne. From there, he issued orders effecting a concentration of the army. Thomas was directed to send Rousseau from Nolensville to Stewart's Creek by nightfall—a march that passed without incident—and McCook to advance on Murfreesboro by way of the Franklin Pike Monday morning.

As darkness fell and the temperature plummeted, Crittenden's infantrymen lay down to rest on their arms, fully expecting that the morning would dawn red with bloodshed. The scattered firing ceased. All along the line, pickets emerged from the woods and—laying down their weapons by mutual consent—walked to the creek's edge for a chat with their opposites. Captain Thomas Wright of the Eighth Kentucky recalled one such exchange:

> Rebel — "What command does you-ens belong to?"
> Federal — "The Third Brigade."
> Rebel — "Who commands that ar brigade?"
> Federal — "Colonel Matthews. What is your command?"
> Rebel — "We ar Wheeler's; an' I believe you-ens are the fellers we fit at Dobbins' Ferry."
> Federal — "You bet we are! What did you think of us?"
> Rebel — "Darned good marksmen; but whar yer fellers tryin' to go ter?"
> Federal — "To Murfreesboro."
> Rebel — "Well, you-ens 'll find that ar a mighty bloody job, sho."

After an exchange of newspapers, the pickets retired to their posts, and all was still.[19]

CHAPTER SIX

THE LINES WERE FORMING

MONDAY, 29 December, dawned bright and chill. A hoarfrost blanketed the fields and turnpike as the infantry of the Left Wing fell anxiously into line. Their commander also was anxious. Expecting opposition, Crittenden directed the eight-gun battery of Lieutenant Charles Parsons to disperse the Rebel pickets across the creek. At 10:00 A.M., after a brief barrage, the Bluecoats splashed into the icy, waist-deep waters of Stewart's Creek, prepared to meet Confederates on the opposite bank.

To their relief, the Yankees found only a corporal's guard of cavalry pickets as they climbed the far bank. Maney had withdrawn his infantry to Murfreesboro under the cover of darkness. Sweeping the startled pickets aside, Crittenden's infantry pushed forward in line of battle "across the fields, over fences, through thickets, and woods, and jungles of woods innumerable." Wheeler's troopers resisted the onslaught as best they could, but they were hopelessly outnumbered. Wheeler could only report at 11:00 A.M. that Crittenden was advancing "very handsomely" near the six-mile post on the Nashville Turnpike, just north of Overall's Creek. A few minutes later, he ordered Pegram and Wharton to fall back with him to Murfreesboro. Left with the field to themselves, the Union infantry waded Overall Creek handily and continued southeast along either side of the Nashville Turnpike.

At 3:00 P.M., with the sun already low and the chill of the winter's eve setting in, the lead elements of the Left Wing caught sight of Breckinridge's Butternuts drawn up on the east bank of Stones River. As neither Palmer nor Wood, the senior officers present, cared to be responsible for bringing about a major battle, they halted their divisions and awaited the arrival of Crittenden.

Palmer and Wood were within two miles of Murfreesboro. Wood's division, in double line of battle, lay on the east side of the turnpike. Hascall's brigade occupied the extreme left, its left resting on Stones River. Next came Harker. His left regiments lay in an open field, those of his right rested in a small wood known locally as the Round Forest, through which passed the Nashville and Chattanooga Railroad. Wagner was astride the turnpike. West of the turnpike, Cruft's brigade of Palmer's division connected with Wagner's right. A fallow field sloped gently upward beyond Cruft's front to the Cowan farm. A few hundred yards beyond the farm, on another elevation, Chalmers's Confederate brigade waited quietly and apparently undetected behind their breastworks. Meanwhile, Grose had come up and formed in a dense cedar brake on Cruft's right, near McFadden's Lane. Negley's division struggled forward through the same cedar brake in the gathering twilight; by nightfall, Negley would join with Grose on his right, their lines connecting obliquely and facing southward into the impenetrable gloom of the forest.[1]

The exhausted Federals welcomed the halt. "Few of us suspected the truth," recalled Corporal Hannaford of the Sixth Ohio, as he and his comrades collapsed on their arms and waited. "We were content to rest here for the night; and while the twilight faded away our mess sat around its bivouac fire discussing the incidents of the day, the probabilities of the morrow, and our suppers."

But the day was not quite over. At dusk, just as Crittenden reached the front, orders came from army headquarters directing the immediate occupation of Murfreesboro with one division. A startled Crittenden soon learned the reason for the order. Two hours earlier, while advancing into position, Palmer had sent word to Rosecrans that the enemy was retreating and that he was in sight of the town. How Palmer mistook the withdrawal of Wheeler's troopers for a general Confederate retreat is a mystery; nevertheless, Palmer filed the report at 3:00 P.M. and, based on this ludicrous assumption, Rosecrans ordered the occupation of Murfreesboro.

Rosecrans's acceptance of Palmer's interpretation of events is understandable. The forty-five-year-old Illinoisan was, generally speaking, one of his more able lieutenants. Although he owed his original commission as colonel of the Fourteenth Illinois Infantry to his political influence within the Prairie State, where he had been instrumental in founding the Illinois Republican Party in 1856, Palmer, unlike most politicians turned soldiers, proved to be a capable fighter whose subsequent promotions were earned by solid performance. Handsome and engaging, Palmer would enjoy a successful political career as governor of Illinois and later as a senator before being defeated in a bid for the presidency on the Gold Democrat ticket in 1896.

Now, at sunset along the west bank of Stones River, he realized the inadvisability of his earlier report. Supported by Wood, Palmer remonstrated with Crittenden against a twilight advance. Both division commanders stressed the hazards involved in a movement after dark over unknown ground toward an enemy of unknown strength. The captious Wood, a thirty-nine-year-old West Point graduate considered by many to be the "military brains" and "military character" behind Crittenden, suggested that his commander might simply ignore the order, as if it had never been delivered. Small of stature and dark-complected, Wood was accustomed to having his way with Crittenden. This time, however, he failed. Crittenden insisted that the order be obeyed. Wood and Palmer wheeled their horses and returned to their commands to make ready. After setting their divisions in motion, they again rode to their commander in a final effort to have the order rescinded. Perhaps Crittenden, watching his infantry disappear into the dark toward the river, was beginning to have second thoughts. Although Crittenden refused to countermand Rosecrans's directive, he agreed to suspend the movement for an hour, while he sought out the commanding general.[2]

At that moment, Rosecrans arrived on the field. He immediately approved Crittenden's suspension of the operation, much to the relief of Wood and Palmer.

But scattered fire from across Stones River indicated that contact already had been made. The engaged units belonged to the brigade of twenty-seven-year-old Colonel Charles Harker. Orphaned as a child, the young Harker became, at age twelve, a clerk in the Mullica Hill, New Jersey, store of N. T. Stratton, a two-term member of Congress who rewarded his employee with an appointment to West Point. Now, just eight years after graduation, the youthful colonel was leading the advance across Stones River. Throwing out a strong skirmish line of two companies per regiment, he crossed the Fifty-first Indiana, Thirteenth Michigan, and Seventy-third Indiana simultaneously at the ford northwest of Wayne's Hill. It was 7:00 P.M., well after nightfall. Flashes of rifle fire greeted Harker's skirmishers as they emerged shivering from the river. They returned fire, not knowing at what or how many they were shooting. The exchange was brisk, but Harker had encountered only the enemy picket line posted along a fence near the bank. After a few minutes the outnumbered Rebels fell back into a cornfield at the base of Wayne's Hill. Harker's skirmishers pursued, only to be halted by fire from infantry concealed among the rows of standing corn. With the approach of Harker's main line, the Confederates fled up the hill to the protection of Cobb's Kentucky battery. Observing the Rebel retreat, Colonel Abel Streight unleashed his Fifty-first Indiana on the double-quick. Streight's Hoosiers climbed undetected in the darkness to within a few yards of the guns and delivered a volley of rifle fire into the unsuspecting artillerymen. For a moment it appeared that the battery would be lost, and with it a key elevation. Cobb rallied his men, but the weight of numbers was beginning to tell. At that moment, Colonel Robert Hunt arrived with his Ninth Kentucky and the Forty-first Alabama, and the balance suddenly shifted. The Fifty-first Indiana, finding itself now outnumbered, stumbled back down the hill and into the cornfield, where it met the Seventy-third Indiana and the Thirteenth Michigan. Here all three regiments remained, concealed among the cornstalks, until their recall at 10:00 P.M.[3]

As they recrossed Stones River, Harker's weary soldiers were unaware how close they had come to taking Wayne's Hill and—had they been supported by the rest of their division—rendering the entire Rebel line on the east side untenable, perhaps altering the shape of the battle to come. Only the initiative of Hunt saved this key hill for the Confederates.[4]

In a larger sense, however, it was Rosecrans, not Bragg, who occupied the more precarious position. Nightfall found only a third of the Army of the Cumberland on the field, opposed by the entire Confederate army. Southwest of Negley's position, between the Wilkinson Turnpike and the Franklin road, Confederate cavalry moved with impunity. McCook's wing, which was to have joined Negley on his right, was at that moment bivouacked astride the Wilkinson Turnpike, on the west bank of Overall Creek. A mile and a half of dense cedar thickets and a creek lay between the Right Wing and the Center.

Not only had McCook failed to reach his objective, but he had been inexcusably silent all day. Neither Rosecrans nor Thomas knew anything of his activities or whereabouts until late afternoon. Although he neglected to tell anyone, McCook had broken camp and taken up the march on the Bole Jack Road shortly after daylight as ordered, Davis's division leading. Zahm's cavalry brigade divided into three parallel columns and screened the infantry. The Third Ohio, in the center, ran into the enemy first, striking Wharton's picket line after just five miles. Minutes later the Fourth and First Ohio, screening the right and left respectively, also ran into Rebel outposts. A spirited, running skirmish continued for three hours and two miles across the entire front. Finally, after launching a brief counterattack to upset the momentum of the Union advance, Wharton withdrew across Overall Creek and made no further effort to develop the strength of the Federals. Credit is due Zahm and his Ohioans who, by aggressively sweeping Wharton before them, prevented him from accurately reconnoitering the Union infantry as it arrived on the field. Bragg was thus unaware of the gap between the Right Wing and Center; had he known of it, he might have launched a decisive attack while the Federal wings were still separated and vulnerable to defeat in detail.

It was late afternoon before the infantry came up. Davis arrived first. While Woodruff's brigade stood guard at the bridge over Overall's Creek, the remainder of the division marched off to the right and bivouacked in line of battle. Sheridan arrived next and filed off to the left. Johnson reached the front at 8:00 P.M., and McCook placed him on Davis's right.

By his own admission, McCook reached the Wilkinson Crossroads with Davis at 4:25 P.M. Although about one hour of twilight remained, he took no further action. Rather, he told his division commanders to bivouac while he awaited orders from Rosecrans. They came an hour later. Aware of the vulnerability of his separated major commands, Rosecrans directed McCook to feel his way forward at once and to continue until he made contact with Negley. For reasons that remain unclear, McCook waited until 10:20 P.M. to acknowledge the order, and then he said only that cavalry had gone out in search of Negley's flank. When Zahm's troopers reported that they had been unable to find it, McCook allowed them to make camp on the old road to Nashville, near his headquarters, and made no further effort to comply with Rosecrans's instructions.[5]

As the night wore on, a cold north wind came up, chilling the men of both armies as it blew through the timber and across the open fields. With the rain-soaked ground their only bed, restless soldiers, too cold to sleep, struck out in search of wood. Cedar boughs, fence rails, underbrush—anything that would burn was gathered to feed the campfires. The Confederates, woefully short of blankets, suffered acutely.[6]

At army headquarters near the Nashville Turnpike, Bragg and his lieutenants prepared for the Union attack they believed would come at dawn, a belief born of incomplete intelligence. By midnight, the Confederate line of battle was essentially complete. That morning, after drawing three days' rations and sending their wagons to the rear, the men of Cheatham's division had taken position behind Withers. Brigadier General Daniel Donelson led his brigade of Tennesseans across the Wilkinson Turnpike bridge to the west side of Stones River. There they bivouacked, some four thousand feet behind Chalmers. Brigadier General Alexander Stewart formed his command on Donelson's left, following a sharp westward bend in the river. West of Stewart's line the river again made a sharp turn, this time to the east. There Maney arrayed his three regiments. Colonel A. J. Vaughan deployed on Maney's left, completing Polk's second line, which now lay some five to eight hundred yards behind Withers. McCown remained with his division on the east bank as the army reserve.

Bragg had deployed his infantry so as to cover all approaches to Murfreesboro; he considered this precaution necessary until the "real point of attack should be developed." For a time during the day, it had appeared as though the attack would come along the Nashville Turnpike and the Lebanon road. Continuing its mediocre performance, Confederate cavalry had exaggerated the size of Hazen's column on the Jefferson Pike two days earlier, leading Bragg to conclude that a significant threat was developing from the direction of Jefferson. He continued to harbor these fears until the morning of 30 December, when it was discovered that Hazen had left the Jefferson Pike to rejoin Crittenden the day before. And while Bragg laid plans to meet this phantom threat to his right, Wharton sent word of McCook's very real appearance along Overall Creek. Now fearing an envelopment of his left should McCook cross the creek, Bragg committed his only reserve, the forty-four-hundred-man division of John P. McCown, to extend that flank across the Franklin road. With his entire army now positioned forward, Bragg went to bed, convinced that he had done everything possible to prepare his command for battle.[7]

Meanwhile, some two and a half miles up the Nashville Turnpike in the dilapidated log cabin that was the forward headquarters of the Army of the Cumberland, it had become apparent to

Rosecrans that McCook had no intention of moving further that night. Exasperated by the delay, Rosecrans summoned his slothful lieutenant shortly after midnight. McCook received the order at 1:00 A.M. and, after groping through the darkness, arrived at headquarters at 3:30. Rosecrans repeated his instructions: McCook was to bring his left to rest on Negley's exposed right, extending his line southward, with his own right to rest on or near the Franklin road, facing east. A chastised McCook returned to his encampment, having promised to cross Overall's Creek at dawn.[8]

As was his custom in the field, Rosecrans rose early Tuesday morning, 30 December. Outside, his staff officers had constructed a makeshift annex to the log cabin headquarters consisting of a fire, a bench, and a canopy of rails with gum blankets overhead. Rosecrans walked over to the fire and sat down, while his staff officers went about their business at a respectful distance, some copying orders, others peering through field glasses in the hope of catching a glimpse of the enemy, a little more than a mile away down the Nashville Turnpike. If they really had expected to see much that morning they were disappointed, as the weather and terrain combined to render the Rebels invisible. From army headquarters the turnpike sloped gently downward, then upward as it neared the Round Forest. At the Round Forest it again dipped, blocking from view what lay beyond. Besides it had rained all night, so that a thick mist veiled the gathering, "obscuring vision and oppressing the senses." All this was of little concern to Rosecrans as he conferred with Crittenden by the fire, despite the interest of his staff in the matter. What occupied his mind at the moment was not the enemy to the southeast but rather the progress of McCook's infantry along Overall Creek.

Fortunately for McCook, Rosecrans was unaware of the Right Wing's lack of progress. Although his troops had been awakened at 3:00 A.M., McCook dallied, waiting until 9:30 to begin the advance. When the Right Wing finally did move, it was Sheridan who led the way. Screened by a regiment of cavalry, the Irishman's division crossed Overall's Creek in column, followed by Davis and Johnson. At first the Federals encountered only sporadic resistance from pickets ensconced in the cedars east of the bridge. But with each step deeper into the woods the opposition grew heavier until, by the time Sheridan reached the Gresham farm, the combined efforts of his lead regiments, the Twenty-second and Forty-second Illinois, were needed to dislodge the enemy. As artillery was now being brought to bear against his advance as well, McCook thought it prudent to halt and deploy Sheridan's division in line of battle, ready to resume the advance upon Davis's arrival.

McCook fed Davis's infantry into line on Sheridan's right as it came up. Davis conducted a left wheel, Sheridan swung Sill's brigade eastward, and the two divisions made contact near the Harding house. Leaving Johnson's division in reserve (less the brigade of Edward Kirk, which had been sent forward to extend Davis's right), McCook threw out a strong skirmish line and recommenced the advance at 2:00 P.M. Immediately the Federals came under fire from McCown's skirmishers, posted in a belt of timber to the southeast. Eager to gain cover, McCook's infantry crossed the open fields rapidly and in good order, only to face a new peril as they tried to pry the enemy from among the cedars and limestone outcrops. Sergeant Lewis Day of the One Hundred First Ohio likened the fighting to a "cat and mouse" game in which the defender had the advantage, as he generally caught sight of his opponent first. The outcome of such a contest, noted Day, "depended largely on nerve and dexterity after discovery."[9]

The men of the Twenty-first Illinois had an opportunity to demonstrate their nerve and dexterity, if not good judgment, as they pushed toward the Widow Smith house. While the remainder of their brigade halted two hundred yards short of the house, the Illinoisans kept on, seizing the six Napolean guns of Felix Robertson in a gallant rush. But it was a fleeting triumph. A sudden volley from McNair's front rank, concealed behind the split-rail fences near the Widow Smith house, drove the Twenty-first back across the field and into the woods.[10]

As the twilight melted into darkness an uneasy silence fell across the lines. Only seven hundred yards separated McCook's wing, now in position, from Withers's front line. North of the Wilkinson Turnpike, Negley's division, having clawed its way through cedar brakes dense even in winter and over outcrops the height of a man, was also up and fronted east, about the same distance from Cheatham. Rousseau arrived at 4:00. Having no place to insert him, Thomas ordered Rousseau to bivouac in a small wood near Rosecrans's headquarters.[11]

On the left, where Crittenden had moved into position the night before, the day passed quietly. His men had little to do but sit or stand in line in the face of a driving rain. James Barnes of the Eighty-sixth Indiana has left a moving portrayal of that dismal Tuesday, passed in "anxious suspense" as the Hoosiers "stood shivering in the lines" near Stones River. Holding their rifles away from the rain, Barnes and his comrades watched as all around them the familiar yet foreboding preparations for battle went on: "The orders were to be ready at a moment's notice. The lines were forming. Batteries were being placed into position. Dark columns stood noiseless in the rain. Hospitals were established in the rear, and the musicians and other non-combatants were detailed to bear the stretchers and attend the ambulances. Medical stores were unpacked and countless rolls of bandages placed at hand for use. Provision trains were brought up and rations issued."[12]

The anxiety was greater still down the Nashville Turnpike, where Bragg spent the day in the saddle, listening intently as the firing on his left grew louder, heralding the advance of McCook. In view of the relative quiet on the right, Bragg interpreted the Federal movement on his left as the prelude to a general attack in that sector. He was troubled. Terminating on the Franklin road, his left flank was in danger of being enveloped, should McCook choose to press his advantage. Consequently, he dispatched John McCown's division—his only real reserve—to this threatened part of the field with orders to extend the Confederate line below the Franklin road.[13]

As the afternoon wore on and the skirmishing to the south continued to grow in intensity, Bragg directed Hardee, then on the east bank of Stones River, to proceed at once to the left with Cleburne and his division and take charge of McCown's command as well. Hardee obeyed, but not before reminding Breckinridge that he alone was now responsible for the integrity of the army's right, to which Wayne's Hill was the key. The Kentuckian understood. He ordered the remainder of the Orphan Brigade to join their comrades of the Fourth Kentucky, who by their impetuosity had saved the hill the night before, and detailed one two-gun section from the Washington Artillery and another from Lumsden's battery to reinforce Cobb. Dan Adams's brigade came over from the extreme right to fill the gap created by Hanson's movement, and Preston and Palmer each shook out a company of skirmishers.[14]

Hardee arrived on the left at sundown to find McCown and Cheatham at odds over the nature of the ground to their front and how best to defend it. Perhaps because he had served longer with Cheatham, Hardee accepted his opinion and, after accompanying the two on a twilight inspection of the lines, ordered McCown to bring Brigadier General Evander McNair's brigade even with the left flank of Colonel J. Q. Loomis's Alabama-Louisiana brigade.

Fearful of provoking a night engagement should he advance McNair, McCown demurred, suggesting instead that Hardee position the brigade personally or, at the very least, that he instruct Cheatham to point out the desired location. Hardee agreed to the latter request, and the two division commanders rode forward into the gathering darkness. Cheatham showed McCown the spot— a small, triangular field bordered on the north and west by the Franklin road and on the south and east by a small cedar thicket. McCown rode to McNair and, after talking briefly, ordered him forward. The Arkansans picked their way two hundred yards through the timber to the opposite edge of the thicket. Here they halted, their right refused along the woodline. Although his right was not where Hardee and Cheatham had hoped it would be, McNair was in contact with Loomis and within three hundred yards of the Federal picket line. Although Bragg would censure McCown for holding back McNair's right, arguing that McCown wasted precious minutes the following morning in bringing up these units, Ector and McNair agreed with their division commander that any further movement that night most certainly would have brought about a general engagement.

McNair's Arkansans also objected to the movement, though for different reasons. In their new forward position, they were prohibited from kindling fires. Having left their blankets in the rear, the Arkansans suffered severely. But as in any army at any time, orders were made to be broken. "I got between two rocks, in the bushes, built me a fire, and in company with ten or twelve men, spread my blanket for sleep," recalled the semiliterate but eminently resourceful Washington Gammage.[15]

With McCown's position at least partially corrected, Hardee dispatched staff officers to fetch Cleburne, who had been waiting with his division at the ford near the Franklin road. It was midnight before his four brigades, stumbling through the darkness over unfamiliar ground, were up and in line. Even then Cleburne was not completely certain where he was: "As well as I could judge from the camp fires, my line was a prolongation to the left of Cheatham's line, and was four hundred or five hundred yards in rear of McCown's division."[16]

While Cleburne felt his way into position, Bragg conferred with his corps commanders. Having passed one tension-filled day awaiting a Federal attack that never came, Bragg resolved to seize the initiative. Assuming that Rosecrans had stripped his left to support McCook—from whom Bragg had expected the primary Union

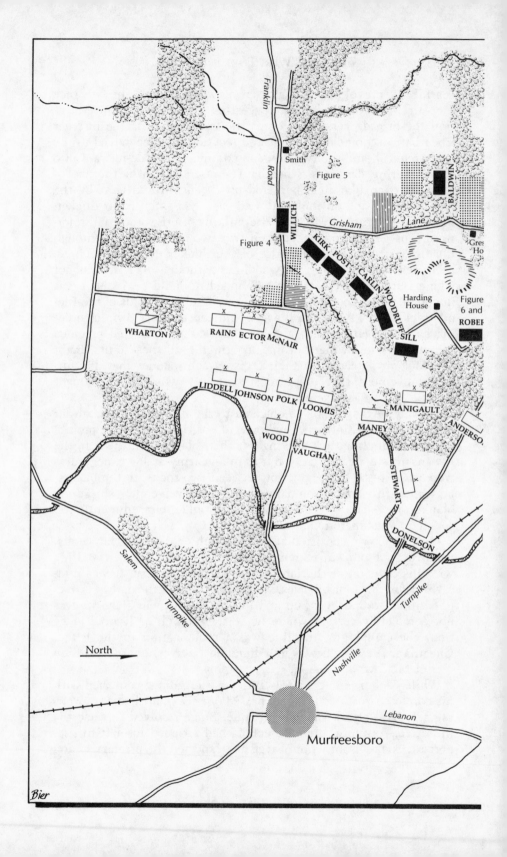

Franklin

Road

Smith

Figure 5

BALDWIN

Grisham   Lane

Gres
Ho

WILLICH

Figure 4

x

KIRK

POST

CARLIN

WOODRUFF

Harding
House

Figure
6 and

SILL

ROBER

x

WHARTON

x
RAINS

x
ECTOR

x
McNAIR

x
LIDDELL

x
JOHNSON

x
POLK

x
LOOMIS

MANIGAULT

ANDERSO

x
WOOD

MANEY

x
VAUGHAN

STEWART

x

DONELSON

Salem

Turnpike

Nashville

Turnpike

Lebanon

North

Murfreesboro

Bier

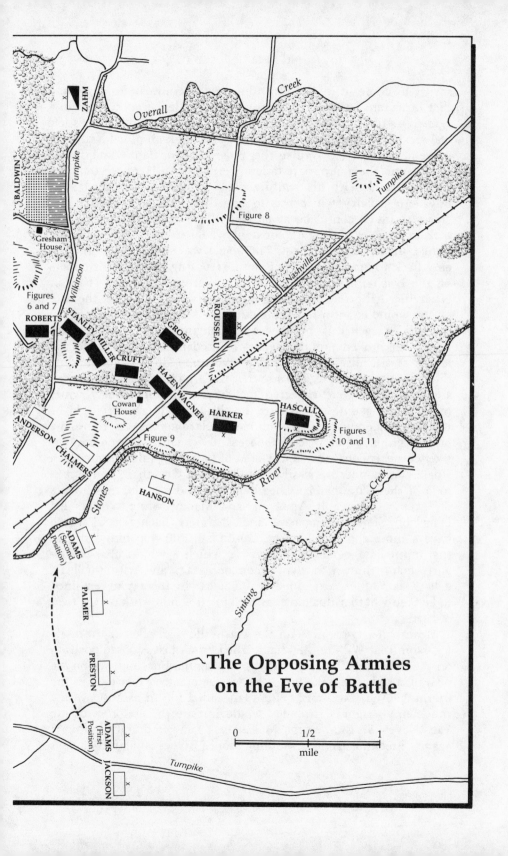

**The Opposing Armies
on the Eve of Battle**

ZAHM

BALDWIN

Overall   Creek

Turnpike

Figure 8   Turnpike

Gresham
House

Nashville

Figures
6 and 7

ROBERTS   STANLEY
MILLER   GROSE   ROUSSEAU

CRUFT

HAZEN   WAGNER

Cowan   HARKER   HASCALL
House

ANDERSON   Figure 9   Figures
10 and 11

CHALMERS

Stones   River   Creek

HANSON

ADAMS
(Second
Position)

Sinking

PALMER

PRESTON

ADAMS
(First
Position)   0   1/2   1

JACKSON   mile

Turnpike

thrust to come—the Army of Tennessee's commander suggested that Rosecrans be attacked along the Nashville Turnpike. Polk disagreed. As the transfer of McCown and Cleburne to the army's left had greatly extended that part of the line, Polk proposed a turning movement directed against the Federal right flank. Bragg concurred, and the appropriate orders were drafted. Hardee would begin the attack with his two divisions of infantry and Wharton's brigade of cavalry, which was to gain the Federal rear rapidly and create as much confusion as possible. Polk would take up the attack in turn, executing a "constant wheel to the right" with his right flank acting as a pivot. The object was simple: Push the enemy back to Stones River and, by interposing Wharton's troopers on the Nashville Turnpike, cut him off from his supply base at Nashville. All present—except perhaps Bragg—knew that the execution would be infinitely more difficult. A wheeling movement of the sort Bragg had in mind was challenging enough in open terrain; over broken ground laced with cedar thickets and cut by fences and farms it might well prove impossible. Compounding the difficulty was Bragg's desire that the attack be made in successive lines that were expected to advance simultaneously while maintaining a uniform spacing. Lastly, his lieutenants would be working under unfamiliar command relationships. As the same broken ground that made a successful wheeling movement unlikely also rendered the supervision of four front-line brigades by a single commander impossible, Withers and Cheatham had agreed to split their commands: Cheatham would direct the movements of Loomis, Manigault, Vaughan, and Maney, while Withers led Donelson, Stewart, Anderson, and Chalmers. Each general would have a more compact force to command, allowing him "to give that immediate, personal supervision which would insure the supports being thrown forward when necessary and with the least delay," as Withers explained it.[17] Logical in theory, it remained to be seen whether this novel arrangement would work on the field of battle.

Meanwhile, two miles up the Nashville Turnpike in the little log cabin that William Bickham called "the most exposed position on the battlefield," Rosecrans was putting the final touches on his own plan of battle. Like Bragg, he was determined to attack in the morning. And like Bragg's, his plan called for an assault against the enemy's right. Crittenden would initiate the action, crossing Van Cleve's division at the McFadden's Lane ford and sending it against Breckinridge. After fording Stones River just above Wayne's

Hill, Wood was to join the advancing Van Cleve on his right and assist him in driving the enemy onto Murfreesboro. This done, Wood's artillery would unlimber on Wayne's Hill and pour an enfilading fire into the Confederates posted across the river; meanwhile, Palmer and Thomas would press them from the west, sweeping them across Stones River and through Murfreesboro. While Crittenden and Thomas crushed the Confederate right and center, McCook was to occupy the best defensive positions he could find, refuse his right, and accept Bragg's attack; if none came, he was to engage the enemy to his front with a force sufficient to prevent its movement to other parts of the field.

His plan of battle formulated to his satisfaction, Rosecrans awaited the arrival of his lieutenants, whom he had summoned earlier. Thomas came first. After receiving his orders, he related to Rosecrans his belief that the enemy was preparing to attack McCook. Already concerned himself with the vulnerability of the Right Wing, Rosecrans sent a message to McCook at 6:00 P.M., directing him to build "large and extended" campfires beyond his right so as to give the impression of a large troop concentration. His business now completed, Thomas retired for the night. Crittenden, with whom Rosecrans had spoken at length during the afternoon, was "excused at the request of his chief of staff, who sent word that he was very much fatigued and was asleep." McCook rode up at 9:00, accompanied by Captain Gates Thruston, his ordnance officer, and General Stanley. Waiting outside, Stanley and Thruston listened intently to the conversation between Rosecrans and McCook. According to Thruston, Rosecrans articulated his desires methodically, underscoring the need for McCook to hold his ground for at least three hours.

"You know the ground; you have fought over it; you know its difficulties. Can you hold your present position for three hours?" Rosecrans was skeptical.

"Yes; I think I can," McCook answered.

"I don't like the facing so much to the east, but must confide that to you, who know the ground," added Rosecrans. "If you don't think your present the best position, change it. It is only necessary for you to make things sure."

With that the conference adjourned, and the three officers returned to the Right Wing.[18]

Alone now with his staff, Rosecrans reflected on his plans and composed a lofty exhortation to the army. Composed as a general order, it read, in part, as follows:

Soldiers, the eyes of the whole nation are upon you; the very fate of the nation may be said to hang on the issue of this day's battle. Be true, then, to yourselves, true to your own manly character and soldierly reputation, true to the love of your dear ones at home, whose prayers ascend to God this day for your success.

Be cool! I need not ask you to be brave. Keep ranks. Do not throw away your fire. Fire slowly, deliberately; above all, fire low, and be always sure of your aim. Close steadily in upon the enemy, and, when you get within charging distance, rush on him with the bayonet. Do this, and the victory will certainly be yours.

Rosecrans's general order never reached the men of Johnson's division, out on the far right of the Army of the Cumberland. Perhaps it was just as well, as they would never have a chance to execute it.[19]

The weather worsened as the night deepened. A northerly wind whipped up, chilling the moist air and whistling dismally through the trees. Rosecrans's Bluecoats, already soaked to the skin, wrapped themselves tighter in their equally wet blankets. An intrepid few started fires, playing a sort of cat-and-mouse game with their officers: "No sooner had the fires been started when they were discovered and an order immediately followed 'put out those fires.' Many of the men, however, did not propose to miss their coffee, so picked up burnt embers, held their cans over this, blowing the coal to keep it alive, they succeeded in boiling their much needed stimulant."[20]

Up and down the line, units prepared for battle. The thoroughness of a unit's preparations depended on the ability and concern of its commanding officer. On the left, Wood directed that three days' rations and an additional twenty rounds of ammunition be distributed to every man in the division. In the center, Thomas ordered Rousseau to break camp no later than 6:00 A.M.; he wanted the Kentuckian ready to move in behind Negley at a moment's notice.[21] But on the right, where the need for vigilance was the greatest, an air of indifference had taken hold. Perhaps it was their ignorance of the strength and dispositions of the Confederate infantry laying a mere three hundred yards away that paralyzed the generals of the Right Wing and prevented them from taking reasonable precautions, or perhaps it was their certainty that Crittenden's attack would eliminate any threat to their end of the line. Whatever the reason, there were indications of the whirlwind to come. That afternoon, Stanley had sent McCook a garrulous and apparently cooperative civilian, discovered near his home on the

Franklin road, who provided surprisingly accurate intelligence. "I was up to the enemy's line of battle twice yesterday and once this morning," he told McCook. "The right of Cheatham's division rests on the Wilkinson pike; Withers is on Cheatham's left, with his left resting on the Franklin road; Hardee's corps is entirely beyond that road, and his left extending toward the Salem pike." McCook sent the man to army headquarters and, now somewhat concerned for his extreme right, directed Johnson to deploy Willich's brigade beside Kirk's. But apart from this, McCook took no other action except to assemble his division commanders long enough to relay Rosecrans's plan of battle.

Ominous sounds drifted through the cedars and across the fields, warning all who cared to listen. Out on the picket line of Carlin's brigade, Sergeant Lewis Day of the One Hundred First Ohio heard troops and artillery pass by all night long. Day and his comrades relayed the information rearward. "To this day, it seems strange that no attention was given to this matter," Day later wrote. Others recalled similar experiences. Colonel Michael Gooding of the Twenty-second Indiana, in the second line of Post's brigade, claimed to have heard the murmur of voices from the Rebel positions. Even Johnson's chief surgeon, Solon Marks, deep in the rear at the division hospital along Overall Creek, distinctly heard the rumbling of moving artillery.[22]

The meaning of this was clear to at least one troop commander of the Right Wing. As the sound of marching troops continued unabated across the narrow valley to his front, Brigadier General Joshua Sill grew increasing restive until, at 2:00 A.M., his anxiety got the better of him and he turned his horse rearward in search of his division commander, West Point classmate Phil Sheridan. Sill found him asleep at his headquarters, the trunk of a large fallen tree, some distance behind Schaefer's brigade. Sheridan listened patiently as his "modest and courageous" subordinate conveyed his fear of a Confederate troop concentration against his right flank, then walked with him across the open field south of the Harding house and into the tangled forest where the Thirty-sixth Illinois and Twenty-fourth Wisconsin rested. They paused along the picket line to hear the unmistakable sounds of moving artillery and infantry, then, returning to their mounts, rode to McCook's headquarters near the Gresham house. The Right Wing commander was asleep on a bale of straw. Sheridan awoke him and, with Sill, proceeded to explain the threat as they perceived it. McCook dismissed their concerns on the grounds that Crittenden's early morning attack would put a swift end to any Confederate designs against the Union right.

Sheridan and Sill were not convinced. Back at division headquarters, the two sat on the fallen tree and continued to ponder their dilemma. Sill's agitation grew with each passing minute. To calm him, Sheridan directed the Fifteenth Missouri and Forty-fourth Illinois forward to reinforce his brigade. Steadied somewhat, Sill returned to his command to place his two newly acquired regiments in line. Sheridan watched him go, then quietly began walking from regiment to regiment, personally waking each commander and seeing that he had his men under arms long before daylight.[23]

Out on the extreme right the mood of indifference continued. Colonel William Gibson of the Thirty-ninth Indiana, acting on his own volition, sent forward a company-sized reconnaissance patrol at 3:00. They returned to report that they had neither seen nor heard anything. Meanwhile, Kirk had dispatched two staff officers, Captain C. P. Edsall and Lieutenant A. T. Baldwin, to check the brigade outposts. They also found only silence. The monotonous firing between the picket lines had subsided and now, at 4:00 A.M., "all the recent signs of activity in the enemy's camp were hushed. A death-like stillness prevailed in the cedars to our front." In less than three hours it would be shattered with a fury that none who survived would ever forget.[24]

CHAPTER SEVEN

BOYS, THIS IS FUN

MORNING came. The darkness melted into a cold, gray mist that dampened the air and depressed the senses. At five o'clock Johnson's division was quietly awakened, and the long blue line came slowly to life as sixty-two hundred drowsy, shivering infantrymen rose from the frozen ground to build their breakfast fires and boil their coffee. It was their first opportunity to evaluate their positions by daylight, and the men of Willich's brigade may have paused a moment to inspect the surrounding countryside. Perhaps what they saw comforted them. There was ample cover to be had, a clear field of fire to the front, and a trail known locally as Gresham Lane running to the rear, should the need arise for a hasty movement in that direction. Eight yards wide as it bisected Willich's line from north to south, Gresham Lane ended at the Franklin road, which in turn followed the trace of the Union line from east to west and was bordered by a wooden fence. On the west side of Gresham Lane, in the angle where the two roads met, lay an open wood three hundred thirty square yards. Surrounding it were cleared fields, the largest extending southward some twelve hundred yards.

More by chance than design, Willich's brigade was deployed so as to avail itself of the natural cover. In line behind the split-rail fence, fronting south, were the reserve companies of the Thirty-ninth and Thirty-second Indiana; the remainder of both regiments were on brigade picket duty seven hundred yards to the south. Next came the Forty-ninth Ohio. It lay within the wood, the regimental front some thirty yards north of the Franklin road. Formed in double column and closed in mass, the Eighty-ninth Illinois rested behind the Ohioans. Willich had placed his remaining units so as to protect the brigade flank: on the western edge of the wood, perpendicular to the Forty-ninth, was the Fifteenth Ohio; wedged between the Buckeye State regiments was Battery A, First Ohio, four of its six guns trained westward.

Arrayed along a narrow belt of timber on Willich's left were the four front-line regiments of Kirk's brigade. Their alignment was flawed. Only the Thirty-fourth Illinois, on the brigade right just north of the Franklin road, had a clear field of fire; the remaining three regiments of infantry—the Twenty-ninth and Thirtieth Indiana and Seventy-seventh Pennsylvania—found themselves locked within the dense cedar brake, their visibility restricted to the line of trees and underbrush to their immediate front. Why Kirk took no action to advance his line is perplexing. That it could be done without bringing on an engagement had already been demonstrated: Kirk's pickets had advanced to the glade's edge without encountering a single Rebel. What's more, Kirk had been ordered into position early in the afternoon the day before, leaving ample daylight for such adjustments. But Kirk, like his division and corps commanders, continued to display a singular lack of concern for preparedness, and the brigade remained as it had been.[1]

It was now half past five. Breakfast fires burned heartily. Huddled in small groups, the men sipped coffee and discussed the chances of battle being joined before the day's end. Officers handled their units as though they were a reserve posted safely in the rear, rather than a dangerously exposed army flank resting within seven hundred yards of the enemy. As the minutes passed and the silence remained unbroken, the sense of peril seems actually to have diminished. Unable to find water during the night, Captain Warren Edgarton of Battery E, First Ohio, released half a battery of horses five hundred yards to the rear at daylight to a recently discovered stream. At his campsite near the Gresham house, McCook enjoyed a leisurely shave. Lieutenant J. H. Woodward, continuing his informal inspection of the Federal right, encountered Willich at breakfast. Woodward dismounted to join him. He found the Prussion relaxed and jovial. "They are so quiet out there that I guess they are all no more here," was Willich's reply to a dispatch from Johnson reminding him to have his men up and at arms before daybreak. "His whole manner impressed me with the feeling that he had no apprehension of an attack upon his front," recalled Woodward.

Willich should have known better. At fifty-two he was among

the eldest and most experienced officers in the Army of the Cumberland. His military education had begun in 1822 when at the age of twelve the Koenigsberg, Prussia, native entered the academy at Potsdam; six years later he was commissioned a second lieutenant in the royal artillery. Willich's unabashedly republican sentiments assured the failure of his military career: thirteen years passed before his promotion to captain; his attempted resignation five years later met with a transfer to a lonely outpost in Pomerania. But the Prussian perservered. He continued submitting his resignation until he was at last court-martialed and discharged from the army. Joining the revolutionists, Willich rose to corps command before defeat at the battle of Candarn caused him to flee to Switzerland. In 1853 Willich arrived penniless on the eastern shore of the United States; within five years he had risen to editorship of a leading German language newspaper in Cincinnati. At the outbreak of the Civil War the indomitable Prussian joined the Ninth Ohio as a private. His talents were quickly recognized, and he was given a brigade command shortly after Shiloh.

Finishing his breakfast, Willich left Woodward and rode rearward to confer with Johnson. On his way he met Colonel William Gibson of the Forty-ninth Ohio. The two talked briefly. Willich remarked that he would be absent from the front, and that if anything were to occur beyond the picket line, the Thirty-ninth and Thirty-second Indiana's reserve companies should be advanced to its support. Gibson acknowledged the order, and Willich continued on his way.[2]

Out on the picket line all was quiet. Perched atop split-rail fences or reclining against cedars, the sentinels gazed absently into the twilight. And then, at 6:22 A.M., they saw it.

Emerging from the gray fog was a wall of Butternut: forty-four hundred men of McCown's division, mostly battle-hardened Texans and Arkansans arrayed in a long double line with the division of Pat Cleburne trailing five hundred yards to the rear.

Rising at the first hint of dawn, they had formed ranks quietly and without breakfast—or for that matter any sustenance at all, save a small but well-received ration of whiskey. "Be quiet—get your men in line—see that their guns are in order—let there be no talking or laughing," were the commands whispered along the ranks. All equipment except haversacks and canteens was shed. A nervous tension gripped the men as the final preparations were made. Two days of inactivity, of lying still in the cold and dampness, had taxed their patience to the limit. Any movement was welcome.

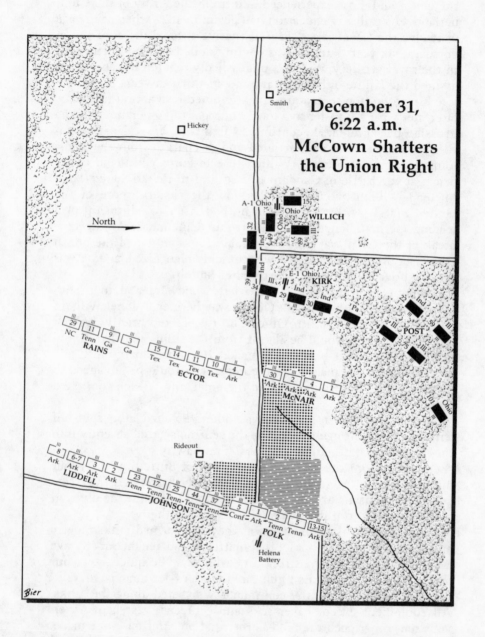

December 31,
6:22 a.m.
McCown Shatters
the Union Right

North

Smith

Hickey

A-1 Ohio

Ohio

Ohio

15

WILLICH

32

Ind

49

89

Ind

39

34

Ind

E-1 Ohio

Ind

Ind

29

30

77

Pa

KIRK

23

Ind

58

74

POST

75

Ohio

29

NC

11

Tenn

9

Ga

3

Ga

RAINS

15

Tex

14

Tex

11

Tex

10

Tex

4

Ark

ECTOR

30

Ark

2

Ark

4

Ark

1

Ark

McNAIR

8

Ark

6-7

Ark

3

Ark

2

Ark

23

Tenn

17

Tenn

25

Tenn

44

Tenn

37

Tenn

Conf

1

Ark

5

Tenn

5

Tenn

13-15

Ark

LIDDELL

JOHNSON

POLK

Rideout

Helena
Battery

Bier

"When the orders came that the command would move forward," recalled Colonel M. F. Locke of the Tenth Texas, "it was difficult to restrain the expression of joy . . . manifested by the men at the opportunity being presented upon an open field . . . of relieving ourselves from this unhappy condition." McNair brought forward his right-flank regiment one hundred fifty yards to correct his alignment. McCown ordered skirmishers shaken out fifty paces in advance of the main body. A final command not to fire until ordered was issued, and the Butternut ranks rose to their feet and surged forward.

On they came with deliberate and measured steps. Brigadier General James Rains's brigade occupied the left, the dismounted Texas cavalrymen of M. D. Ector held the center, and the dilatory McNair was on the right. A spattering of musketry finally rattled from the dazed Union picket line, startling Willich and Johnson, who had been talking at division headquarters, but drawing no response from the advancing Confederate wave, now within two hundred yards of Kirk's lines. After frantically calling back his horses from the rear, Edgarton opened on Ector with a volley of canister. With that the Texan ordered his men forward at the double quick, and the Union picket line disintegrated.

Among the first to fall was young John Gorgas of Company A, Thirty-fourth Illinois. Abandoning his post on the picket line at the first sign of the approaching Confederates, Gorgas was running rearward when struck in the hip by a minie ball. But his desire to escape the Rebels was greater than the pain, and he continued despite being hit by a second round that pierced the left side of his neck. A call from behind of "halt, you Yankee" caused him to look over his shoulder in time to catch the ball in the side that finally knocked him down. Miraculously, Gorgas survived.

Ector was now closing fast, and Edgarton's horses still had not returned. Faced with the imminent loss of his artillery, Kirk turned to Colonel Dodge and ordered him and his Thirty-fourth Illinois into the cornfield to meet the enemy and buy time for Edgarton. It was a gallant but fruitless gesture: the hopelessly outnumbered Thirty-fourth pushed forward just seventy-five yards before a volley from the Tenth Texas halted it. That was enough to convince Dodge—who had already lost his stomach for the obviously uneven fight—to order a withdrawal back to Edgarton's battery. His men reached it to find that "everything was confusion"; nevertheless, they made a stand around the guns. Five blueclad color-bearers fell before Locke's Texans finally seized the standard and the Thirty-fourth collapsed. Left without infantry support, the Ohio artillerymen could manage only one more volley of canister before the Confederates surged past the guns. The entire battery fell, but it was a prize dearly won: the Thirtieth Arkansas lost seven of ten company commanders in the initial advance and the highly regarded Colonel J. C. Burks was mortally wounded in the final rush. Hiding his wound, he continued at the head of his regiment until, weak from loss of blood, he tumbled from his mount and died.

Only five minutes had passed since the opening volley, yet everywhere Kirk's line was crumbling. Kirk himself was down, struck in the thigh by a minie ball. Captured as his brigade abandoned the field, the Illinois brigadier would be exchanged the following year and taken to his home in Sterling, where he would linger for seven months before dying from the effects of his wound.

Brigade command now passed to Colonel Dodge, but it was an empty honor. Dodge could only watch helplessly as McNair, moving by the left flank, slammed into the Thirtieth and Twenty-ninth Indiana. Neither regiment gave a good account of itself. Lieutenant Colonel Orin Hurd withdrew his men as soon as the picket line was hit, despite having lost only two men from his reserve companies. Captain John Lavender of the Fourth Arkansas vividly recalled the collapse of the Thirtieth Indiana: "The line . . . raised a yell and charged the Feds like a storm taking them completely by surprise. . . . Their coffee pots was on the fire frying their meal, guns in stacks." The Twenty-ninth fared little better. Although the Hoosiers tried to hold their ground and engage McNair, they found their field of fire—such as it was in the dense thicket—blocked by the regiment's own skirmishers. Not until McNair's infantry was within twenty yards were the men of the Twenty-ninth able to deliver a volley. Although well-directed, it produced "no visible effect." By this time Ector had gained their rear, and Dodge ordered a retreat.

Only the Seventy-seventh Pennsylvania remained on the field. Having moved laterally by the left flank in order to engage the Twenty-ninth and Thirtieth Indiana with superior firepower, McNair was able to bring only his right-flank regiment, the First Arkansas, to bear on the Pennsylvanians. In one of the morning's few equal contests, the Seventy-seventh bested the Arkansans, driving them through the cornfields and back onto the narrow stream west of the Widow Smith house. The Pennsylvanians continued their pursuit until, isolated by the retreat of the Thirtieth Indiana, they too withdrew, falling back one hundred fifty yards to join Post's brigade.[3]

With Kirk swept from the field, McCown turned his attention to Willich. The first indication Willich's infantrymen had of the impending onslaught was the sound of rapid firing from Kirk's front that came "while we were blowing our coffee cool enough to drink," recalled a veteran of the Fifteenth Ohio. Colonel Gibson, in temporary command of the brigade in Willich's absence, heard the firing too; glancing at his watch, he noted the hour as 6:25. He sent a staff officer after Willich and then prepared to receive the attack.

Gibson's troops were no more ready for battle than Kirk's had been. Although the Confederates were sweeping down on them from the southeast, four of the five Union regiments fronted southward, leaving their flanks exposed to an oblique attack. And like the cannoneers of Kirk's brigade, the men of Battery A, First Ohio, had unhitched the horses from their limbers; when the attack came, the drivers were grazing them in the field west of their position. But it was the disintegration of Kirk that really made the defeat of Willich inevitable: even with these liabilities of position and preparedness, Willich may have been able to offer a respectable challenge to McCown's Rebels had it not been for the refugees from Kirk's shattered regiments streaming through his lines and obscuring the fields of fire of his infantry.

The Thirty-ninth and Thirty-second Indiana, hit first, were swept from the field as much by the weight of Kirk's panicked soldiers as by the Confederates. On the picket line when Ector struck his regiment, Lieutenant Colonel Fielder Jones looked back to see his reserve companies melt away as the pursuing Texans interposed themselves between his pickets and the brigade main body. The pickets of the Thirty-second Indiana found themselves in a similar predicament as Lieutenant Colonel Frank Erdelmeyer was unable to draw them in or assemble his seven remaining companies before they too were stampeded.

The Forty-ninth Ohio collapsed next. The Ohioans' rifles were stacked and empty when Ector struck, and he swept them aside with ease while Rains gained their rear. "Oh such a sight I never want to see again," Private James Cole confessed to a friend after the battle. "Just think ... men running every way and no one knew where to go but to try and get out of danger."

While Ector's left rolled up the Forty-ninth Ohio, his right confronted the Eighty-ninth Illinois. Lieutenant Colonel Charles

Hotchkiss had had his men lie down while the shattered regiments passed through his ranks, and so was ready for the Confederates. Rising up, the soldiers of the Eighty-ninth delivered a volley that temporarily halted the Rebels, now within fifty yards. A spirited exchange followed before Hotchkiss—having no orders and seeing the brigade crumble around his regiment—reluctantly directed a withdrawal by the right flank.

Hotchkiss had received no orders because the brigade was without a commander: Gibson had been dismounted and isolated from his staff; Willich had returned from division headquarters only to fall captive—in his haste to rally his troops the excited Prussian had blundered into the midst of Ector's Texans.

Only the Fifteenth Ohio remained to put up a stand that was as comical as it was brief. Through a series of intricate maneuvers better suited to the parade ground, its commander tried to bring the regiment around to face the attacking Rebels. Having stepped a few paces forward, the men were attempting a countermarch when they were greeted by the stunned and bleeding survivors of the Forty-ninth Ohio. Ranks intermingled, the Confederates surged past their flanks, and the retreat began. "We stood to deliver our fire and say good morning, then took to our heels and ran," gibed Private Robert Stewart.[4]

McCown now had the field, along with eight guns—Edgarton's entire battery and two pieces from Battery A of the First Ohio— and some one thousand prisoners. His men did not halt, except perhaps to snatch a bit of hardtack or bacon from the still-burning breakfast fires or rummage the haversack of a fallen Yankee, but continued on after the rapidly scattering remnants of Johnson's front-line brigades.

There was little organization to the Federal retreat, and no unified command. Regiments—or more often bits of regiments— made brief stands behind fences or among farmhouses and outbuildings. The Fifteenth Ohio kept together until it ran into the picket fence along the eastern edge of the Smith farm. Here panic broke out. Trapped in an open field with a fence too high to scale readily to their front and Ector's Texans firing into their backs, the Ohioans tried frantically to pry apart the posts and rails. Here and there a gap was found, and the more fortunate slipped through, discarding rifles and haversacks in their haste, and ran toward Overall Creek. Others were less successful or less tenacious—Sergeant Alexis Cope claimed that over one hundred of his comrades surrendered rather than be shot in the back searching for a way through the fence. Cope was more persistent. Unable to get over or under the fence, he jogged south toward the gate and the enemy. Passing through the gate and into the Smith house unmolested, he emerged on the west side only to be struck by a minie ball that jarred his rifle from his grasp; without missing a stride he picked it up and continued running toward Overall Creek. Cope was lucky. Not only did he successfully run the gauntlet of pursuing Confederates, but the ball that had struck his arm was spent, leaving only a painful bruise beneath his heavy overcoat.

While Cope made good his escape through the Smith house, Robert Stewart crouched outside behind the chimney and defiantly fired a few shots at the Rebels. "I do not know that I hurt anybody," he admitted. "I am not sure that I shot at anybody in particular, but it was a good thing to do. It made me feel better." John Rennard of Company K also fought back, but with less success. While ramming home a charge from behind the fence he was struck in the thigh. "I threw my gun in one direction and the ramrod in another, spread my arms, a black curtain came before my eyes, and I fell on my side." Rennard awoke to find himself behind enemy lines.

Other regiments dissolved in much the same fashion as the Fifteenth Ohio. Colonel Erdelmeyer of the Thirty-second Indiana found himself separated from all but two hundred of his men during the retreat, and it was not until they reached Overall Creek that Erdelmeyer was able to rally even this remnant for a brief stand. Although his Eighty-ninth Illinois had begun its withdrawal in good order, after just four hundred yards Colonel Hotchkiss was left with only four companies; with these he retired across Overall Creek to join Erdelmeyer and his little band, as well as a few companies of the Forty-ninth and Fifteenth Ohio. Hotchkiss and Erdelmeyer were fortunate. Captain Alexander Dysart, the senior officer left standing in the Thirty-fourth Illinois, never had more than fifty men at his side the remainder of the day.[5]

As McCown's Southerners drove the survivors of Kirk's and Willich's brigades, the Confederate offensive showed its first sign of unraveling. Although Rosecrans would later censure these units for inclining "too far to the west" in their withdrawal, the route spontaneously chosen by the fleeing Federals actually assisted the Union defense by throwing McCown's brigades off course and slowing Cleburne, who unexpectedly found himself in the front line. Rains made the first error in judgment. Instead of inclining northward as part of the general right wheel prescribed by Bragg, he led his brigade westward toward Overall Creek in pursuit of Willich's Federals. Not until he reached the creek did Rains change direction. Ector also moved off toward Overall Creek after punching through the open wood at the angle of the Franklin road and Gresham Lane. The Texas brigadier aligned his brigade with Rains's right as the latter advanced northward along the east bank of the creek, only to discover that he had lost contact with McNair in the process.

Cleburne, meanwhile, had his supporting line in motion. As McCown's infantry disappeared into the twilight mist to join battle with Willich and Kirk, Cleburne's veterans stepped "short upon the right and full upon the left, so as to swing round my left as directed," in the words of their division commander. It was an uneven movement. Brigadier General St. John Liddell's Arkansans, as the left-flank brigade, found themselves literally running to maintain the right wheel while Bushrod Johnson and his Tennesseans, in the center, crossed the fields south of the Franklin road at a walk. On the right, Brigadier General Lucius Polk, the twenty-nine-year-old nephew of Bishop Polk, faced an equally exasperating and potentially more serious problem. Cheatham's left-flank units had not started concurrently with Polk's brigade as ordered, creating a gap that widened as the young brigadier advanced. Polk had risen rapidly through the ranks from private in the Yell Rifles—of which Pat Cleburne was once captain—to general, succeeding his fiery Irish mentor to brigade command just eighteen days before Stones River. His boyish good looks and easy manner—as "simple and guileless as a child"—quickly won for him the devotion of his troops. But Polk was inexperienced as a brigade commander. He was in a quandary. If the advance were continued, his right flank would become increasingly exposed; should he halt so as to keep with Cheatham, he would become hopelessly separated from his division. Fortunately, the decision was made for him. Noticing the inactivity on Cheatham's front, Hardee directed the brigade of S. A. M. Wood forward from its position in the divisional rear to extend the right. His flank secure, Polk resumed the advance.

Johnson and Liddell by this time had crossed the half-mile of open ground between their line of departure and the Franklin road, all the while assuming that their units were tucked safely behind McCown's frontline brigades. Even the rattle of small-arms fire to their front and exploding shells overhead did not unduly concern

Cleburne and his brigadiers. Unable to see through the twilight mist, they assumed the firing meant that McCown was in contact ahead of their division, that is, until men began dropping in the front ranks. Cleburne had struck Davis's division, although at that moment he knew only that "I was, in reality, the foremost line on this part of the field, and that McCown's line had unaccountably disappeared from my front." Cleburne shook out his skirmishers and elected to continue the right wheel.[6]

There is no evidence that Hardee attempted to correct the drift of McCown, or that he was even aware of it. In any event, it is doubtful that Hardee would have been able to restore the original two-wave alignment, had he tried. Cleburne was virtually on top of Davis before he discovered he was out in front, leaving no room to reinstate McCown in the front line. Had Cleburne disengaged and retired to await McCown's return, Davis would have been better prepared to meet the Confederate attack when it did come, and more of Johnson's division might have rallied. There is no doubt, however, that McCown's drift was a costly error. Had the original alignment been maintained, Sheridan would have been struck by an overwhelming and probably irresistible force, and the final drive against the Nashville Turnpike could have been made by a comparatively fresh second-line division, rather than by four fagged and disorganized brigades.

Like Cleburne, Davis found himself in an unexpected position. Now in command of what had become the right-flank division of the army, he used the delay between McCown's attack on Johnson and the appearance of Cleburne to withdraw Colonel P. Sidney Post's brigade to a more defensible position. The former Illinois attorney had begun the action on Kirk's left, his brigade fronting east in a thicket so dense that his men could not even see the fight between Kirk and McNair. His new position was markedly superior. All four regiments were on line, facing south toward the Franklin road a half mile away, and had unobstructed fields of fire. The Seventy-fourth and Seventy-fifth Illinois—both organized just three months earlier—steeled themselves from behind a split-rail fence at the timber's edge on the east side of Gresham Lane. The remainder of the brigade was drawn up in fallow fields to the west, the Fifth Wisconsin Artillery of Captain Oscar Pinney unlimbering between the Fifty-ninth Illinois and Twenty-second Indiana. Kirk's Seventy-seventh Pennsylvania, still intact, lined up on the brigade right. Colonel Philemon Baldwin's reserve brigade of Johnson's division rested four hundred yards to Post's right rear.

Scarcely had Post taken position and deployed his skirmishers when the brigade of Bushrod Johnson emerged from the open woods and cedar glades on either side of Gresham Lane. It was a disjointed movement. The Thirty-seventh and Forty-fourth Tennessee struggled slowly through narrow, overgrown pasture below the Seventy-fourth and Seventy-fifth Illinois, the Twenty-fifth Tennessee straddled the lane, and the Seventeenth and Twenty-third Tennessee stepped freely through cleared fields on the west side.

Captain Pinney watched impatiently behind his guns as the Rebels neared. Earlier that day, Post had had to restrain Pinney. In his enthusiasm to kill Confederates, the Wisconsin artilleryman had almost fired on friendly pickets, having mistaken them for McNair's Arkansans in the dark and tangled cedar glade. But now, with a clear field of fire, there was no mistaking the enemy. Pinney's Parrott guns roared, and Johnson's line recoiled. The Twenty-fifth Tennessee, astride the lane, was raked by the enfilading cannonade. Hard hit too was the Seventeenth Tennessee. Despite the loss of their commander, the Tennesseans pressed forward until a volley from the Fifty-ninth Illinois halted them a mere one hundred fifty yards short of Pinney's guns. Here they dropped to the ground to return the fire. Bushrod Johnson at once called upon Captain Putnam Darden and his Jefferson Flying Artillery to silence the Federal guns. Darden's Mississippians unlimbered their pieces amid a shower of canister from the Yankee Parrotts, and a twenty-minute artillery duel ensued. Although unable to fire canister for fear of striking the men of the Seventeenth, Darden's gunners eventually silenced their opponents with a steady barrage of shot and shell. As Pinney began limbering his pieces to prevent their capture, the Tennesseans, sensing a chance to seize a Yankee battery, rose to their feet and surged forward. The Twenty-second Indiana joined in the fray, and more Tennesseans went down—twelve company officers and over one hundred enlisted men in all. But this time the Seventeenth kept going. Returning the fire on the run, they dropped Federal artillery horses by the score. The Fifty-ninth Illinois now broke off fire as its commander, Captain Hendrick Paine—a martinet known as "buck and gag" after his preferred method of punishment—directed the regiment to save the battery. With upbraiding from Paine the Fifty-ninth successfully dragged five guns off the field.

The withdrawal of Pinney's guns spelled the end of Federal resistance to Johnson's attack on the west side of Gresham Lane. Left

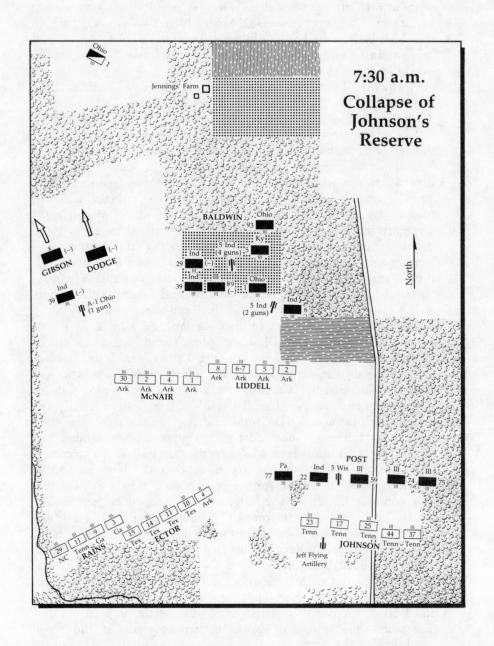

7:30 a.m.

Collapse of Johnson's Reserve

Jennings' Farm

North

Ohio 1

BALDWIN
Ohio 93
5 Ind (4 guns) Ky 5
Ind 29 (–)
Ind 39 89 (–) Ohio
GIBSON (–) DODGE (–)
Ind 39 (–)
A-1 Ohio (1 gun)
Ind 6
5 Ind (2 guns)

30 Ark 2 Ark 4 Ark 1 Ark 8 Ark 6-7 Ark 5 Ark 2 Ark
McNAIR LIDDELL

POST
77 Pa 22 Ind 5 Wis 59 74 75
ECTOR
4 Ark 10 Tex 11 Tex 14 Tex 15 Tex 3 Ga 9 Tenn 11 Tenn 29 NC
RAINS
23 Tenn 17 Tenn 25 Tenn 44 Tenn 37 Tenn
JOHNSON
Jeff Flying Artillery

without artillery support, the Twenty-second Indiana gave way in confusion. The Seventy-seventh Pennsylvania followed. Struck in the thigh by a minie ball while searching in vain for troops to pull his remaining gun, Captain Pinney fell as Johnson's Tennesseans overran his position.[7]

Meanwhile, Johnson's attack on the east side of Gresham Lane had stalled. The Twenty-fifth, Forty-fourth, and Thirty-seventh Tennessee had intermingled as they crowded into the narrow field. A lack of artillery support and the tenacity of the Yankee skirmishers compounded the Confederates' difficulties. So too did a breakdown in command as key officers fell. In some thirty minutes of bitter fighting the Thirty-seventh Tennessee lost its colonel and lieutenant-colonel, the Twenty-fifth its colonel and six company-grade officers, and the Forty-fourth its major and eight company-grade officers. Although they succeeded in closing the distance between themselves and the enemy, the Tennesseans were unable to carry the field until the retreat of the Fifty-ninth Illinois exposed the right flank of the defending Federals. Their position now untenable, the Seventy-fourth and Seventy-fifth Illinois at last retired into the cedars, and the Tennesseans pursued.[8]

While Johnson struggled to dislodge Post, St. John Liddell, advancing northward beyond Johnson's left, found himself locked in an equally desperate contest with the Union brigade of Colonel Philemon Baldwin. Here Liddell was joined by McNair, who had halted in the open fields east of Overall Creek after losing sight of Rains and Ector, only to find his flank balanced precariously between Baldwin on his right front and Post on his right rear. The North Carolinian at once fell back to protect his wounded and meet Liddell. Minutes later McCown rode up to find the two brigadiers locked in a passionate argument over the best method of attacking Baldwin. Not surprisingly, McCown sided with his brigade commander; citing the fatigue of his men, he begged Liddell to take up the advance in front of McNair. Liddell was of a different mind. Pointing out the strength of Baldwin's line, he suggested instead a combined effort by the two brigades attacking on line. McCown agreed, and the movement was made.

While the Confederate generals argued, Baldwin adjusted his regiments. Although his men—having watched as the attack on Kirk and Willich unfolded to their front—were better prepared for the impending onslaught than had been their comrades in the front-line brigades, the predawn call to arms nonetheless found the units badly scattered. "Before sunrise, the long roll beat, causing a great commotion throughout the regiment," recalled Levi Wagner of the First Ohio. "Some were still sound asleep, some were preparing their breakfast, others had gone . . . after water; so but a few were ready when ordered to fall into line."

The brigade formed initially along the southern edge of the large belt of timber below the Wilkinson Pike. The Fifth Kentucky, First Ohio, and Sixth Indiana constituted the first line; the Ninety-third Ohio and the Fifth Indiana Artillery lay in support. Here they remained until shortly after seven o'clock when Johnson, who had taken refuge behind his reserve brigade at the first sound of firing that morning, waved them forward to meet the approaching Confederates. In compliance with his division commander's orders, Baldwin threw the First Ohio across the cornfield to its southern edge. Here the Ohioans halted to take cover behind a rail fence and among the broken stalks and scattered limestone boulders. "And right here," Wagner noted, "if you were inclined to smile at the idea of a rail fence being any protection during a battle, if you could just for a few moments transport yourself to the opposite side of that fence and view the bullet holes those rails contain, you would see that a very light obstruction often saves a life." The Sixth Indiana came up next, settling in behind the fence to the left of the First Ohio. Seventy-five yards behind the Ohioans the Fifth Kentucky formed and the Ninety-third Ohio remained in the woods as the brigade reserve. Captain Peter Simonson split his battery. He placed his two light twelve-pounders seventy-five yards in advance of the Sixth Indiana and kept the remaining four Parrott guns in the cornfield behind the First Ohio.

Bits and pieces of the shattered brigades of Kirk and Willich paused in their rearward flight to extend Baldwin's line. Colonel Dodge gathered a handful of survivors from the Thirtieth Indiana along the fence to the right of the First Ohio; Major Joseph Collins, meanwhile, pieced together a fragment of his Twenty-ninth Indiana behind Dodge. Near the east bank of Overall Creek, Colonel Gibson prepared to make a stand with a corporal's guard of the Thirty-ninth Indiana and an artillery piece.[9]

It was 7:30 A.M. Crouched behind the split-rail fence, Baldwin's infantrymen watched as the Rebel line neared. It was a colorful spectacle. "The men were good-sized, healthy, and well clothed," noted one observer, "but without any attempt at uniformity in color or cut." Out in front was their commander, Brigadier General St. John Richardson Liddell, wildly waving his cap. This was the forty-seven-year-old Mississippian's third battle as a troop leader.

He had begun the war as a volunteer aide-de-camp to Hardee, later serving as confidential courier to General Albert Sidney Johnston before being rewarded with a brigade command at Corinth. Liddell's formal military education had been limited to one year at West Point, his resignation from the Military Academy presumably a result of his low class standing. But even four years of West Point pedantry would have left him unprepared for what he encountered here at Stones River. "Could I have dreamt that such scenes would await me," he later wrote his wife, "I would have fled."

On came the Arkansans. At one hundred fifty yards Simonson's guns and the First Ohio opened fire, and Liddell's left recoiled. At one hundred yards the Sixth Indiana released its first volley, and Liddell's right ground to a halt. Falling to the ground, the Arkansans traded volleys with their Yankee tormentors. Their plight was desperate. Liddell had struck the Union line unsupported, McNair having lagged behind on the left. To make matters worse, Lieutenant H. Shannon, Liddell's artillery commander, engaged Simonson with counterbattery fire that proved worse than ineffective: while trying to sight over their heads, Shannon's gunners killed or maimed several members of the Sixth and Seventh Arkansas.

As Liddell's regiments wavered, McNair belatedly attacked the patchwork lines of Dodge and Gibson. McNair's men ran the three hundred yards to the Federal positions, slamming into and knocking down the intervening split-rail fences without missing a stride. With seventy-five yards to go, the Confederates steeled themselves for the hand-to-hand combat all dreaded, yet expected. But bayonet fighting was a rarity in the Civil War. The destructive accuracy of the rifle usually decided the outcome of a charge before the attackers could close with the enemy. McNair's attack was no exception. The defenders scattered long before McNair's men reached their lines. That they did not give a better account of themselves is hardly surprising in view of the thrashing they had received an hour earlier. The men simply had lost the will to resist. Even the Seventy-ninth Illinois, coming up fresh from overnight guard duty in the rear, crumbled after its colonel was struck down in the initial Rebel volley. Only the gunners of the Fifth Indiana stood their ground, and all that was gained by their gallantry in the face of the Fourth Arkansas was the loss of two guns and twenty-four men.

Clearing the now abandoned rail fence, McNair's Arkansans pursued the Federals as they fled, individually or by squad, through the cotton field and into the woods along the Wilkinson Pike. Midway through the field McNair broke off the pursuit, turning his attention instead to the exposed right flank of the First Ohio.

Major Jacob Stafford and his Buckeye State volunteers were fighting splendidly, having held three Rebel regiments at bay for twenty minutes—"the fiercest engagement," claimed Levi Wagner, "for its short duration of any we experienced while in the service." But, with McNair rapidly gaining his rear, Stafford knew that to continue the fight would be to sacrifice his regiment. Accordingly, he barked out the order to retreat. In the din, it was not heard. He repeated the command. Again there was no response. Stafford screamed the command a third time in "such forcible language that to ignore it would have been an act of rashness." The Ohioans fell back into the right flank of the Fifth Kentucky as it attempted a change of front to the west. In the confusion, the First Ohio disintegrated.

The collapse of the First Ohio emboldened Liddell's Arkansans. Within minutes the men of the Second and Fifth Arkansas had risen to their feet and charged the Sixth Indiana. Left without support on the right and with the Seventeenth and Twenty-third Tennessee already along the fence to the left, the Sixth began leaking men rearward. Like Major Stafford of the First Ohio, Colonel Hagerman Tripp saw that further resistance was futile. With the Second and Fifth Arkansas now only twenty-five yards away and the Sixth and Seventh Arkansas already one hundred yards in his rear, he wisely ordered a withdrawal. The Fifth Kentucky, alone now in the cornfield, also bid a hasty retreat. Only the Ninety-third Ohio remained. Their commander, Colonel Charles Anderson, had thrice called for orders. None came. Finally in frustration he began deploying his skirmishers to cover the withdrawal of the units to his front. Just then Baldwin rode up and instructed him to fall back. Anderson complied, though he later made the strange complaint in his report that he had been denied a meaningful role in the battle.

As the Federals fled into and through the timber without a fight, some of Liddell's veterans momentarily forgot their hatred of the Northerners. John Berry of the Seventh Arkansas recalled a brief but poignant encounter with a wounded Federal at the wood's edge. Stopping to place a piece of wood under the Yankee's shattered leg, Berry remarked that he was "nearly dead for water." The grateful soldier offered Berry his canteen. He declined, reminding the Federal that he would need it for himself. But the soldier insisted, and so Berry took a few swallows of "the best water, it seemed, that I ever drank. If that man is still alive," Berry later wrote in *Confederate Veteran*, "I should like to hear from him."[10]

On the east side of Gresham Lane, meanwhile, Cleburne's remaining brigades encountered opposition as determined as that which Liddell and Johnson faced. Their two units moving together smartly into the cedar glade opposite the Widow Smith house, S. A. M. Wood and Lucius Polk entered the woods confident that McCown had swept the area clean. They were wrong. Lying undetected behind the outcrop to their front was the One Hundred First Ohio of Colonel William P. Carlin's brigade. The Ohioans waited patiently as the Confederates penetrated deeper into the cedar brake, a brake so dense that company commanders could not see the length of their lines. Then, with Wood's Butternuts just a few yards away, the One Hundred First opened fire. The stunned Confederates returned fire, but it's doubtful they hit anything, given the element of surprise and the natural cover enjoyed by the Federals. The struggle was brief. Having studied law in Murfreesboro before the war, Wood was familiar enough with the countryside to know the futility of continuing such an unequal contest deep in a cedar thicket and so ordered a cease-fire and withdrew his brigade.

Polk received an equally warm welcome on entering the cedars. He had advanced only seven hundred yards when the colonel of the Fifth Tennessee sent word that the brigade right was engaged. Polk was incredulous. "I did not believe at first that the enemy could be so near us," he later admitted, "having understood that we were supporting General McCown." Riding to the sound of the fighting, Polk was greeted with a volley that unhorsed his orderly and removed all doubt as to the source of the firing. The young brigadier quickly issued orders bringing his remaining regiments across the Franklin road and into a right wheel against Carlin's flank.

But the ten-year veteran of the regular service had forseen Polk's turning movement. Like Post moments earlier, Carlin seized the opportunity presented by the confusion in the Rebel ranks to withdraw his units to more tenable positions. The Twenty-first Illinois moved to cover the brigade right rear. Carlin pulled back the One Hundred First Ohio from its exposed position forty yards in advance of the brigade to a limestone outcrop alongside the Second Minnesota Artillery. The Fifteenth Wisconsin retired fifty yards to a rail fence and the Thirty-eighth Illinois lined up on its left.

Advancing a second time, Polk and Wood struck Carlin's new line together. The One Hundred First Ohio wavered first as Polk, moving on the Twenty-first Illinois, gained its rear. Carlin tried to compensate, but Colonel John Alexander of the Twenty-first declined his request to bring his regiment on line with the Ohioans, pointing out that he was just as hotly engaged.

Carlin began to despair. An ominous silence beyond his right told him Post had quit the field. Rather than see his brigade enveloped and destroyed piecemeal, Carlin decided to withdraw by the left flank. But before he could relay the order he was unhorsed, then struck by a Rebel bullet. Within minutes Carlin's entire staff was either killed, wounded, unhorsed, or engaged elsewhere, and he could only watch as the fighting raged about him and the retreat he had tried to direct began spontaneously.

With the stubborn Colonel Alexander down and severely wounded, the Twenty-first Illinois collapsed first. Next to go was the One Hundred First Ohio. Their withdrawal, begun in disorder, deteriorated into a route as first Colonel Stem, then Lieutenant Colonel Moses Wooster fell mortally wounded. "Of course, everything was perfect confusion," Private Jay Butler of Company B admitted after the battle in a letter home, "men and horses running in every direction and Rebels after us, firing upon us and yelling like Indians." In their haste to escape, the Ohioans abandoned to the Rebels property more highly prized than regimental colors. Recalled Butler: "When we got back as far as my knapsack, I picked it up and attempted to carry it and did so for a quarter of a mile when I found that I was getting behind and that the bullets came nearer and thicker, so I dropped it, took out my rubber blanket and went on my way feeling very down hearted at leaving so many good and useful articles to the enemy that were fast coming upon us, such as my sleeping cap, shirts, dressing case, nice, new stockings, etc."

The withdrawal of the Thirty-eighth Illinois minutes later left only Hans Heg and his Fifteenth Wisconsin to cover the brigade's retreat. Heg's was a regiment recruited largely from communities of German and Scandinavian immigrants in Wisconsin, Illinois, Iowa, and Minnesota. The moving force behind the organization of the unit in the fall of 1861, Heg reflected the hardihood and spirit of independence typical of its members. Leaving his native Norway to cross the Atlantic with his parents at age eleven, Heg was in California panning gold with the Forty-niners just nine years later. On receiving word of his father's death in 1851, Heg returned home to Wisconsin. The two years spent in the goldfields had apparently satisfied his wanderlust, as the young Norwegian settled down to farm, became active in state politics, and won election as the Wisconsin prison commissioner on the Republican ticket in 1859. His appearance and manners were typically Scandinavian: "Tall and straight, heavily bearded, strong and vigorous," Heg was of a "quiet demeanor, taciturn manner, and sternness." Drawing on these qualities here at Stones River, Heg kept his regiment intact long enough for the brigade to retire without the loss of a single artillery piece.

While the fighting raged on around him, Heg crouched behind a small tree and listened as ball after ball struck the opposite side. He returned to the spot after the battle to count five rounds imbedded in the trunk.

Finally the Fifteenth Wisconsin yielded, and the victorious Confederates surged over the split-rail fence in pursuit. Some found it impossible to contain their enthusiasm. None was more ecstatic than young William Matthews, a color-bearer in the First Arkansas for whom Stones River was his first battle. "Boys, this is fun," he yelled as the Arkansans chased the fleeing Yankees. "Stripes, don't be so quick," advised a veteran, "this is not over; you may get a ninety-day furlough yet."

Twenty minutes later, Matthews's exuberance turned to agony as a minie ball shattered his arm.[11]

Major General William Starke Rosecrans
(United States Army Military History Institute)

Major General Alexander McDowell McCook
(United States Army Military History Institute)

Major General George Henry Thomas
(United States Army Military History Institute)

Major General Thomas Leonidas Crittenden
(United States Army Military History Institute)

Brigadier General Philip Henry Sheridan
(United States Army Military History Institute)

General Braxton Bragg
(United States Army Military History Institute)

Lieutenant General Leonidas Polk
(From a contemporary engraving)

Lieutenant General William Joseph Hardee
(United States Army Military History Institute)

Major General John Cabell Breckinridge
(United States Army Military History Institute)

Major General Patrick Ronayne Cleburne
(United States Army Military History Institute)

CHAPTER EIGHT

MATTERS LOOKED PRETTY BLUE NOW

FIVE Union brigades were in full retreat, and the battle was hardly an hour old. Confusion and panic gripped the men, paralyzing what few efforts were made to resist the Confederate attack west of Gresham Lane. There was no sign of McCook, nor of Johnson, nor of any leadership above the regimental—or occasionally brigade—level.

The completeness of the Federal collapse surprised everyone, Blue and Gray alike, but no one was more shocked by its speed than Solon Marks, chief medical officer of Johnson's division. Marks had set up the division hospital at the General Smith plantation near Overall Creek the night before and was at headquarters when the battle began. The first shots sent him back to the hospital, where a growing stream of wounded were converging on the manor. Slipping inside, Marks lost himself in the grizzly work of amputation until a frightened orderly whispered that the division was falling back. Supposing Johnson to be withdrawing deliberately in accordance with orders, Marks assured the orderly that the enemy advance would be arrested long before it might threaten the hospital. Apparently calmed, the soldier went outside to attend to the incoming wounded. But a moment later he was back, insisting that Marks come and see for himself. He did, and what the surgeon saw stunned him: "As I stepped from among the buildings, where I could look to the front, I confess that I was not only surprised but paralyzed. Johnson's men were falling back as fast as their legs could carry them, in the greatest possible confusion, followed by the enemy in perfect lines of battle, outflanking them at least a quarter of a mile. . . . It was evident that our position must shortly fall into the hands of the enemy."

Marks's first thoughts were of the wounded still on the field. Confident that his brigade and regimental surgeons could manage without him, Marks mounted to ride forward. But before he could leave, his surgeons surrounded the horse, looking up at him expectantly for orders. Marks explained his purpose, then called for volunteers to remain behind. Not surprisingly, none came forward. Marks tried a different approach. Dismounting, he announced that he would stay; they could remain or leave as they saw fit. "To their credit," Marks later attested, "every surgeon returned to his duty, and stood bravely at his post during the trying ordeal which followed. In a few minutes our troops had fallen back past our position, and we were between the two armies." The Butternut ranks of Rains and Ector swept past, and the hospital was behind enemy lines. "Our hospital was at once surrounded by skulkers, to be found in all armies, ever ready to fall out of line of battle and wander over the field, robbing the dead and wounded," recalled a disgusted Marks.[1]

Eight hundred yards to the east, near the Gresham house, the scene was repeated. Here Carlin and Post struggled to piece together their shattered commands for a final stand. Despite their pleas, only a corporal's guard rallied around the colors. Colonel Heg fell in with just one hundred troops on hand; Major Isaac Kirby of the One Hundred First Ohio arrived with half that number. In the orchard west of the Gresham house, Lieutenant S. M. Jones was a little more fortunate. He had stemmed the retreat of the Seventy-fourth and Seventy-fifth Illinois, gathering enough volunteers to make a respectable stand. Joined by bits of the Fifth Kentucky and First and Ninety-third Ohio, the Illinoisans turned and faced forward for the last time that day.

On came the Confederates. East of Gresham Lane, Polk and Wood rolled over the plowed fields of cotton and corn for a rematch with Carlin. A severe and unexpected enfilading fire from two artillery batteries belonging to the division of Phil Sheridan and posted on a knoll to Wood's right caused him to call a halt, although the Sixteenth Alabama kept on alone for nearly a mile before being pulled back into line. Polk, who escaped the shelling, pushed on, his left covered by Bushrod Johnson as he closed with Carlin's ragtag line.

The final heave of resistance by Johnson and Davis south of the Wilkinson Pike hardly slowed the Confederates. Baldwin's regiments scarcely had reformed when "some general" (perhaps Johnson) ordered them to fall back. Although the order caused resentment among the brigade staff, it was for the best. As the commander of the Ninety-third Ohio noted, the brigade was out-flanked on the right by McNair, whose line extended several hundred yards beyond Baldwin's toward Overall Creek. Post's men gave way at about the same time, after firing only a few ragged volleys. Left without support on his right and finding Polk in his rear, Carlin too withdrew across the pike.

Like Solon Marks, Dr. Charles Doolittle, volunteering to stay behind with the wounded at the Gresham house, found himself trapped between the lines as his brigade disintegrated. He later recalled: "The bullets flew so thick, it seemed as if one had only to hold out his hand to catch it full of them. There were two killed in the yard to the house where I was and another in the hall. There were a great many killed along side of the fences around the house. The whole thing was one magnificent exhibition of human passion."

A few tense moments passed, and then the Rebels came up. The ration of whiskey delivered at dawn had gotten the better of the weary and famished Southerners, and they were in ill humor; according to Doolittle, their drinking "seemed but to increase their hatred and bloodthirstiness." Doolittle had hoped that the arrival of their brigade commander, St. John Liddell, would help curb their anger, but he was wrong. A request that Liddell order a cease-fire, so that the wounded might be spared death in the crossfire, met with an impassioned rebuttal. After retorting that he personally would rather die than fall prisoner to the Yankees, Liddell "cursed us for everything that was mean under the sun." Earlier, he had heaped invective upon the heads of a group of captured Federal pickets who begged the general for mercy, "telling them they were fine fellows, invading our country and then asking pardon." Liddell had reason beyond mere antipathy to Northerners to be angry. Of the seven staff officers who began the day at Liddell's side, four already were wounded. And, just moments before Liddell met Doolittle, someone told him that his son Willie had been killed.[2]

After refilling their cartridge boxes from McCown's ammunition train, Liddell's Arkansans disappeared into the timber north of the pike, much to the relief of Doolittle and his patients. In the dark and tangled cedar glades, Liddell immediately lost his way, leaving the rest of the division far behind as he veered to the northwest.

Like Rains's earlier detour, the drifting of Liddell's brigade demonstrates how quickly the Confederate attack unraveled amid the patchwork of murky forests, overgrown fields, and split-rail fences below the Wilkinson Pike. Units broke up and reformed as much by chance as by design, as the movements of McCown's brigades illustrate. Separated from the remainder of the division and finding his men and ammunition nearly spent, McNair halted his brigade in the orchard along the pike. While his soldiers refilled their cartridge boxes, McNair, troubled again by an illness that had left him bedridden most of the month, yielded brigade command to Colonel R. W. Harper of the First Arkansas Mounted Rifles and with McCown's permission returned to camp. As the ailing general rode rearward, the brigades of Rains and Ector chanced upon his Arkansans. Surprised to find themselves reunited with Harper, they too stopped to draw ammunition and dispatch their prisoners to the rear. Delighted to have his three brigades together again, McCown was content to await further orders.

The temporary halt of McCown and Liddell offered the fleeing Federals no respite; instead, a new threat appeared in the form of John Wharton and his veteran cavalry. Like everyone else, Wharton had been unprepared for the speed of McCown's advance. "So vigorous was the attack of our left upon the enemy's right, proceeding first at a trot and then at a gallop, I had to travel a distance of two and a half miles before I reached the enemy rear," he later admitted. Once clear of friendly infantry, Wharton found his way blocked by Zahm's Ohio cavalry brigade. Zahm repulsed Wharton's lead units, forcing him to call up Captain T. F. White's Tennessee battery. Zahm had no artillery with which to return White's fire, and so was forced to withdraw across the Wilkinson Pike.

Wharton now turned his attention to the remnants of Johnson's infantry division. Wharton planted his brigade colors astride the pike, then ordered Colonel John Cox and his First Confederate Cavalry to charge the Federals. Cox's troopers faced little opposition. Whole units surrendered without a fight. The Seventy-fifth Illinois was taken en masse, but most subsequently escaped. Colonel Gibson, taken along with a portion of the Thirty-ninth Indiana, was about to surrender his sword when a detachment of Federal cavalry launched a counterattack that allowed him and the Hoosiers to fight their way out. Less fortunate was General Kirk. Badly wounded but conscious, Kirk was in an ambulance making its way rearward when Wharton struck. "Boys, get out of here as soon as possible, or you will all be captured," he told his escort. They did and slipped away, but Kirk fell into Confederate hands.[3]

While Wharton's troopers were netting hundreds of prisoners below the Wilkinson Pike, a prize far greater than frightened infantrymen or wounded generals awaited them near the Gresham house, where the seventy-six heavily laden wagons of McCook's ammunition train were drawn up, ripe for the picking. Only one infantry company of seventy-five men stood guard over the train, and the officer-in-charge, Captain Gates P. Thruston, was absent, having hurried to the front with two wagonloads of ammunition as the first scattered shots broke the predawn stillness. Thruston had emerged from the timber near Baldwin's position to find that brigade melting away. Surmising the "critical position of our army" and by inference that of his train, Thruston galloped back to the Gresham house, only to find everything in disarray. A group of Rebel cavalrymen were leading away McCook's supply and personal baggage trains, while a second made ready to seize Thruston's ordnance wagons. "I had no special orders and just what to do was something of a problem," the Ohioan admitted; but orders or no orders, Thruston knew he had to do something, and do it quickly. After repelling the detachment of Rebel cavalry Thruston led the train north into the cedars above the Wilkinson Pike. Thruston, his seventy-six drivers, and their infantry escort struggled through a half mile of thickets, ravines, and fencerows before reaching the open ground south of the Widow Burris (or Burrows) farm. Here a scene equally desperate greeted them. Thruston recounted: "The whole area in rear between our right and left was a scene of strife and confusion that beggars description. Stragglers from the front, teamsters, couriers, negro servants, hospital attendants, ambulances added to the turmoil. Wounded and riderless horses and cattle wild with fright rushed frantically over the field."

Here too they met the Confederate cavalry in force. Faced with the imminent loss of the train, Thruston appealed to every Union cavalry officer in the area for help. Colonel Zahm responded first, sending Major John Pugh and some three hundred men of the Fourth Ohio Cavalry into line on the left flank of the train, fronting west toward the enemy. They looked menacing, but they were not up to the duty. A few well-placed rounds from Wharton's artillery scattered them, and a charge by his troopers sent them rearward "at a pretty lively gait." Wharton next turned his guns on the Second Tennessee Cavalry, a green regiment that had been organized at Murfreesboro only five months earlier, and, according to Zahm, they broke and fled "like sheep." This left Zahm with only two regiments, his own Third Ohio and Colonel Minor Milliken's

First Ohio. But before Zahm could organize a coordinated defense, Millikin and his horsemen were off. "The very acme of Colonel Millikin's ambition had been to have the regiment make a sabre charge," a member of the unit recalled, "and now the supreme opportunity had arrived." Galloping across the sodden sward, Millikin slashed his way into the midst of Wharton's ranks, throwing the Eighth Texas momentarily into disorder. Close combat followed, "in which the revolver was used with deadly effect." Deadly indeed: Milliken toppled off his horse mortally wounded, shot through the neck by a revolver-wielding Texan. With their leader down, the fight went out of the Federals (who probably did not want to be there to begin with), and they tried to retrace their steps. But Wharton had them surrounded, and over one hundred fell prisoner while trying to cut their way out.

Thruston and his party had watched the affair. Anticipating the outcome, most of the teamsters had stampeded, leaving the wagons "high and dry" in the cornfields. Thruston and the infantrymen were right behind them. They fired a parting volley, then fled to the nearest cedar glade.

"Matters looked pretty blue now," Zahm admitted later in a classic bit of understatement. Zahm himself had been swept from the field with his three regiments, and the Third Ohio, finding itself alone, immediately fell back from its perimeter around the outbuildings of the Widow Burris farm. The field theirs, Wharton's troopers began leading away Thruston's wagons.

"Happily this appalling state of affairs did not last long," wrote Thruston. Federal cavalry launched a surprise countercharge that caught Wharton's men unprepared. At the head of the attack was Colonel John Kennett, commander of the division of which Zahm's hapless brigade was a part. Uncertain of the extent of the disaster that had befallen McCook but worried nonetheless, Rosecrans earlier had urged Kennett to gather all idle cavalry from along the Nashville Turnpike and ride at once to the right. Kennett found only one squadron of the Third Kentucky, but orders were orders, and so with this tiny column he galloped toward the retreating Union infantry.

As he led his ragtag force across the turnpike, perhaps Kennett wondered where Stanley was and why he had done nothing to challenge Wharton's rampaging Butternuts. The answer, had he known it, would have infuriated Kennett.

After his visit to army headquarters the night before, Stanley had returned to his bivouac and quickly fallen fast asleep. A little after midnight, he was awakened and an order from Garesche was thrust in his hand. It related Wheeler's attacks on supply trains along the Wilkinson Pike and directed Stanley to ride at once to Stewart's Creek to take charge of the defense of army trains parked there.

Stanley arrived at Stewart's Creek an hour before daylight to find the trains safe and the commander of the guard, Colonel Joe Burke of the Tenth Ohio, hard at work on a bottle of Irish whiskey. Forgetting the threat to the Union right, which had so occupied his thoughts before midnight, Stanley dismounted and joined Burke and his chaplain for "hot punch and delicate breakfast." Stanley was still enjoying Burke's hospitality when a courier from Garesche galloped up with word of McCook's defeat and an order to "hasten to the right and do your best to restore order." Stanley mounted and cantered south, only to become lost in a sea of stragglers surging up the Nashville Turnpike. It was late afternoon before Stanley reached the battlefield, by which time the Confederate cavalry attack had played itself out.

Rosecrans clearly is to be criticized for sending his chief of cavalry to do the work of a brigade commander, particularly on the eve of a major battle. Stanley, however, must share in the blame. He must have known his place was at the front on the morning of 31 December, and he should have reminded Rosecrans of this when awakened by Garesche's order.

Back at the front, Kennett's luck changed as he rode south. Captain Elmer Otis fell in with six companies of his unattached Fourth United States Cavalry, and the Third Ohio managed to halt its retreat and rally. Kennett ordered his reinforced command to dismount behind a fence south of the Nashville Turnpike. From there they drove away Wharton's startled troopers, who thought they had seen the last of organized resistance. As the Confederates withdrew, two squadrons from the Third Ohio deployed to screen the train and hold Wharton in check while Thruston patched up the disabled wagons and reorganized the train. Train guards and stragglers were enlisted to ride the lead horses of each team, and the train creaked toward the turnpike. After evading Cleburne's artillery and a final charge by Wharton, Thruston brought his wagons safely to rest on the west bank of Stones River near army headquarters.

Thruston's exploits did not go unnoticed. While he supervised the parking of the train, Thruston was greeted by Captain Charles Thompson of the general staff, who congratulated him on his escape. Thompson remarked that the commanding general had heard that Thruston had been captured along with the entire train. "No, my ammunition train is safe," came the emphatic reply. Thompson left to pass the welcome news on to Rosecrans, who rode up moments later.

"Are you the officer who says McCook's ammunition train was saved?" shouted Rosecrans.

"Yes, sir," Thruston responded with a salute.

"How do you know it?"

"I had charge of it, sir."

"Where is it?" Thruston led Rosecrans a few yards to the opposite side of a cedar glade, and pointed it out. "How did you manage to get it away over here?"

"Well, general," said Thruston, "we did some sharp fighting, but a great deal more running."

Rosecrans was delighted. Slapping the young captain on the shoulder, he exclaimed: "Captain, consider yourself a major from today." The general kept his word. Not only was Thruston cited for conspicuous gallantry and promoted, but he was appointed senior aide-de-camp to the commanding general.[4]

So, even amidst the confusion and ignominy of that dark December morning, reputations were made as a select few overcame the panic that gripped the Right Wing of the Army of the Cumberland. While a weary but elated Thruston parked his wagons, some two miles to the southeast among the rolling fields and scattered thickets near the Harding house another officer was winning immortality for himself and his division. There fiery Phil Sheridan was about to hand Bragg his first defeat of the day.

CHAPTER NINE

THE REBELS WERE FALLING LIKE LEAVES OF AUTMN

THE first indication Bragg had that his attack was not going as planned came just moments after McCown struck Johnson's picket line. A courier from Hardee brought word that Cheatham had yet to advance and that, as a consequence, Cleburne's right was exposed. (This was the delay that troubled Lucius Polk in the opening minutes of the battle.) Concerned but not yet alarmed, Bragg dispatched a messenger to Cheatham with a rebuke and an order to get moving. The Tennessean responded to the order, but Bragg's troubles with him were far from over. In the weeks following Stones River, Cheatham would be among the most outspoken in calling for Bragg's resignation. Throughout the day Cheatham acted rashly and recklessly, sacrificing hundreds of irreplaceable veterans in poorly coordinated charges. Apologists later attributed the Tennessean's impulsive behavior to his natural combativeness; critics, however, suggested that Cheatham, like so many of the men in ranks, was drunk. Rumormongers whispered after the battle that the general had had trouble just staying on his horse.[1]

Sober or drunk, at 7:00 Cheatham moved to the attack. But instead of continuing the right wheel with a general advance of both his lines—however impractical this tactic ultimately proved—the Tennessean committed his brigades piecemeal, allowing Sheridan to deploy and redeploy his units so as to repel each attack in turn.

Deas' brigade, led by Colonel J. Q. Loomis, opened the action. The odds were against Loomis's Alabamians, and they knew it. Three hundred yards of open cornfields separated them from Colonel William Woodruff's three Union regiments, which lay on a ridge behind a fence. "Covered with a dense growth of rough

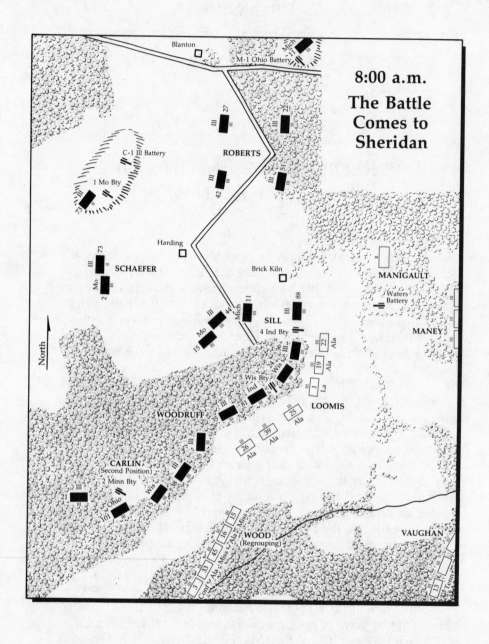

8:00 a.m.
The Battle Comes to Sheridan

cedars," the Federalist position offered a clear field of fire all the way to Rebel lines. The weakest link was Woodruff's left flank, which rested in a field. Woodruff had moved three guns belonging to the Eighth Wisconsin Artillery into the meadow at daybreak, but he still felt uneasy. Woodruff explained his fears to Sill, whose brigade lay to his left, and Sill spoke with Sheridan, who ordered the Fifteenth Missouri and Forty-fourth Illinois forward from their positions in reserve. (Sheridan had detailed these regiments to Sill the night before. Not needed then, they had returned to their former positions at dawn.) Just before Loomis attacked, however, the Missourians and Illinoisans again abandoned the line, leaving Sill with his original four regiments to face the Confederates. In the front line, from left to right, were the Eighty-eighth and Thirty-sixth Illinois and Twenty-fourth Wisconsin; the Twenty-first Michigan rested behind the Eighty-eighth.

Loomis's Butternuts slogged through the sodden field in good order, conducting a right wheel as they neared the enemy. But once within range of the Yankee rifles, the brigade separated: the three regiments on the left struck the Twenty-fifth Illinois and Eighty-first Indiana, while the remainder drifted to the north, hitting Sill's right.

The Alabamians enjoyed early success on the left, the Twenty-fifth Illinois and Eighty-first Indiana recoiling into the woods as the Rebels neared the fence. Colonel Thomas Williams of the Twenty-fifth tried desperately but unsuccessfully to stem the rearward flow of Bluecoats. Grabbing the regimental colors, he yelled out: "We will plant it here, boys, and rally the old Twenty-fifth around it; and here we will die." And there he did die. A bullet pierced his chest as he finished his speech, and he sank to the ground, dying instantly. Around his body and the fallen colors, the bloodletting went on. While the infantry ran, the artillerymen of the Eighth Wisconsin fought on alone until the Rebels enveloped them and their battery commander, Captain Stephen Carpenter, fell dead across a Parrott gun.

Loomis's Alabamians were punishing Woodruff's Bluecoats, but in pressing their advantage they pushed too far. Not content to stop at the rail fence, they jumped it and darted blindly past the Thirty-fifth Illinois, exposing their left flank as they ran by. It was more than the commander of the Thirty-fifth could resist. He gave the order to fire, and his Prairie State farm boys released a volley that, in the words of the unlucky colonel of the Twenty-sixth Alabama, "raked down our lines with heavy damage to us." The

Twenty-sixth melted away, and the Twenty-fifth Illinois and Eighty-first Indiana, taking heart, counterattacked to regain the fence and send their tormentors reeling across the valley.

On the right, the story was the same. The withdrawal of Woodruff's two left regiments exposed the right flank of the Twenty-fourth Wisconsin, a green regiment organized just four months earlier in Milwaukee. Charging up the boulder-strewn slope, the First Louisiana struck it and struck hard, first startling, then panicking the Yankees. After firing only a few scattered shots, the regiment crumbled. Major Elisha Hubbard directed his men to break contact and retire by companies, but the order was lost in the noise and confusion, and the men broke contact as it suited them.

The collapse of the Twenty-fourth Wisconsin now left the Thirty-sixth Illinois with its right in the air. But unlike Hubbard, Colonel Nicholas Greusel was equal to the challenge; besides, he led a crack outfit that had distinguished itself at Pea Ridge and Perryville. Fixing bayonets, his Illinoisans held their fire until the Stars and Bars came within fifty yards, then unleashed a volley that slammed the Nineteenth Alabama to a halt. For thirty minutes the Illinoisans and Alabamians slugged it out, trading fire and peering through the smoke for a sign that the other was wavering. Neither regiment did, that is until the batteries of Hescock and Houghtalling were brought to bear. Then, slowly at first, Southern infantrymen began trickling rearward, dodging the sabre strokes and turning a deaf ear to the cries of their furious officers. Sensing the moment to be at hand, Greusel ordered a counterattack. The timing was perfect. The Rebel left already had disintegrated before the determined defense of Woodruff and, with Loomis struck down by a falling limb, the brigade right was without a commander. Raising a cheer and surging forward, the Illinoisans swept away the Nineteenth Alabama, pursuing it down the slope and into the cornfield until Greusel called his enthusiastic infantrymen back into line.

The First Louisiana, meanwhile, had continued its advance against the Twenty-fourth Wisconsin. When a brigade staff officer delivered the order to retire, Captain Taylor Beatty was surprised, for his men had enjoyed only success. But it was a success dearly won, as even Beatty later admitted. Of the two hundred thirty-one men he had taken into action, only one hundred twenty-seven re-crossed the valley with the Louisiana captain.

In halting this first Rebel attack the Federals too had paid a heavy price. Sill was dead. A bullet had gored his upper lip, passing into his brain and emerging at the base of the skull. Lieutenant John Mitchell, on the staff of the brigadier, recalled the moment of death:

At this critical juncture, a general charge was ordered which was bravely responded to. Sill sent me along the line to aid in the movement. Hurrying back, I came across the brigade adjutant; he had just seen the general's horse galloping to the rear. In our search for Sill we almost stumbled over his prostrate body. A bullet had penetrated his brain; he had tumbled from his horse without even a friendly arm to ease his fall. He lay unconscious and alone, bubbling out his last breaths through the blood that thickly flowed over his fair face and silky beard. Two stragglers were with difficulty persuaded to aid in taking his body in a blanket to a farmhouse nearby. Thus died a model of martial virtues, the gentle and chivalric Sill. This scene and its dread surroundings horrified me with war.[2]

Brigade command now passed to Greusel, and Major Silas Miller took charge of the Thirty-sixth Illinois, its ranks already two hundred thirty men thinner. Placing the Fifteenth Missouri and Forty-fourth Illinois into the gap created by the flight of the Twenty-fourth Wisconsin, Greusel reformed his line and awaited the next Confederate onslaught, which came just moments later. While Cheatham reorganized Loomis's shattered brigade, Brigadier General Alfred Vaughan moved to the attack over the same blood-stained and trampled earth covered by the Alabamians. "Our men would guy and jeer the Alabamians for taking the back track as they passed through our line," recalled Private A. H. Brown of Memphis as he and his fellow Tennesseans marched into the cornfield. But the jeering stopped when one angry Alabamian pointed toward Woodruff's line and yelled: "Yes, and you'll find it the hottest place that you ever struck in a little while." "His remark was about right," remembered Brown.

Vaughan's attack began inauspiciously. With Wood masking its left and Maney uncomfortably close on its right, Vaughan's brigade quickly lost its alignment as it tried to squeeze into the valley. To relieve the congestion, Vaughan directed the Ninth Texas to break off and advance with Wood. After the Texans got under way, Vaughan led his remaining five regiments forward northeast of the Widow Smith house. Stumbling up the slippery slope, Vaughan's men righted themselves at the top and attacked with a fury that sent the hapless Twenty-fifth Illinois and Eighty-first Indiana reeling from the fence a second time. With Colonel Williams of the

Twenty-fifth dead, his leaderless regiment withdrew one hundred fifty paces before Captain Weford Taggart was able to rally it. The Eighty-first Indiana reappeared on its right, and the two commands fixed bayonets and charged to reclaim their positions. Vaughan did not contest their advance. Colonel A. M. Manigault, who moved against Greusel minutes after Vaughan struck Woodruff, had failed to press his attack, leaving Vaughan's right open to envelopment. Vaughan gave the inevitable command, and his Tennesseans withdrew.

Not all the Confederates fell back. Colonel William Young and his Ninth Texas, unaware of what had happened to the brigade, continued to claw forward among the limestone outcrops after Vaughan had fallen back to regroup for a second attack. The Texans actually had been fighting alone for some time. After they bid farewell to their Tennessee comrades and attached themselves to Wood's right, the Texans pressed on into the woodline on the opposite side of the valley, only to find it empty. While their adoptive brigade grappled with Carlin's Bluecoats, the Ninth searched for a solo engagement, Texas-style. They found it with the Thirty-fifth Illinois, two hundred yards away on their right. The Texans opened fire, but their bullets spattered harmlessly against the intervening trees. Realizing the futility of continuing the fight at this distance, Young pushed his regiment forward a hundred yards by the right flank to a tall fence, from which they reopened fire. Still their bullets missed the target. Young grew impatient. He yelled at his men to scale the fence and close with the Illinoisans. In the din, his command was misunderstood; the Texans scaled the fence, but then stopped after only fifty yards, again falling to the ground to engage the enemy. Suddenly, the sound of firing erupted from the rear. The Ninth was in trouble. The Texans inadvertantly had wedged themselves between the Thirty-fifth Illinois and Carlin's Thirty-eighth Illinois, still in position in their rear. For five minutes the Texans endured a withering crossfire as Young rode frantically about, trying to make himself heard. Men dropped all around him—over one hundred in less than thirty minutes. Young himself went down, his horse shot from beneath him. But his resolve to charge was unbroken. Running up and down the line, he grabbed each company commander in turn to explain his intention. Then, to ensure their response, the colonel seized the regimental colors and, in his own words, importuned his men to "move forward with a shout, both of which they did a la Texas." The Illinoisans gave way, and the Texans sprinted after them.

Their charge was well timed, coming just as Carlin retreated and Vaughan closed on the Twenty-fifth Illinois and Eighty-first Indiana for the second and final time. Although men fell in wind-rows—56 percent of the Twelfth Tennessee dropped dead or wounded, and Bishop Polk, in this long day of costly charges, would later single out Vaughan and his troops for special praise—the Tennesseans kept on coming. Woodruff's line crumbled, not to be reformed. Woodruff later implied that he directed the with-drawal that followed, but the weight of evidence suggests rather that his soldiers, low on ammunition and isolated, took matters into their own hands. The Thirty-fifth Illinois was already gone, and the Twenty-fifth was not far behind. Captain Taggart led his regiment first to safety behind the batteries of Hescock and Houghtalling, and next across the Wilkinson Pike and out of the battle. Then the Eighty-first Indiana withdrew, and only Carpenter's Wisconsin battery was left on the field. Woodruff had instructed Carpenter to cover the Hoosiers' withdrawal from a position near the Harding house, but the young artilleryman was killed before he could comply. Lieutenant Henry Stiles took charge, unlimbered the guns as ordered, and held Vaughan in check long enough for the infantry to make good its escape. Woodruff, meanwhile, was waiting on the Wilkinson Pike to gather up his fleeing soldiers and throw them into line west of the Blanton house.[3]

While Woodruff's brigade and the Thirty-sixth Illinois struggled with Vaughan, Greusel faced his first direct atttack. The time was 8:00 A.M. Like Loomis and Vaughan, Cheatham's third brigade commander, Colonel A. M. Manigault, attacked late and unsup-ported. A thirty-nine-year-old South Carolina businessman whose formal education had ended with elementary school, Manigault had spent all but two of his thirty-six years before the war in Charleston, leaving the port city just long enough to see limited service as a lieutenant with the Palmetto Regiment in Mexico. As a lieutenant colonel on the staff of General Beauregard, Manigault was present at the bombardment of Fort Sumter and remained in Charleston until the summer of 1862, when he was ordered, along with his Tenth South Carolina, to join the Army of the Missis-sippi. Manigault went on to serve with distinction in every major campaign through Franklin, where a head wound sent him back to South Carolina. Here at Stones River, the balding, sharp-eyed South Carolinian would lead his own Tenth, along with the Nine-teenth South Carolina and three Alabama regiments, in some of the bloodiest charges of the battle.

Across the valley, the men of Colonel Francis Sherman's Eighty-eighth Illinois lay quietly watching the Stars and Bars draw nearer, unaware that less than a mile behind them the divisions of Johnson and Davis were in a confused and panicked flight northward. For a moment, their attention was drawn from the approaching enemy to a phenomenon recorded by several soldiers in the ranks. The racket raised by Vaughan and Woodruff in the thicket to Greusel's right had driven scores of dazed rabbits from their nests, and they now took the Illinoisans from the flank, "nestling under their coats and creeping under their legs in a state of utter confusion." "They hopped over the field like toads," recalled William Bickham, "and as perfectly tamed by fright as household pets. Many officers witnessed it, remarking it as one of the most curious spectacles ever seen upon a battle-field."

The boom of their own guns, as Houghtalling and Hescock lobbed shells into Manigault's ranks, shook the Illinoisans back to the reality of battle. With the Rebels now just fifty yards away, the Eighty-eighth rose up and, after its skirmishers cleared the front line, joined in the firing. Manigault's infantry came no closer, but halted, wavered, and broke to the rear.

As Manigault withdrew to the sound of cheering from the Union ranks, the first of Sheridan's regiments to have been engaged found itself with empty cartridge boxes. With its acting commander, Major Silas Miller, badly wounded, the Thirty-sixth Illinois received permission to leave the front line and retire north of the Wilkinson Pike to draw ammunition. The Thirty-sixth had fought splendidly, as its losses attested. Forty-six Illinoisans were dead, another one hundred fifty-one lay wounded, and fifteen more were missing. Although the regiment would go on to participate in every major battle in the West, it was at Stones River that it suffered its heaviest losses. Only one hundred forty survivors answered muster as their adjutant searched for ammunition. He found none: the men needed .67 caliber, but Sheridan's wagons could offer only .58. At this point McCook rode up and ordered the regiment back to the Nashville Turnpike, where it remained until reunited with the brigade that afternoon.[4]

This rare appearance of McCook was typical of his role, or rather lack of a role, in the early hours of the battle. He was as invisible as Sheridan was ubiquitous. Instead of helping his finest division commander rally survivors for a stand near the Harding farm, McCook seems to have drifted aimlessly in the rear of his fast-disintegrating command, stepping in only to order regiments still

engaged to give up and retreat, as if the shock of battle had overcome his own will to resist.

But with or without McCook, Sheridan aimed to fight on. While
Manigault prepared to renew the attack, Sheridan reformed his
lines to conform to the second positions of what remained of the
brigades of Woodruff, Carlin, Post, and Baldwin. He withdrew his
right-flank regiments, the Eighty-eighth Illinois and Twenty-first
Michigan, to the outbuildings of the Harding farm on the north
side of a narrow country lane. Then he moved the Fifteenth Missouri and Forty-fourth Illinois, both woefully short of ammunition, to a place of relative safety behind Hescock's battery. Bush,
meanwhile, unlimbered his guns near the Harding house in support of Greusel, while Houghtalling abandoned the elevation in favor of a small neck of wood six hundred yards northeast of Bush,
on the dirt lane just below the Wilkinson Pike.

Manigault struck Sheridan's second position at 8:30 A.M. This
time he had support. Cheatham had committed George Maney's
brigade, his last. Like Cheatham, Maney was a Tennessean, raised
in nearby Franklin and schooled at the University of Nashville.
Maney served briefly with Tennessee volunteers in the Mexican
War, then returned to Nashville to practice law until he was
elected colonel of the First Tennessee in 1861. Maney survived the
war and seems to have reconstructed quickly, as he campaigned
unsuccessfully for the governorship of Tennessee on the Republican ticket in 1876. Afterwards he tried his hand at diplomacy,
serving as American consul in Colombia, Bolivia, Paraguay, and
Uruguay before his death in Washington D.C. in 1901.

But all that was years in the future. Maney's sole concern for the
moment was to guide his men safely across the valley behind
Manigault, whose brigade was again crumbling under a murderous
converging fire from Bush and Houghtalling. Colonel George Roberts, his brigade as yet unbloodied, saw in Manigault's stalled attack a chance to swing the momentum of the battle in favor of the
Federals. Encountering Sheridan behind Hescock's guns, Roberts
begged permission to counterattack. The colonel's enthusiasm was
contagious, and Sheridan immediately approved the plan. Roberts
wasted no time in carrying it out. His Illinoisans lined up in the
field south of the Blanton house, "as if on parade," recalled Alexander Stevenson of the Forty-second Illinois, the right-flank regiment in the brigade front line. On its left was the Fifty-first
Illinois, behind it the Twenty-second Illinois. The soldiers fixed
bayonets, the officers reminded them not to fire until ordered, the

command "Forward, march!" rang out, and the brigade lurched forward. Roberts's adjutant galloped ahead to ask Colonel Sherman of the Eighty-eighth to tear down the fence that stood between the brigade and Manigault's Confederates, but his words were lost in the din. Undaunted, the adjutant rode to the fence and, through a variety of gestures, convinced the soldiers to level it, cease firing, and lie down. Right behind came the Forty-second which, after passing over the Eighty-eighth, aligned itself and prepared to charge. From his place in the ranks Alexander Stevenson recalled the scene that followed: "Suddenly the grand form of Colonel Roberts could be seen riding in rear of the regiment, telling the officers not to let a shot be fired; then, wheeling around the left wing, he rode in front of the regiment along the whole line, with his cap in his hand, cheering the men to endless enthusiasm and shouting to them: 'Don't fire a shot! Drive them with the bayonet!' " The command "Charge!" followed, and the Forty-second surged forward with a cheer, leaving behind the Fifty-first, its way blocked by a neck of cedars. Manigault's men were too badly shaken by the artillery fire to resist even a single regiment of infantry, and they retreated back to their line of departure, the Forty-second Illinois following them as far as the rail fence previously held by the Twenty-fourth Wisconsin. The impetuous Illinoisans in turn found themselves surrounded by a swarm of Southerners—Polk and Wood had swept through the fields to their rear. Sheridan recalled the regiment at once.[5]

Manigault falling back with his brigade met Maney and his Tennesseans coming up. The two conferred. Manigault outlined the Federal dispositions, then subjected the Tennessean to an impassioned account of the havoc Bush and Houghtalling had wrought on his brigade, explaining that their synchronized, mutually supporting fire made an attack against just one impossible, as it would expose the flank of the attacking force to destruction by the other battery.

Manigault's analysis may have surprised Maney, but his troops already understood the destructive power of the Federal guns. As they lay in the fields southeast of the Brick Kiln, they spent twenty harrowing minutes dodging incoming rounds while their commander listened to Manigault. Finally Manigault finished, and Maney agreed to his plan. Each would move against one battery in a simultaneous assault. Manigault chose Houghtalling's battery; Maney, that of Bush. The two generals returned to their commands. Manigault changed front to the right so as to face Houghtalling, and Maney advanced to Manigault's left.[6]

Sheridan, meanwhile, was availing himself of this second lull to modify his lines. Again it was the failure of the commands on his right to resist Cleburne and Vaughan that forced Sheridan to withdraw. Roberts's brigade would be the anchor of this, Sheridan's third position. Sheridan had ordered him into the timber along the Wilkinson Pike after his successful counterattack. In compliance with orders, Roberts inserted the Twenty-second Illinois behind and to the left of Houghtalling, then placed the Forty-second Illinois to the left of the Twenty-second. Due north of Houghtalling and across the pike rested the Fifty-first and Twenty-seventh Illinois, fronting south. With Roberts in position, Sheridan reeled in Schaefer and Greusel. The former joined Roberts's right with the Second Missouri and the Seventy-third Illinois, the Fifteenth Missouri and Forty-fourth Illinois having left the line in search of ammunition; Greusel, meanwhile, sent a staff officer to Colonel Sherman with instructions to fall back alongside the Twenty-fourth Wisconsin, which had reformed west of the Blanton house, and another to the commander of the Twenty-first Michigan with orders to redeploy in support of Hescock. Even with this, however, the Missouri artillerymen could not stay long on the high ground, where they presented Vaughan's sharpshooters with an easy target. Accordingly, Sheridan dispatched them to the small knoll that lay in advance of Negley's right. It was a position of great natural strength, commanding the open fields to the east and the cedar belt to the south. After detaching his two-gun section of Parrotts under Lieutenant R. C. M. Taliaferro to shore up Houghtalling, Hescock rode to the knoll with his remaining four pieces.[7]

While Sheridan organized his third position, Maney prepared to seize Bush's battery and drive away the Eighty-eighth Illinois and Twenty-first Michigan, as yet unmoved from behind the rail fence near the Harding house. Supposing Manigault to be ready, Maney sent the Sixth and Ninth Tennessee Consolidated sprinting ahead to occupy the edge of a cedar thicket three hundred yards to their front or, if no enemy were found, to rejoin the main body. Meanwhile, the Fourth Confederate and First and Twenty-seventh Tennessee Consolidated waded through cotton fields earlier trampled into a pasty ooze by Manigault's Alabamians. As they right-wheeled south of the Brick Kiln, Bush withdrew to join Hescock on the knoll, their infantry support to the Wilkinson Pike. Raising a cheer, the Confederates ascended the ridge only to find that, silhouetted between the Harding house and the Brick Kiln, they presented Houghtalling with a shooting-gallery target. Out on the skirmish line the startled Butternuts, unable to believe that Manigault had failed to clear away the Federal guns, cried "Cease firing! Cease firing! You are firing on your own men!" Back on the ridge, where "the Rebels were falling like leaves of autumn," Houghtalling's shelling froze Maney and his lieutenants with indecision. Like his skirmishers, the Tennessean believed that Manigault had done his part in dislodging Houghtalling and thus assumed the fire to be friendly. But friendly fire or not, men were dying, and so, while their leaders hesitated, the soldiers fell to the ground.

Sam Watkins, out on the skirmish line, had another explanation for the failure of Confederate leadership at this critical juncture: "John Barleycorn was general in chief. Our generals, and colonels and captains, had kissed John a little too often. They couldn't see straight. It was said to be buckeye whiskey. They couldn't tell our own men from the Yankees. The private could, but he was no general, you see."

Whatever the cause of the officers' indecision, it was clear that the identity of the guns had to be established—and quickly. Colonel H. R. Field of the First and Twenty-seventh Tennessee Consolidated understood this, and he sent Lieutenant R. F. James of his staff forward on horseback to reconnoiter the battery. James made it to within fifty yards of the guns before Roberts's Bluecoats shot him dead. Maney still doubted that the guns were hostile. A second officer rode out. He came within forty yards of Houghtalling's battery before Roberts's infantry again rose and fired. This time the bullets missed their mark, and the officer wheeled his horse and escaped unharmed. Field, at least, was convinced that the guns and their infantry support were Yankee. His men happily obeyed the order to return fire.

Amazingly, Maney's other regimental commanders continued to harbor doubts, that is, until two color-bearers volunteered their lives to put an end to the uncertainty. The color sergeant of the Fourth Tennessee acted first. Marching ten paces forward, he raised the flag and waved it. For ten minutes he drew fire from the Forty-second Illinois before returning to the line, his colonel convinced and the colors considerably more tattered. Sergeant M. C. Hooks of the Sixth and Ninth Tennessee Consolidated, which had rejoined the brigade on its left, advanced next with his unit's

colors, placing them atop a feed crib. Adjusting range and elevation, Houghtalling's gunners blasted the crib but missed the sergeant. It was enough, however, to convince everyone the guns were
unfriendly.

Certain now that Manigault had failed to move as agreed,
Maney brought up the two Napoleans and two twelve-pounders of
Smith's battery. Battery commander William Turner unlimbered
near the spot that Bush had vacated, and opened on Houghtalling
with "terrible effect."[8]

While Turner and Houghtalling pounded one another, Vaughan's
Tennesseans emerged from the timber south of the Harding house
and approached Maney's left. Unlike Maney, Vaughan never had
any doubt that the artillerymen who were raking his lines with
solid shot were Yankees. Stopping short of Maney's left, Vaughan
wisely ordered his men to take cover on the west side of the ridge
while he awaited instructions from Cheatham.

Sheridan now confronted three Confederate brigades from his
position along the Wilkinson Pike: Manigault and Maney opposite
Roberts, Vaughan opposite Schaefer and Greusel. As before, it was
not the forces to his front that troubled Sheridan most, but rather
those beyond his right, where the patchwork Union line was again
crumbling. This time the little Irishman decided to see for himself
what was happening to Davis's division. He galloped past Woodruff
to Carlin, who with Davis was trying in vain to rally his brigade.
The contrast in their behavior under fire surprised the Ohioan:
"The calm and cool appearance of Carlin, who at the time was
smoking a stumpy pipe, had some effect," Sheridan noted, "and
was in strong contrast to the excited manner of Davis, who seemed
overpowered by the disaster that had befallen his command." But
even Carlin's coolness could not stem the retreat—the men simply
were too demoralized to turn and fight. A cursory inspection of
Carlin's disintegrating line was enough to convince Sheridan that
he would have to draw in his right still further. Turning his horse,
he retraced the route to his division. What Sheridan saw as he
passed Woodruff only added to his dismay. Only seven days in
command, Woodruff was just sitting and staring as his men
streamed rearward. "There seemed to be no fear, no panic, but a
stout indifference, which was unaccountable," Woodruff recalled.
"Officers and men passed to the rear; no words or exhortation
could prevent them." On their heels came the brigades of Wood,
Polk, and Johnson, right-wheeling as they neared the Wilkinson Pike.

Rejoining his command, Sheridan instructed Greusel and Schaefer, whose troops were woefully low on ammunition, to withdraw from the pike and into the cedars just as Polk bore down on them from the west, Johnson in echelon to his left, Wood in line to his right. Greusel, with only the Eighty-eighth Illinois and Twenty-fourth Wisconsin remaining under his direct command, retired into the timber north of the Blanton house. To his left, Schaefer reconstructed his brigade. The Fifteenth Missouri deployed to the left of the Twenty-fourth Wisconsin, and the Forty-fourth Illinois wedged itself into line between the Fifteenth Missouri and one battalion each from the Second Missouri and the Seventy-third Illinois: the second battalion of Missourians was shaken out as brigade skirmishers; the second battalion of the Seventy-third had become separated from the brigade during the withdrawal, to be picked up by Rousseau as his division moved up on Sheridan's right.

"In falling back, we found the cedar woods so thick, and so filled with rock and caverns and fallen trees, that it was almost impossible to get through it," remembered one member of the Seventy-third Illinois. "The history of the combat in those dark cedar thickets will never be known. No man could see even the whole of his own regiment," maintained a veteran of the Thirty-sixth Illinois.[9] His observation is still true today. The events of the next two hours remain shrouded in uncertainty: the tangled cedar glades and the smoke of battle obscured the precise movements of units Blue and Gray, resulting in after-action reports that are vague and often contradictory. The final movements of Greusel and Schaefer are speculative; only the final stand of Roberts's brigade can be recreated with certainty. And as for the succession of Confederate attacks against Sheridan's final stronghold by Wood, Polk, Johnson, Manigault, and Anderson, all that can be said without fear of contradiction is that they were launched within minutes of one another, but with an unaccountable lack of coordination.

S. A. M. Wood, it seems, was the first to encounter Sheridan's salient. Although Wood had entered the timber northeast of the Gresham house supported by Polk on the left and Vaughan on the right, Vaughan's decision to halt behind the ridge near Maney left Wood's flank in the air as he pursued the remnants of Woodruff's brigade across the Wilkinson Pike and into the field west of the Blanton house. Houghtalling's busy gunners, joined by those of Taliaferro and Lieutenant D. Flansburg (leader of a two-gun section from Bush's battery detailed to reinforce Houghtalling), wheeled their pieces and opened on this new target. Wood charged. His Alabamians came within two hundred yards of the guns before a murderous converging fire from Schaefer's brigade and Roberts's Twenty-seventh Illinois stopped them. Left standing in an open field, the Alabamians had no chance against an enemy invisible among sink holes and outcrops, and so Wood ordered them to fall back seventy-five yards to the left of the batteries of J. H. Calvert and Putnam Darden, which Cleburne had called on to silence the Federal artillery. There Wood held on for perhaps an hour. His men kept up a steady fire, digging deeper and deeper into their cartridge boxes until, ammunition exhausted, they left the battle in search of the division ordnance train. "After this," notes Alexander Stevenson, "there was but little firing for some time; it was the calm—warning of the approaching storm."[10]

This lull, welcome to the exhausted Federals, was not calculated; rather, it was the by-product of confusion among the Confederate commanders. The determined resistance of Sheridan—as fierce as it was unexpected—had splintered the attacking Gray lines, so that now at 9:00 Vaughan, Maney, and Manigault languished in the fields south of the Wilkinson Pike waiting for someone to bring order to the confusion, while Cleburne's brigadiers found themselves suddenly isolated, far in front of the remainder of the Confederate left. Thus exposed, Wood had been mauled. Now Polk, advancing in his stead, faced the same fate as he neared the pike. Hardee's whereabouts were unknown, and Bragg was out of touch with the tactical situation. Only Cleburne was on hand and had the presence of mind to halt the North Carolinian below the pike. While Darden and Calvert kept Houghtalling occupied, orders went out to Bushrod Johnson directing him to realign and advance his command to assist Polk.

The Tennessean did his best to comply. He marched his brigade by the left flank across the pike and into the cedars northwest of the Blanton house, then eastward up a rock-strewn slope until he reached what he thought was Polk's left. But as he stopped the brigade his skirmish line opened on a file of dark forms that were drifting silently across their front. Thinking he had come up behind Polk rather than on his left, Johnson rode forward and ordered his skirmishers to cease firing. He no sooner had quieted his skirmish line when the rattle of musketry erupted from out beyond his right front, toppling Major J. T. McReynolds, the last field-grade officer in the Thirty-seventh Tennessee. His regiment returned the fire until Johnson withdrew the brigade south of the pike. Although he later reported that a heavy force had been encountered flanking his right, what the Tennessean actually had stumbled upon was Greusel in his final position. Far from trying to turn Johnson's flank, Greusel's weary Bluecoats were merely conserving what little strength—and ammunition—they had left to hold their own line; consequently, little real damage was done Johnson's brigade. In twenty minutes of desultory fighting with a largely invisible foe, only the Thirty-seventh Tennessee suffered significant losses. The Twenty-fifth, occupying the brigade center, did not lose a single man.

But what of Lucius Polk during all this? Johnson had not found Polk because the North Carolinian, after detaching his two smallest regiments to support Darden and Calvert, had disappeared into the smoke-blanketed cedars to do battle with Schaefer. Johnson drifted past Polk, leaving him to fight Schaefer alone and outnumbered.[11]

While Polk and Schaefer sparred among the cedars and limestone outcrops north of the Wilkinson Pike, Manigault belatedly led his brigade against Roberts's stronghold. The situation had changed appreciably since the South Carolinian had convinced Maney to attack Bush's battery. Bush was now posted beside Hescock, on the knoll at the junction of the Wilkinson Pike and McFadden's Lane. Manigault made this new concentration of Federal artillery his objective, sending his Alabamians against the guns and their infantry support, the Twenty-second and Forty-second Illinois, from the south. The Rebels came close, but ultimately the results were the same. "So dense were the cedar bushes in front of the Forty-second Illinois," remembered one veteran, "that they were not aware of the approach of the enemy until they saw their glistening bayonets a few feet from them." The ensuing struggle was bitter but brief, as for a third time the Alabamians stumbled rearward through the cedars.

If Manigault were to take the guns, he would need help. And so, shortly after 9:00, he rode to the commander of the as yet uncommitted brigade to his right, Brigadier General Patton Anderson. Like Maney, Anderson agreed to help Manigault and his Alabamians. At his command the Forty-fifth Alabama and Twenty-fourth Mississippi left their temporary breastworks and formed on Manigault's right for a second charge from the south. Ten minutes later they too met with a bloody repulse as Houghtalling, Hescock, and Bush combined their fire to rake the entire Confederate line.

Two attempts to dislodge Bush and Hescock from the flank having failed, Anderson and division commander Jones Withers agreed to apply direct pressure. The forty-three-year-old Tennessean committed his three remaining regiments to take the batteries from the front, "if necessary," while he moved the Alabama battery of Captain David Waters to their left in support of the attack.

Lieutenant Colonel J. J. Scales of the Thirtieth Mississippi found the discretionary order to seize the knoll superfluous: "It was impossible indeed at that juncture to move forward without taking it," he later wrote, adding that "we therefore attempted what I candidly confess, not knowing at the time that I had any support, appeared to me a hopeless undertaking."

But Colonel W. F. Brantly, in command of the Thirtieth, felt otherwise, and the Mississippians marched forward. The line unraveled as the regiment trampled through the tangled thicket that lay between it and the guns. Unit integrity was lost, although not a shot had been fired. When the skirmishers came within range of the batteries, it was as if a wire had been tripped, and "every step from this time forth was marked by a terrific shower of grape, canister, and shell," recalled Scales, who suddenly found himself in command as Colonel Brantly was felled by the concussion of an exploding shell. Bursting shells and falling limbs were claiming Mississippians by the score, and those not struck were beginning to scatter in search of cover, threatening to end the attack before it could be pressed home. Realizing that it would be suicide in such a state of confusion to give up the comparative safety of the thicket for the open field that spread between his regiment and the Federal guns, Scales halted to reform. While his troops dodged shells and dressed ranks, a courier from brigade headquarters brought new instructions: the batteries were to be taken "at all hazards." Apparently the punishment that Sheridan's gunners were wreaking upon Scales and his Mississippians was enough to convince Anderson that any assault that did not have as its objective the knoll was pointless, as well as suicidal. Satisfied that order had been restored, Scales resumed the advance until his regiment stood poised at the wood's edge. Two hundred yards of open ground, punctuated only by brittle cornstalks and shallow middles between the rows, stood between it and the guns. The Mississippians stepped into view, and the Federal fire doubled in intensity as the Forty-second Illinois, Twenty-first Michigan, and the Eleventh Michigan of Stanley's brigade opened fire in support of the cannoneers.

Pandemonium followed. As the Mississippians pressed on, slower now, through the corn rows "men fell around on every side like autumn leaves and every foot of soil over which we passed

seemed dyed with the life blood of some one or more of the gallant
spirits whom I had the honor to command," wrote Scales. Finally
the Butternuts could stand it no longer. Instinctively they fell to
the ground, oblivious to Scales's frantic cries of "forward." The
regiment lay frozen, a mere seventy-five yards from the muzzles of
Sheridan's artillery. Turning to those nearest him, Scales pleaded
for help in making his commands heard. What followed filled the
lieutenant colonel with pride and horror:

> Asking several around me to aid in shouting "forward" Private Mc-
> Gregor, Company A, an old man, after doing so at the top of his lungs
> in vain rushed ahead of the line crying "follow me boys, follow me."
> He then roused several officers, shouting "the colonel commands
> forward," this was repeated by them, but all lost amidst the deafening
> thunder around us. To lie there was death to the last man, but my
> order to retreat repeated again and again met with the same fate, and
> there lay these noble men and loaded and fired—fought and died as
> heroically as men ever did and in a manner worthy of the first great
> cause at stake.

At long last, by shouting the command to those around him and
having them repeat it to the next man and so on down the line,
Scales was able to extricate his regiment from the slaughter. Stumbling back across the field and through the cedar thicket to their
breastworks, now occupied by A. P. Stewart's brigade, the Mississippians gathered around Scales to rest and regroup. The thinness
of their ranks reflected what they had suffered: by nightfall only
two hundred remained of the four hundred who had answered roll
that morning. Riding through the wood the next day along the
route taken by Scales, Bishop Polk was moved to write: "Such evidence of destructive firing as were left on the forest ... have
rarely, if ever been seen. The timber was torn and crushed."

Meanwhile, on the right of the Thirtieth, the Twenty-ninth Mississippi had been dealt a blow equally severe. Its predicament was
more troublesome even than that of the Thirtieth, as its path of
advance took the regiment under Sheridan and Negley's guns from
the moment it left its breastworks. The Bluecoats held their fire as
the Thirtieth struggled through the corn rows, following the Mississippians down their cannon barrels and through their rifle
sights. At thirty yards the command "fire" rang out, and the Rebel
line melted as men dropped to embrace the earth. Young J. E.
Robuck of Company A had been irritated by the deep furrows that
separated the rows of corn when the charge began—jumping them
winded him. Now, trying to escape the hail of bullets, he found

them far too shallow. "I would have liked it better had they been four feet deep," he admitted later. Mercifully the command to retreat was given, and the regiment hurried back to the breastworks. By Robuck's estimate the entire affair lasted just fifteen minutes, during which time two hundred one men fell dead or wounded on one acre of ground.

The last of Anderson's regiments, the Twenty-seventh Mississippi, fared a little better. While the Twenty-ninth and Thirtieth were being thrown back to the breastworks, Lieutenant Colonel James Autry was able to guide his men out of the field by the left flank and into the protective cover of a wood, where they fell in alongside the Twenty-fourth Mississippi, before he was shot through the head.[12]

As the last of the attackers retreated out of range, the thickets and fields on Roberts's front again fell silent, the stillness broken only by the groans of the wounded. His brigade and Hescock and Bush's gunners were the fulcrum of the Federal defense. With Greusel and Schaefer they had fought seven Confederate brigades—almost half of all Southern units on the west side of Stones River—to a standstill in ninety minutes of desperate combat. Some later would call it the most determined stand of the entire war. Aging veterans would write with pride of the part they had played in the "struggle in the cedars." But for the moment, as they reached into their boxes to remove their final cartridge and searched those of the dead for more, many of Roberts's Bluecoats must have wondered if the next fight would be their last.

CHAPTER TEN

ROSECRANS RALLIES THE RIGHT

THE muffled, faraway rattle of gunfire greeted the men of the Left Wing as they prepared to wade Stones River. At first, no one attached any importance to the clatter: after all, McCook had been fighting his way into position since the day before, and the plan of battle called for him to receive the attack of the enemy. Confident that McCook could contain the Rebels, Crittenden told Van Cleve to begin crossing as ordered at 7:00 A.M. Sam Beatty forded without incident and deployed along the east bank. Price followed. But as Colonel James Fyffe waited his turn and Hascall herded his own regiments into column, the firing drew suddenly nearer and heavier. The crossing continued, but now "the most terrible state of suspense pervaded the entire left," recalled Hascall, "as it became more and more evident that the right was being driven rapidly back on us." Lieutenant John Yaryan of Wood's staff reached the same conclusion: "The noise of battle was nearing too rapidly. McCook is certainly not going to hold the enemy in his front three hours at this rate. Not only did the sound travel too rapidly, but it broke out too much to the north and curled around to our rear with infernal speed and intensity. Men looked at each other for an explanation that each one knew for himself but dreaded to speak."[1]

Although his soldiers feared the worst, the approaching thunder initially left Rosecrans unmoved. The Ohioan's lack of concern was a consequence of poor reporting by McCook's staff. The first courier from the troubled right had told the commanding general only that McCook was "heavily pressed and needed assistance"; he said nothing of the collapse of Willich and Kirk. Lacking this information, Rosecrans merely sent the officer on his way with an empty admonition to McCook to "hold his ground obstinately." A second staff officer, however, had the good sense to render an account of Johnson's defeat. It was "a fact that was but too manifest," Rosecrans conceded, "by the rapid movement of the noise of battle toward the north."

This second report threw Rosecrans into one of his famed fits of nervous hyperactivity. He would remain this way until dusk, and from his agitation came a flood of orders, far too many, Sheridan and Crittenden thought, for troops struggling for survival to carry out. Rosecrans directed brigades, regiments, companies, any body of men he could admonish into his ragtag line. Sometimes his orders countermanded the efforts of subordinates trying to piece together their shattered units. Rosecrans would meet a brigadier, bark out a command, ride a few hundred feet, spot a regimental commander, then order him elsewhere. Such meddling only added to the prevailing confusion. His frenzy completely overcame his better judgment. Without regard for his safety, Rosecrans rode repeatedly to the muzzles of his frontline units and often beyond. (Perhaps he reasoned that, should the army be crushed, it would be better to be a fallen hero than a living scapegoat.) But whatever the wisdom of a commanding general exposing himself to direct individual brigades and regiments, it must be conceded that Rosecrans's presence helped restore the morale of those around him at a moment of supreme crisis. Numerous letters after the battle attest to this, and most men offered only their highest praise for a commander willing to share the risks of combat with them. Sergeant Henry Freeman of the Pioneer Brigade expressed the prevailing feeling: "The crisis seemed to rouse his every energy, and he appeared the embodiment of strength, courage, coolness, and determination as he directed the organization of his new line." Recalled a member of the Seventy-fourth Illinois: "The men, reassured by their leader's serenity, felt that he was the man for the hour, and could be observed scanning eagerly their general's face, as if to read in its quiet lines whose plans which wrought success." Not all wrote such hyperbole. The more discerning, peering beneath the veneer, saw Rosecrans's actions for what they were: the groping to do something, anything, of a man too stunned to seize control of events. Reflecting on the battle years later, the historian of the Forty-first Ohio wrote: "At Stone River . . . Rosecrans in person put the Forty-first in position at one time. This was while the hazard of the day was still undecided, and when the ablest commander might well have been overburdened with weightier affairs than posting a single regiment, and that for a duty not the most important conceivable. He failed to produce an impression as one who grasped the whole momentous situation with the hand of a master."[2]

Fortunately for the army, Rosecrans issued a number of timely orders before succumbing to his anxiety, orders second only to Sheridan's stand in their impact on the outcome of the battle.

Thomas received the first order. Through him, Rosecrans directed Rousseau's three brigades, then bivouacked in a grove midway between army headquarters and the Round Forest, into the cedars to sustain Sheridan's exposed right. Next, he commanded Crittenden to suspend Van Cleve's crossing and to instead deploy Price behind McFadden's Ford while retaining Fyffe and Sam Beatty in reserve along the railroad for deployment as needed.

No sooner had Rosecrans issued these instructions than a rabble of dazed infantry stumbled out of the cedars west of the turnpike; a most disgraceful scene, recounted Yaryan: "Soon fugitives and stragglers emerged from the cedars in full view, and came toward us on the run, followed by confused masses of panic-stricken troops firing their muskets in the air, or back in the faces of their comrades, following them."

With the collapse of McCook now painfully evident, Rosecrans abandoned any hope of retaining a reserve and instead mustered every available unit to piece together a new front line west of the Nashville Turnpike. Van Cleve's wet and shivering infantry, tramping toward the railroad, suddenly found themselves running into the cedars to extend Rousseau's right, and Hascall's idle brigade received orders to march up the turnpike as far as army headquarters, then turn to the southwest and press forward with Van Cleve until Rebels were encountered. The ever-present Rosecrans issued Harker similar instructions in person.

Beatty, Fyffe, and Harker swung north through a growing throng of wagons and demoralized troops. Despite the congestion they eventually reached their destination. Not so Hascall. Starting last, his men found the way blocked after moving just two hundred yards. A nightmare of confusion lay before them: "Shot and shell from the Rebel batteries were plowing up the ground all around us," recalled a veteran, "and wagons, teams, ambulances were flying about seeking places of safety." Unable to advance, Hascall likewise sought a place of safety, placing his brigade behind the Round Forest in reserve—a wise decision, as his command would prove indispensable in repelling a series of afternoon assaults against the wooded salient.

Rosecrans's next decision was his wisest of the day as well. Aware that his patchwork line could not hold indefinitely and that a Confederate drive against the turnpike itself was likely, he placed Morton's Pioneer Brigade and Captain James Stokes's Chicago Board of Trade Battery on a commanding rise near army headquarters. From there, the Chicagoans could train their guns on any Confederates attempting to cross the eight hundred yards of open ground between the eastern edge of the cedars and the turnpike.

To stem the flow of demoralized soldiers up the turnpike and out of the battle, Rosecrans directed Lieutenant Colonel John Parkhurst to form a stragglers' line north of headquarters with his Ninth Michigan Infantry. As commander of Thomas's provost guard, Parkhurst was experienced in collecting skulkers, and so took the assignment philosophically; until, that is, he saw the magnitude of his task. A leaderless transportation train, its drivers "in the most rapid retreat, throwing away their arms and accouterments, and apparently in the most frightful state of mind, crying 'We are all lost,'" nearly trampled Parkhurst's men before he was able to deploy them astride the turnpike on the north side of Overall Creek. Once formed, they netted several hundred cavalrymen, seven artillery pieces, and two regiments of infantry in a matter of minutes. With these, Parkhurst recrossed the creek and shook out his stragglers' line behind army headquarters as ordered.[3]

Meanwhile, to the west, Rousseau's division had joined the fray. "The ground was new and unknown to us," wrote Rousseau, "the woods were almost impassable to infantry." Still, by 9:30 A.M. his men had joined Sheridan's right in good order, Colonel John Beatty's brigade touching Greusel's flank and fronting southwest, Lieutenant Colonel Oliver Shephard's seven battalions of regular infantry falling in on Beatty's right, and Colonel Benjamin Scribner's five-regiment brigade coming to rest in line of battle one hundred yards to the rear. Now in position, Rousseau's men lost no time in preparing for the enemy. Skirmishers disappeared into the cedars, fallen trees became breastworks, and blue forms scrambled for cover as the Confederates, now only a few hundred yards away, closed rapidly.[4]

The Rebels were showing signs of life on Sheridan's front as well. His piecemeal assaults having accomplished nothing, Patton Anderson now called upon Brigadier General Alexander Stewart, whose brigade occupied the earthworks the Mississippians had va-

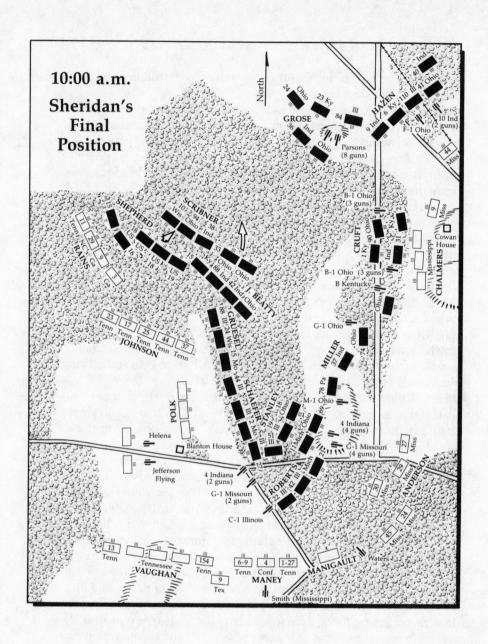

10:00 a.m.

Sheridan's Final Position

North

GROSE

24 Ohio   23 Ky   III   84   III
36 Ind   9 Ind   HAZEN   6 Ky / 110   41 Ohio
         Ohio   Ind   40
                    Parsons   F-1 Ohio   10 Ind
                    (8 guns)   (2 guns)

                                                        44
                                                        Miss

SHEPHERD
11   III
US   29   III
Tenn US   9   B-1 Ohio
      US   III   (3 guns)   9
RAINS   3   Miss
      16   18   SCRIBNER   38   92 III   CRUFT
      US   US   10   III   Wis Ohio Ind   90 Ohio   31
            19   15   33   III   1 Ky   III   Cowan
            US   Ohio Ohio   2   J. BEATTY   House
                        15   Ky 88 Ind 42 Ind Ohio   CHALMERS
                        III   B-1 Ohio (3 guns)   9
                                                           B Kentucky   Miss
                  23   17   25   44   37   G-1 Ohio
                  Tenn Tenn Tenn Tenn Tenn   III   Ohio
                        JOHNSON   GRUESEL   74   III
                                             88   III   MILLER III
                                             24 Wis   37 Ind
                                             15 Mo 44 III
                                      POLK   SCHAEFER   78 Pa
                                      III   73 III   III
                                      III   2 Mo   69   M-1 Ohio
                                                    III   STANLEY III
                              Helena   19 III   51 Michy Ohio   4 Indiana
                              III   III   III   (4 guns)
                        Blanton House   36 III   11 Michy Ohio   G-1 Missouri
                  III   (4 guns)
                  III   Jefferson   22 Mich   27   III
                        Flying   4 Indiana   III   ROBERTS   Miss   ANDERSON
                                      (2 guns)   42 III III   29   III
                                      G-1 Missouri   22 III   Miss   III
                                      (2 guns)   30   III
                                      C-1 Illinois   Miss
                                                                                      45   III   24   III
                                                                                      Miss   Miss
      13   III   Waters
      Tenn III   III   154   III   6-9   III   4   III   1-27 III   x
            Tennessee   Tenn   Tenn Conf   Tenn MANIGAULT
      VAUGHAN   9   III   MANEY
                         Tex   Smith (Mississippi)

cated, to commit two regiments in support of a second run at the Yankees. Stewart refused. A talented officer who would rise to corps command before the war's end, Stewart had no intention of repeating Anderson's mistake; rather, after conferring with Withers, he chose to throw his entire brigade simultaneously against the Federals.

Stewart's thoughtful decision spelled the end of Sheridan's stronghold. Within minutes of this final attack Roberts was dead; just moments after assuming brigade command, Colonel F. A. Harrington of the Twenty-seventh Illinois died instantly as a shell fragment tore away his jaw; and, after watching nearly all of his artillery horses fall, Captain Houghtalling went down, severely wounded.

The Federals may have overcome the loss of their officers, but they could not fight without cartridges. "There was no sign of faltering with the men," Sheridan would later boast, "the only cry being for more ammunition, which unfortunately could not be supplied." And as it could not be supplied, Sheridan prepared to withdraw. He began by riding to the heavily engaged Forty-second Illinois and summarizing the division's plight to its colonel: the division—or more correctly what remained of it—was nearly surrounded, the ammunition train was gone, and there was no hope of resupply. In short, it was time to leave. Sheridan pointed over his shoulder toward the northeast, and the Forty-second backed out of the fight. The Twenty-second Illinois followed.

From across the field northwest of the Harding house, Maney and Manigault watched the Illinoisans disappear into the timbers north of the Wilkinson Pike. Ben Cheatham saw them go too and decided to follow. As Sam Watkins recalled: "The impression that General Frank Cheatham made upon my mind, leading the charge on the Wilkinson Pike, I will never forget. I saw either victory or death written on his face. When I saw him leading our brigade . . . I felt sorry for him, he seemed so earnest and concerned, and as he was passing me I said, 'Well, General, if you are determined to die, I'll die with you.' Then it was that I saw the power of one man, born to command, over a multitude of men then almost routed and demoralized."

Watkins's narrative makes good reading, but it is as far from the truth as is his mistaking Cheatham's drunkenness for courage and clarity of thought. In reality, by the time Cheatham reorganized his command (placing Manigault on Maney's left) and led it—or reeled alongside it—across the pike, only dead and wounded Federals remained to greet him. Meddling in the affairs of Sheridan, his most capable division commander, McCook had reappeared at the front long enough to order Greusel to break contact and fall back to the Nashville Turnpike. Greusel's ill-timed withdrawal allowed Lucius Polk to completely overrun Houghtalling's battery, and all six guns fell to the Arkansans and Tennesseans. With their right now in the air, the Twenty-seventh and Fifty-first Illinois fell back, dragging Hescock's battery and all but two of Bush's guns with them. After covering the retreat of Bradley (now in command of Roberts's brigade), Schaefer broke contact and turned northward at 10:45.

"I cannot remember now or ever seeing more dead men and horses and captured cannon, all jumbled together," recalled Watkins as he stood at the center of what had been Roberts's final position. But Watkin's horror was fleeting. Noticing a dead Yankee colonel nearby (perhaps Harrington), Watkins's gaze was drawn to the officer's fine riding boots. The bitter cold stung more than his conscience, and so, taking hold of a foot, Watkins tugged at the boot. Midway through his labors, Watkins happened to glance at the colonel's face. He "had his eyes wide open, and seemed to be looking at me. He was stone dead, but I dropped that foot quick. It was my first and last attempt to rob a dead Yankee."

As horrendous as were Sheridan's losses in officers, men, and equipment, the Confederates had suffered more. Nine Butternut brigades had been thrown against Sheridan at one time or another—only Maney's had emerged with casualties anything less than severe. And beyond the dead and wounded were countless soldiers who, pushed to the limits of their endurance, simply fell out and drifted to the rear. J. E. Robuck of the Twenty-ninth Mississippi, detailed to escort prisoners to a division collection point, ran across one such soldier named, ironically, Joe Coward. Robuck, evidently trying to bait him, asked Coward if he were lost. No, he was not. Adding a bit of poetic advice, perhaps embellished by Robuck, Coward replied: "He who fights and runs away, may live to fight another day; but he who is in battle slain, will never live to fight again."[5]

With Sheridan at last defeated, Hardee was able once again to turn his attention to the Nashville Turnpike and the Union rear, blocked only by Rousseau's now isolated division. The task of removing Rousseau fell to McCown, whose units were resting and drawing ammunition near the Gresham house. As Rains's brigade was the strongest, having suffered only a handful of casualties, Mc-

Cown moved it from the division left to the right, with orders to take Rousseau from the front while Ector and Colonel Robert Harper (in command of McNair's brigade as the latter had taken ill and left the field) drove past his right flank toward the turnpike. Rains responded quickly. He marched his brigade to the edge of the cedars, reformed his regiments so that the Eleventh Tennessee and Twenty-ninth North Carolina traded places, then awaited the order to charge.

McCown's plan for gaining the Union rear, simple in design and seemingly guaranteed success, failed to allow for the generalship of Lovell Rousseau, a citizen soldier who made up in enthusiasm what he lacked in formal military training. In fact, this "natural leader," as William Shanks styled him, threw himself so ardently into his new calling that, at Stones River, he was already among the most highly regarded generals in the army.

Rousseau's entire life had been one of self-education, and the parallels with Lincoln were not lost to contemporaries. Rousseau too was tall, nearly six-foot two. And, like Lincoln, he was born into poverty, a poverty deepened by his father's death during a cholera epidemic. The sole provider of his family at age fifteen, Rousseau labored by day and, we are told, devoted himself with Lincolnian energy toward self-improvement by night as, with book in hand, he "sat by the log-fire, its blaze his only lamp, and slowly but surely mastered not only the common but the higher branches of English classics." Having taught himself all he could, Rousseau moved to Michigan to complete his education and obtain a law degree. After a term in the Indiana state legislature and brief volunteer service in Mexico, Rousseau—now a Whig—returned to Kentucky to throw himself against the tide of "Know-Nothingism" that was rising within the party. Stepping between a German immigrant attempting to vote and a mob determined to stop him during the height of Know-Nothing frenzy in Louisville, Rousseau took a bullet in the abdomen. Undaunted, he continued to oppose the Know-Nothings from his sickbed until, when their influence at last subsided and he recovered, an appreciative citizenry elected him to the state legislature. There he became an outspoken critic of secession until his resignation to join the Union army in 1861.

Here at Stones River, amid the tangled thickets west of the Nashville Turnpike, Rousseau realized even before the blow fell that his isolated command could not hope to hold out. As the scattered popping of rifle fire announced the approach of Rains's skirmishers, the Kentuckian wheeled his horse and rode off in search of a fallback position along the turnpike. Encountering Battery A, First Michigan Artillery, as it struggled over limestone outcrops behind Scribner's infantry, Rousseau told Lieutenant George Van Pelt to turn his limbers around and find firing positions near the turnpike.

Lieutenant Alfred Pirtle, Rousseau's ordnance officer, had just parked his train on the high ground between the railroad and the turnpike that today marks the national cemetery when Van Pelt's battery emerged from the timber "at a walk, in perfect order." Right behind came Rousseau. Judging that the battle might soon overtake his train, Pirtle rode forward to help Rousseau place the guns, suggesting that they might replace his vulnerable wagons on what was ideal artillery ground. Rousseau concurred and disappeared into the timber. Pirtle led Van Pelt up the slope, placed his guns where they could sweep the four hundred yards of open field west of the turnpike, then quickly moved his wagons into a small hollow behind the knoll.

Rousseau, meanwhile, had returned to find his line already engaged. Thanks to poor communications within the brigade, Shephard's right battalions (First Battalion, Fifteenth United States Infantry, and First Battalion, Sixteenth United States Infantry) had missed the order to halt and instead continued deeper into the woods, enticed by Rebels clad in Union blue. According to Captain Jessee Fulmer of the Fifteenth United States, the Confederates, who "feigned to be us," led his skirmishers to within a few yards of their main body. A spattering of fire grew to a sudden crescendo. The deception succeeded. The skirmishers collapsed on the battalion line, and Captain Fulmer, noticing that the Eleventh Tennessee had skirted past his right, withdrew his unit after firing just one volley. The Sixteenth fared a little better. Sheltered behind a limestone outcrop, Captain Robert Crofton's regulars challenged the advancing Twenty-ninth North Carolina to what that regiment's commander called "the struggle of the day." Crofton contested the first seventy-five yards inch by inch, and his men even halted the North Carolinians momentarily. But the hasty retreat of the Fifteenth left him alone, and Crofton was compelled to withdraw his battalion by the right of companies.[6]

Crofton had been more isolated than he thought. Rousseau, after posting Van Pelt's battery, had decided to deploy his entire division along the high ground near the turnpike. As Shephard's remaining battalions were not engaged when Rousseau returned to the front, the Kentuckian ordered them to retire with Lieutenant Francis

Guenther's Battery H, Fifth United States Artillery, to join Van Pelt. The Second and Thirty-third Ohio, meanwhile, had withdrawn to support Van Pelt—apparently at Rousseau's command, although he makes no mention of it in his report of the battle. Left with only three regiments, Scribner passed a worrisome twenty minutes until word came for these to be withdrawn as well.

Lieutenant Pirtle was surprised at the disorder of Scribner's retreat, particularly as the men had not been engaged: "Across the cotton field a few men straggled in leisurely fashion toward the rear; an ambulance came into view; a squad of soldiers moved rather rapidly from the front; I saw more unhurt men every moment; it looked badly to me as the crowd grew larger and larger; a color-bearer with the colors thrown carelessly over his shoulder moved to the rear, and the space was filled with an unorganized mob, so numerous that I thought I was about to see another Bull Run."

Scribner too was mortified by the impression his troops made as they fled across the cotton field, the more so as General Thomas was watching the spectacle from a point near Pirtle's train. Seeing his reputation dissolve with his command, Scribner galloped to join Thomas. His men had not been driven from the cedars, he explained emphatically; rather, they had been ordered out and at his command had dispersed upon entering the field so as to present Rebel sharpshooters a scattered target. Looking over his shoulder, Scribner was relieved to see his brigade rally along the turnpike.

"And now, General, you see they are re-forming," Scribner added, in case Thomas misinterpreted the obvious. "Have you any further orders?"

"No, re-form on the pike," replied Thomas.

Had Thomas looked more closely at the drama unfolding along the turnpike, he may have noticed that a third of Rousseau's command was unaccounted for. While Shephard and Scribner reformed under the safety of Van Pelt and Guenther's batteries, John Beatty remained in the cedars, fighting the better part of a Confederate division without knowing that he fought alone. Beatty's ignorance of the fate of the rest of the division is understandable: his own brigade had formed in a thicket "so dense as to render it impossible to see the length of a regiment." But there is no satisfactory explanation for Rousseau's failure to inform Beatty of his decision to withdraw. Perhaps hoping to draw attention away from the incident, Rousseau made no mention of it, or of Beatty's subsequent stand, in his report of the battle. For his part, Beatty said only that he last saw his division commander at 9:00, when the Kentuckian enjoined him to hold his line "until hell freezes over."

Hell began freezing over the moment the Ohioan halted in the timber. Reinforced with two regiments detached earlier in support of the division artillery, Lucius Polk's Butternuts struck Beatty's right center while the Federals were frantically building breastworks from logs and underbrush.

Beatty initially had the upper hand. An open wood lay between the two brigades, and the Confederates, attempting to cross it, suffered terribly. Polk pushed his men forward until, convinced by the growing carpet of Butternut that a frontal assault was futile, he changed course and tried to envelop Beatty's right. Again he miscalculated. Instead of gliding unopposed past the Federal right, his men ran into the Fifteenth Kentucky, hidden behind the many limestone boulders that dotted the Federal right. The Kentuckians held until their colonel fell, but even their retreat failed to turn the tide. Anticipating their collapse, Beatty had wheeled his remaining units to the right, and they now opened with an enfilading fire that eventually forced Polk to break contact.

The lull that followed gave Beatty time to evaluate his situation. Having noted an absence of firing from beyond his flanks during the fighting, Beatty sent one staff officer to report the brigade's position to Rousseau, a second in search of Shephard, and a third to look for Van Pelt's battery, which Rousseau had assured Beatty would support him. All three returned with the same news: There was no one left on the field but their brigade and the Confederates. "I conclude that the contingency to which General Rousseau referred—that is to say, that hell has frozen over—and about face my brigade and march to the rear," Beatty wrote wryly, adding that he feared the prospect of pulling his men out of the cedars: "A retrograde movement under fire must necessarily be extremely hazardous. It demoralizes your men, who cannot, at the moment, understand the purpose of the movement, while it encourages the enemy."

He was right. Polk chose precisely the moment of Beatty's withdrawal to renew his assault. Vaughan's brigade, ordered to his support by Cheatham, joined Polk on the right. And S. A. M. Wood, whose men had just refilled their cartridge boxes, may have fallen in on his left, though reports are unclear on this point. In any event, the pressure was enough to panic the Federals and, despite

Beatty's efforts at rallying them for a final stand at the northeast
ern edge of the cedar brake, they swept past into the cotton field.
There Beatty again tried to steady them, only to have his horse
killed. "Before I have time to recover my feet, my troops, with
thousands of others, sweep in disorder to the rear, and I am left
standing alone." Beatty threw a final defiant glance at the Confederates, then gathered up his sword and ran toward the turnpike to
join his command.[7]

Hardee now had cleared all but a portion of one Federal brigade
from the thicket north of the Wilkinson Pike that today consti-
tutes the southern limit of the Stones River National Battlefield.
Only Colonel Wiliam Grose's Sixth Ohio and Thirty-sixth Indiana stood between Rains and the turnpike. Rains charged the
Midwesterners.

Grose's infantry had had plenty of time to ponder their fate.
Fearing that the struggle on Sheridan's front might soon envelop
his rear, the Hoosier colonel had changed front at 8:00. With Palmer's concurrence, Grose realigned his brigade so as to form a "V"
with Hazen. The Sixth Ohio and Thirty-sixth Indiana constituted
the front line; the Twenty-third Kentucky and Eighty-fourth Illinois, a new regiment, formed the second line; the Twenty-fourth
Ohio faced northwest and covered the right rear; and Captain
Charles Parsons placed Batteries H and M, Fourth United States
Artillery, on a slight rise between the frontline regiments so that
they had a clear field of fire across the cotton field.

At 9:00, after Rousseau's columns double-timed past his regiments into the cedars, Grose ordered the Thirty-sixth Indiana and
Sixth Ohio forward two hundred yards to better support Shephard's regulars. Assuming Shephard to be holding his own, neither
regimental commander deployed skirmishers. They were wrong.
Advancing blindly, their troops were wholly unprepared for the
confusion that greeted them as they neared Shephard's rear. Corporal Hannaford of the Sixth Ohio recalled his surprise: "The line in
advance of us, a brigade that had passed us only a few minutes
before, had been crushed and beaten back, and were drifting toward
us in utter confusion. Organization and discipline were forgotten;
they were fleeing for their lives . . . and almost before I had time to
comprehend its meaning, the rebel bullets were hissing all about
us. We were in action."

Hannaford's commander, Colonel Nicholas Anderson, was
equally stunned. By the time the regulars cleared his ranks, Rains

was only one hundred yards away. The Rebels delivered the first volley, and Anderson's ranks quivered. His men recovered and returned the fire, and for twenty minutes the two lines traded fire until Anderson, for reasons known only to him, decided to fix bayonets and charge. But before he could carry out this reckless maneuver his attention was drawn to his left flank company, the object of a deadly oblique fire from Lucius Polk's ubiquitous Butternuts.

Hannaford saw them too. As he turned his head toward the left, "a whistling volley of bullets came over from that new enemy, and for me the battle was over." The Ohioan had been hit: "I remember no acute sensation of pain, not even any distinct shock, only an instantaneous consciousness of having been struck; then my breath came hard and laboured, with a crouplike sound, and with a dull, aching feeling in my right shoulder, my arm fell powerless at my side, and the Enfield dropped from my grasp. I threw my left hand up to my throat and withdrew it covered with the warm, bright-red blood. The end had come at last." Hannaford's most immediate fear was of being trampled in the confusion. Wanting only to "die in peace," he crawled between two large boulders, spread out his rubber blanket, and lay down—as he then imagined—to die.[8]

Meanwhile, Anderson had instructed his men to about-face, fire by the rear rank, and then fall back. They emerged from the timber in good order, having held forty minutes, and reformed behind Parsons.

For the Thirty-sixth Indiana, the story was much the same. Shephard's regulars blocked the Hoosiers' field of fire so effectively that the Twenty-ninth North Carolina and Eleventh Tennessee were on top of them before they could fire a shot. Major Isaac Kinley, the acting commander, was wounded almost immediately, and within minutes every mounted officer but the adjutant had lost his horse. Companies A and C collapsed first, swept away with the panicked regulars; then the remaining eight companies broke contact and scattered. The last Union infantry to leave the cedars, they stopped running only after they had cleared Rousseau's batteries.

For a moment there was silence. All eyes turned toward the timber. Lieutenant Pirtle continues the story: "As I looked on, an officer on foot, sword in hand, sprang into view with a shout; in an instant the edge of the timber was alive with a mass of arms, heads, legs, guns, swords, gray coats, brown hats, shirt sleeves, and the enemy were upon us, yelling, leaping, running. Not a shot from them for a few jumps, then one or two paused to throw up their guns, fire and yell, and then run forward to try to gain the front."

At that instant the batteries that Pirtle had helped place roared into action, and the cotton field was blanketed in smoke. Rains had stumbled into a hornet's nest. At least four Union regiments—the Eighty-fourth Illinois, Twenty-fourth Ohio, Twenty-third Kentucky, and, at the wood's edge, the Ninety-fourth Ohio—joined Van Pelt, Guenther, and Parsons in decimating the exposed Confederates. Rains fell with a bullet through his heart. His men held on ten minutes until—hungry, exhausted, and leaderless—they melted back into the woods. Only dead and wounded remained among the boulders and furrows of the cotton field.[9]

As the survivors, now nominally under the command of Colonel Robert Vance of the Twenty-ninth North Carolina, stumbled toward the Wilkinson Pike, they encountered the equally exhausted men of Cleburne's division and learned why they had charged the turnpike alone. After prying loose Greusel and rolling up Beatty, Cleburne had discovered a large body of Yankees beyond his right. Rather than expose his already jaded infantry to a flanking fire that might break them, Cleburne pulled Johnson and Polk out of the cedars. After allowing him time to regroup his command, Cleburne ordered Johnson to march by the left flank until he made contact with Liddell, who by this time had drifted nearly a mile to the northwest. Johnson found Liddell along the southern edge of the clearing below the Widow Burris house. Liddell yielded the front to Johnson, who ascended a small hill while Liddell reformed under its brow. Vaughan, still under orders to support Cleburne, and Polk fell in on Johnson's right. Liddell rejoined Johnson's left, and Cleburne again sent his command forward, this time toward the Widow Burrows house and the Nashville Turnpike beyond. Wood's brigade, reduced to five hundred effectives, stayed in the rear to guard the corps ordnance train.[10]

The troops that had convinced Cleburne to change course belonged to Colonel Timothy Stanley. For twenty minutes following Sheridan's departure Stanley's front lay silent. Then Stewart and Anderson, supported by a converging fire from the Jefferson Flying Artillery and Humphrey's Arkansas Battery south of the Wilkinson Pike and Stanford's Mississippi and Barret's Missouri batteries east of McFadden's Lane, slammed into his line. The only instance of effective artillery support provided Rebel infantry during the battle, it devastated Stanley's brigade. Negley called the fire "most destructive." Private Ira Gillaspie of the Eleventh Michigan said that it mowed down his comrades by the score. Even those rounds that sailed overhead took lives, recalled one veteran, as they cut tree limbs, "which, falling, crushed the living and dead alike."

Men reacted differently to the fire. Some hurled insults: "Why don't you come over and take us into camp?" "Hey, Johnny, step along this way, a little quicker!" "Ah, yes, very well aimed, but it never touched me." Others prayed. James Haynie of the Nineteenth Illinois recalled the last act of one man in the ranks. "There is a five-dollar bill in my watch-fob pocket," he told Haynie. "Take it out when I'm done for." A moment later the man was dead.

Badly outnumbered and flanked to the west by Manigault and Maney, Stanley's regiments wavered. The Sixty-ninth Ohio quit the field first, its colonel "so drunk as to be unfitted to command." The remainder of the brigade collapsed more or less simultaneously, leaving three guns to the Confederates.[11]

Stanley's defeat brought the battle to Colonel John Miller, commander of the second of Negley's two brigades. Only thirty-one years old, the South Bend, Indiana, native was among the most promising officers in the army. "There was not perhaps in all the army a brigade . . . having a commander in which it had greater confidence," wrote headquarters clerk Wilson Vance. Although Miller's rise through the ranks would be slowed by a bullet the following June, the postwar years would find him in Washington as a powerful California senator.

Having just received a desperate order from Negley to "hold my position to the last extremity," Miller scrambled to realign the brigade. Positioned to receive an attack from the east, his regiments were painfully vulnerable to an assault from the south, the direction from which the Confederates were coming. Only the Seventy-eighth Pennsylvania, nestled in a limestone outcrop fifty by seventy-five yards in size, was deployed to defend against an attack from that direction; the remainder of the brigade, including two batteries of artillery, fronted the earthworks of Chalmer's Confederate brigade.

Unfortunately for Miller, the enemy struck before he could take any corrective action. Again the guns of Barret and Stanford announced the approach of Withers's infantry. Stewart lapped Miller's right and slowly worked his way into the Hoosier's rear, while Anderson maintained pressure in front. Miller's regiments held firm until their ammunition began to run out. The Thirty-seventh

Indiana wavered first. Backing out of the line, it withdrew a short distance in search of the ammunition train, and the Seventy-fourth Ohio and Seventy-eighth Pennsylvania joined flanks to fill in the interval. The Thirty-seventh returned moments later empty-handed. Its commander informed Miller that the brigade teamsters had fled at the first volley, and the men, gathering what ammunition they could from the boxes of the dead and wounded, returned to the fray.

The Seventy-eighth Pennsylvania faltered next. Engaged on the left, right, and in front, the regiment fell back one hundred yards before Miller personally guided it back into line. No sooner had Miller plugged this gap then the Thirty-seventh Indiana again gave back. The Seventy-fourth Ohio followed. Miller chose to let them go—with Stanley gone and Stewart now entirely in his rear, retreat was inevitable. As the Twenty-first Ohio was still in line, Miller ordered its commander, Colonel James Niebling, to cover the brigade's withdrawal. Although it was their first battle, the Ohioans responded well. Armed with Colt revolving rifles, they halted the Twenty-fourth and Twenty-seventh Mississippi as they struggled across the cornfield to their front. "Give 'em hell by the acre, boys," Niebling shouted as he rode along the line. And give them hell they did, until only the Ohioans and Stanley's Nineteenth Illinois were left on the field. Together they launched a bayonet charge that threw the Confederates off balance long enough for the brigade to break through to the Nashville Turnpike. One entire company of the Twenty-first fell captive to the Twenty-seventh Mississippi before the remainder of the regiment succeeded in cutting through Stewart's ranks to rejoin their comrades along the turnpike.

Miller's artillery fared no better. With nearly all their horses dead, the men of Battery M, First Ohio, were forced to surrender four pieces to the enemy; Battery G, First Ohio, and Nell's Kentucky Battery each left behind one gun. Looking over his shoulder as his regiment retreated, Joseph Gibson of the Seventy-eighth Pennsylvania caught a glimpse of one tragically devoted artilleryman: "One of the last sights witnessed as we entered the cedar woods in our retreat was an artilleryman trying to haul his gun off the field with one horse, the other five having been killed. One wheel of the gun carriage had become fastened between two rocks, and the brave artilleryman was trying with a rail to pry it out."[12]

CHAPTER ELEVEN

OUR BOYS WERE FORCED BACK IN CONFUSION

IT was noon. Six hours earlier a double line of blue had extended from Stones River to the Franklin road. Now only a tangled remnant remained to receive the eleven Butternut brigades approaching the Nashville Turnpike. Should any of them sever that vital artery, it might cost Rosecrans the battle and, conceivably, much of his army.

Rains had lunged at the turnpike alone and met with disaster. Undaunted, Ector was about to repeat that error. His failure to support Rains had doomed the attack; now Harper's inability to keep pace with Ector was to have the same result. McCown either was unaware that the two brigades had separated or was unable to reunite them, and Ector's men stepped out of the cedars alone.

They could not have struck a better-prepared segment of the Union line had Rosecrans guided them in himself. The units facing Ector were virtually the only fresh troops left to Rosecrans. Directly opposite the Texan, on the rise near the Cowan graveyard between the turnpike and the railroad, lay Morton's Pioneers, Stokes's Chicago Board of Trade Battery, and Battery B, Pennsylvania Light Artillery. And in a cedar glade beyond Ector's left, Sam Beatty's as yet uncommitted brigade paused to enfilade the Rebel flank.

Raising the rebel yell, the Texans surged into the open fields. Ector's right regiments enjoyed initial success as they crested the small but commanding knoll on the west side of the turnpike that today marks the battlefield park headquarters. There they settled in to trade blows with Morton's Second and Third battalions. On the left, however, the Texans found trouble the moment they came into range. Lured by the invisibility of Sam Beatty's brigade, the Fifteenth Texas advanced some three hundred yards before its skirmishers uncovered the enemy. The Texans surged forward and chased the Yankee skirmishers another three hundred yards before running into Beatty's main line. Colonel Andrews brought up the remainder of the Fifteenth, and the two lines disappeared in smoke.

Despite the advantages of surprise and cover, Beatty's troops were wavering. The human debris from the Right Wing that Ector had swept before him nearly stampeded them before they were able to form a line of battle. "They broke through the lines of the brigade," complained Beatty, "infantry, cavalry, artillery, ambulances, baggage trains, etc. in the greatest confusion, frequently separating the regiments of the brigade, threatening serious trouble." Major Charles Manderson of the Nineteenth Ohio, in front with the Ninth Kentucky, agreed: "This scene was one of disorder and panic. Regiment after regiment swept our lines in the greatest confusion; but through it all our men preserved an unbroken front." Nerves were less steady in the second line. The Seventy-ninth Indiana, a new three-year regiment in action for the first time, almost collapsed under the weight of the troops retreating through its ranks. Before irreparable damage could be done, Colonel Frederick Knefler wisely instructed his Hoosiers to lie down. The men were grateful, and "they clung a little closer to the bosom of Old Mother earth than they had ever done before."

They held on. On the other side of the field, Colonel Andrews began to despair. Looking about, he could see only his Fifteenth Texas, the Fourteenth Texas, and Federals in the cotton field. Andrews rode to Ector, who was encouraging the Fourteenth in its duel with the Nineteenth Ohio, and asked him if he knew where the remainder of the brigade was. Ector, who had followed the Fourteenth and Fifteenth, said no. At that, Andrews replied that he could not hold out much longer against an entire brigade and two batteries of artillery. Ector thought for a moment, then agreed that both regiments "had better give back." Returning to his command, a relieved Andrews shouted the order to withdraw, only to have his voice drowned out by the clatter of musketry. Andrews tried again, those nearest heard the command and obeyed it, and eventually the entire regiment got the idea. Ector, meanwhile, shepherded the Fourteenth out of the field.

At the command of Lovell Rousseau, who happened to be in the area, the Nineteenth Ohio and Ninth Kentucky pursued the Confederates. They spilled across the field, driving the enemy a quarter of a mile before empty cartridge boxes forced them to halt. At that point Beatty again took charge of his brigade. He directed a passage of lines under fire, a difficult maneuver under the best of circumstances. The Nineteenth Ohio and Ninth Kentucky broke into column, and the second-line regiments—including the green Seventy-ninth Indiana—advanced. The passage went flawlessly, and the brigade resumed its pursuit of Ector, driving him another six hundred yards across a large field and into the timber south of the Widow Burris house.

Major Manderson was grateful that his regiment had been removed from the front line. During the advance he had had his horse shot out from under him; as he tumbled to the ground, his eyeglasses shattered, leaving the battlefield a blur to the nearsighted Ohioan. After mounting a second horse, Manderson dispatched his servant rearward to retrieve his spare pair of eyeglasses. Manderson waited. The afternoon passed, the fighting sputtered out, and Manderson returned to the unit baggage train to search for the eyeglasses himself. Only then did he learn that his servant and glasses had disappeared in the direction of Nashville.

Despite the absence of Ector, the Tenth and Eleventh Texas fought well, not withdrawing until Beatty was deep in their rear. Fortunately Captain Morton crossed the turnpike just far enough to occupy the knoll the Texans had abandoned, and so the two regiments escaped unmolested. Battery B, Pennsylvania Light Artillery, Stokes's Chicagoans, and Rosecrans were right behind. The general paused briefly to tell Stokes that "if he could hold that place for one hour, he would save the day." A flattered Stokes said he would try, and Rosecrans spurred on after Beatty's brigade.[1]

Beatty, meanwhile, had been joined on his right by Fyffe, who took position near the Asbury Church at 1:00 P.M. Harker arrived a few minutes later to extend the line northward as far as the Widow Burris house. The three brigades continued the pursuit of the Fourteenth and Fifteenth Texas until Van Cleve halted them along the southern boundary of a large sward, within sixty yards of the cedars. The next move belonged to the Confederates.

They made it sooner than Van Cleve or his lieutenants expected. Where two regiments had melted into the timber, four brigades emerged, scattering the Federal skirmishers and startling the front-line regiments. "We received such a Southern greeting as we had never before experienced, not even in the bloody forests of Shiloh," remembered a member of Fyffe's staff. The greeting came courtesy

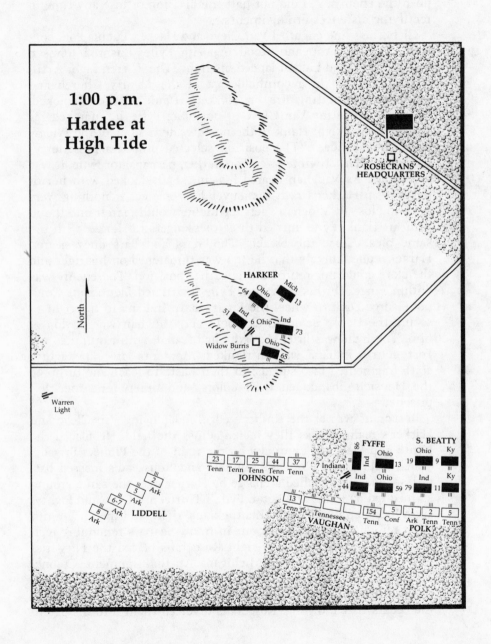

1:00 p.m.
Hardee at
High Tide

North

ROSECRANS'
HEADQUARTERS

XXX

HARKER

Mich
13

64 Ohio

51 Ind   Ind
6 Ohio   73

Ohio
Widow Burris   65

Warren
Light

FYFFE   S. BEATTY

86   Ohio   Ohio   Ky
7 Indiana   Ind   13   19   9
                                Ind Ky
23 17 25 44 37   Ind Ohio 79   11
Tenn Tenn Tenn Tenn Tenn 44   59
JOHNSON

13   154   5   1   2   5
Tenn Tennessee   Tenn Conf Ark Tenn Tenn
      VAUGHAN   POLK

2
Ark

5
Ark

6-7
Ark

8
Ark
LIDDELL

of Pat Cleburne. Cleburne had shattered Davis and pried loose
Sheridan. Now he was after Van Cleve. "My orders," he wrote,
"frequently received from General Hardee during the day, being to
push the enemy . . . I did not halt the division or lose any time in
rectifying distances or alignments."

Cleburne's line engulfed Van Cleve and Harker. Lucius Polk confronted Beatty, Vaughan stood opposite Fyffe, Bushrod Johnson
faced Harker, and Liddell lapped his right. The Warren Light Artillery unlimbered in a cornfield east of the Asbury Church and
opened a devastating fire on Harker's flank. Harker panicked.
Without consulting Van Cleve or notifying Fyffe, he marched his
brigade by the right flank to the northwestern slope of the Widow
Burris house ridge. "The position selected proved a most fortunate one," Harker wrote later. For Harker, perhaps; for Fyffe, it was
disastrous. As Vaughan neared his line, Fyffe looked with horror
on the gap Harker's rash maneuver had created: if nothing were
done to close it, Vaughan's left regiments would march into it and
turn his flank. Fyffe hurried three messengers to Harker with the
same plea: Close the breach. The Stars and Bars drew nearer.
Harker replied merely that he too was threatened on his right and
therefore could not return to his earlier position. The enemy was
within range. On his own now, Fyffe instructed Lieutenant Colonel George Dick to wheel the Eighty-sixth Indiana to the right to
secure the flank. Before Dick could act, Vaughan was on top of
him. The fight was brief. As Fyffe had feared, within minutes the
Forty-fourth Indiana was outflanked. Moments later the Eighty-
sixth fragmented into squads: in their haste to reach the turnpike
the Hoosiers abandoned their colors, and ninety-nine men fell
prisoner.[2]

Rosecrans was at the timber's edge, redeploying Van Cleve and
Harker's regiments as they reeled across the field. He placed the
Ninth and Eleventh Kentucky on the right of the Pioneer Brigade,
which—along with Stokes's gunners and Rousseau's massed batteries—had just repelled a charge by Harper over the same ground
stained red by Rains and Ector. Fyffe's Thirteenth Ohio and Eighty-
sixth Indiana rallied on the Kentuckians' right, and the Fifty-ninth
Ohio remained on the ridge out in front. Beatty's remaining regiments fell in next; on their right Rosecrans placed the Fifty-first
Ohio and the Thirteenth Michigan. At that moment Colonel
Luther Bradley appeared at the head of the Fifty-first and Twenty-
seventh Illinois, in search of ammunition after their long ordeal in
the cedars that morning. Rosecrans diverted them into his patch-

work line; to Bradley's protest that he needed ammunition, the general replied that it was a desperate moment and they must go forward, with or without ammunition.[3]

The situation appeared desperate indeed. As the sun sank beneath the horizon and the chill of a winter's eve set in, Cleburne's seemingly invincible veterans drove toward the Nashville Turnpike and the Union rear. Cleburne's lieutenants were confident of success. So certain was St. John Liddell of the outcome that he paused at the Widow Burris house to chat with Union surgeons. Liddell's frame of mind had improved considerably since his encounter with Surgeon Doolittle that morning. His son was not dead as Liddell had been led to believe, and a trusted staff officer had pulled him off the field and seen him safely to the rear in an ambulance. Liddell this time was happy to accommodate the Federal doctors who begged his protection from prowling Confederate skulkers. He told the chief surgeon to chalk his name on the wall and claim for him the hospital. Then, recalled Liddell, the unbelievable happened: "While this was occurring, which was in an incredibly short space of time, I discovered our lines breaking rapidly to the rear, to head off the stragglers and check the retreat, not knowing what was the cause of this sudden movement. On halting and rallying the stragglers, I found that they were General Johnson's men, who were passing in rear of my line, and were retreating toward my position, on the left."

Liddell stemmed their route, realigned them, then galloped to Johnson to demand an explanation for the miserable performance of the Tennessean's command. Johnson had none. Dumbfounded, he simply pointed to a neck of wood where Liddell's equally demoralized brigade lay cowering. Johnson later wrote of his shock: "The movement was to me totally unexpected, and I have yet to learn that there exists a cause commensurate with the demoralization that ensued. At the moment in which I felt the utmost confidence in the success of our arms I was almost run over by our retreating troops. I contended with the tide step by step, but made no impression on the retreating columns."

What had gone wrong? Why did Cleburne's division crack just as it reached its final objective? The reports of brigade and regimental commanders offer no answer: each blames the other for giving way first. Evidence suggests that Vaughan wavered after taking only a few ragged volleys. And when Bradley's two weary regiments counterattacked with empty cartridge boxes, Vaughan's brigade disintegrated. Polk and Johnson may have held on longer.

George Blakemore, on leave from duties with the garrison at Charleston, South Carolina, witnessed their effort to seize the turnpike from atop a knoll near the Widow Burris house. "Our boys charged repeatedly to capture the annoying guns," he wrote, "but were each time forced back in confusion." Nevertheless their collapse, when it came, was as irredeemable as it was unexpected. Colonel D. C. Govan, acting brigade commander during Liddell's untimely visit to the Union hospital at the Widow Burris house, had halted the brigade a few hundred yards behind Johnson while a staff officer was dispatched to satisfy his regimental commanders' cries for ammunition. Govan joined his subordinates in conversation and awaited the return of his staff officer. To the horror of all, Johnson's Tennesseans came running back in disorder, and their panic threw Liddell's ranks into confusion. Major W. F. Douglas of the Sixth Arkansas was surprised to see them, as the gunfire along the turnpike had seemed light; Lieutenant Colonel John Murray of the Fifth Arkansas was furious, calling the retreat "disorderly and disgraceful." Govan waited until the demoralized Tennesseans cleared his lines, then followed them.

Pat Cleburne offered perhaps the best explanation for the defeat of his men when they appeared to be on the brink of victory. Simple exhaustion and not Yankee bullets had turned the tide: "It was . . . after 3 o'clock; my men had had little or no rest the night before; they had been fighting since dawn, without relief, food, or water; they were comparatively without the support of artillery, for the advance had been too rapid to enable my single battery to get into position and answer the enemy; their ammunition was again nearly exhausted and our ordnance trains could not follow."

Afterwards, Hardee would complain bitterly of the absence of reinforcements at this, the critical moment of the battle. The time Cleburne expended breaking off the pursuit of Rousseau and regrouping prior to attacking Harker and Van Cleve had been excessive but, without fresh units to replace him, unavoidable, reasoned Hardee. It was this delay, he believed, that allowed Rosecrans to patch together a final defensive line near the turnpike.[4]

Hardee's analysis is sound, his criticism justified. To several requests for reinforcements, Bragg responded that none were available. By 3:00 P.M. this was true: Bragg had committed them in a reckless attempt to break the Union salient that had developed around a small copse along the railroad. For four hours this little wood obsessed Bragg, and his obsession cost him the battle.

CHAPTER TWELVE

WHIRLWIND IN THE ROUND FOREST

WILLIAM Babcock Hazen was a soldier's soldier. The army was his life—before, during, and after the war. A boyhood friend of James Garfield and a West Point graduate, Hazen had his first taste of combat chasing Commanches in Texas. There, in 1859, he took a wound that left him on sick leave until the outbreak of the war. Given command of the Forty-first Ohio in October 1861, Hazen went on to distinguish himself in every major action of the Army of the Cumberland, and before the war ended he would earn every brevet through major general in the regular service. After the war, Hazen followed the Germans as an observer during the Franco-Prussian War and later became the U.S. Army's chief signal officer.

Although still a colonel, Hazen at Stones River was among the most experienced and capable commanders in the army. The battle would only add to his reputation, as it fell to him to defend what was to become the most fiercely contested spot on the entire field—a copse of cedar and oak known to posterity as the Round Forest.

A singularly unimpressive bit of timber, the Round Forest at its highest lay only three feet above the fields of cotton and winter wheat that encircled it. From the southeast the charred remains of the Cowan farm, resting on an elevation midway between the lines, dominated it completely. The Round Forest became critical to the Union defenses only through a tactical error.

It took Hazen's division commander, John Palmer, until the morning of the thirty-first to recognize the importance of the Cowan farm and the vulnerability of his own brigades, particularly

Hazen's, which was deployed in the field between the forest (then held by Colonel George Wagner) and the farm. Hazen described the position as "utterly untenable . . . being commanded by ground in all directions with covers of wood, embankment, and palisading at good musket range in front, right, and left."

As the Confederates to his front showed no inclination to attack, Palmer at 8:00 A.M. set his brigades in motion toward the Cowan farm. Negley had agreed to advance with him, but all that emerged from the timber beyond Cruft's right was the echo of heavy firing. Riding down McFadden's Lane, Palmer discovered that Negley, instead of advancing, had retired his lines in response to Cheatham's attack against Sheridan. Staff officers rode at once to halt Cruft and Hazen.

Palmer returned to find his subordinates awaiting orders, their units having covered just one hundred yards. Palmer directed Cruft to retrace his steps into the timber, a movement he accomplished rapidly and in good order. Matters were more complicated on Hazen's front. Wagner had been compelled to pull three of his four regiments out of the Round Forest to extend his line to Stones River and close the gap made by Harker's departure. But in filling the breach on his left, Wagner opened a larger and potentially more dangerous one on his right. Palmer ordered Hazen to fill it. Leaving the Ninth Indiana south of the turnpike, the Ohioan led the remainder of his command into the forest. Colonel Walter Whitaker and his Sixth Kentucky formed line of battle astride the turnpike. The One Hundred Tenth Illinois—another green three-year unit mustered in that summer—settled into the wood itself behind Captain Dan Cockerhill's Battery F, First Ohio Artillery. The Forty-first Ohio rounded out the line in support of the Tenth Indiana Artillery, left behind by Wagner to shore up Hazen's defenses.[1]

Hazen's men fell out to gather logs and rocks for breastworks. Just as quickly they picked up their rifles and fell back in. Scattered firing from the picket line announced the first challenge to the Round Forest salient.

"They moved forward in splended style," Colonel Thomas Sedgewick of the Second Kentucky wrote of the Confederate advance. Brigadier General James Chalmers's two thousand Mississippians may have looked impressive as they passed the Cowan farm, but it is unlikely that they entertained much hope of success. Not only was the brigade fated to cross eight hundred yards of open ground in full view of the enemy, but Chalmers's right-flank regiment, the Forty-fourth Mississippi, went into action virtually

unarmed. According to Major J. O. Thompson, the brigade ordnance officer had gathered all the rifles in Thompson's command
five days earlier for redistribution among the other regiments of
the brigade. Two days later, he returned with several wagonloads of
what Thompson derided as "refuse guns." Inspecting them, Thompson was mortified: "Many of these guns were worthless—some being bent, some cocked could not be pulled down, some whose
hammers had to be carried in the men's pockets until time to
commence firing, others so foul as to render it impossible to ram
home the cartridge, many without ramrods and only one bayonet
in the lot. Even of these poor arms there was not a sufficiency and
after every exertion on my part to procure arms, one half of the
regiment moved out with no other resemblance to a gun than such
sticks as they could gather."

The majority of Chalmers's brigade swung south of the Cowan
farm and into the rifle sights of the Second Kentucky and Thirty-
first Indiana. A few well-aimed volleys from behind boulders and
rail fences sent the Mississippians reeling over the ridge and out of
sight. Almost immediately the Stars and Bars reappeared above the
ridge, and Chalmers led his men through the cotton and winter
wheat to within fifty yards of the Federals. The Confederates held
on longer this time and paid the price. For thirty minutes they
stood in the open, exchanging volleys with the six hundred men
of Cruft's front line. The Rebels fell in windrows. The ground in
front of the Thirty-first Indiana was so heavily blanketed with
dead and wounded that it was later labeled the "Mississippi Half-
Acre." Among the wounded was Chalmers. Struck in the head
by a shell fragment, the thirty-one-year-old attorney was carried
from the field, bleeding and unconscious. Chalmers's staff failed to
inform the next ranking officer, Colonel T. W. White, of the Virginian's wound, and so the brigade fell back to its rifle pits in leaderless disorder.

But not all the Mississippians quit the field. The brigade had
split as it negotiated the outbuildings of the Cowan farm: while
most followed Chalmers, the Ninth Mississippi and Thompson's
Forty-fourth drifted north. Although the Ninth remained near the
farm, the Forty-fourth continued on to within two hundred yards
of the Forty-first Ohio and the Round Forest, stopping on a small
rise that commanded the Union lines. After clearing away the Federal skirmishers, Thompson's men deployed behind what cover
they could find, and those with serviceable weapons opened fire
on the Ohioans. After an hour the Forty-first withdrew in search of

ammunition, and the Ninth Indiana took their place. This new regiment proved too much for the Mississippians, who crawled behind a small dip in the ground in front of the Hoosiers. Here Thompson and his men remained until sunset, watching as brigade after brigade swept by them in fruitless assaults against the Round Forest.[2]

It was 9:30 when the last of Chalmers's units broke contact. No fresh troops appeared to renew the attack, and a lull fell over the field. Grateful for the respite, Cruft and Hazen adjusted their defenses. The former conducted a passage of lines, replacing the Thirty-first Indiana and Second Kentucky with the First Kentucky and Nineteenth Ohio; a few minutes later, Hazen reinserted the Forty-first Ohio into the front line.

At 10:00 Brigadier General Daniel Donelson led the last uncommitted Confederate brigade on the west side of Stones River into action. Donelson, at sixty-two the oldest troop commander in the army, and his Tennesseans began the day in reserve near Bragg's headquarters, moving forward at 9:00 to occupy the rifle pits abandoned by Chalmers. There they witnessed the Mississippians' attack on the Round Forest. "It soon became apparent to everyone that Chalmers's brigade was giving way," noted Lieutenant Colonel John Anderson of the Eighth Tennessee, "for it was with great difficulty that I could keep his men from running over my men; they came running back in squads and companies." As the last of the Mississippians cleared his front, Donelson gave the order to charge. The command echoed from company to company, the men raised a cheer, and the long Butternut line surged out of the rifle pits.

Donelson went down in the first volley, his horse shot out from under him. But the old Tennessean was unhurt. Rising to his feet, he led his men into the garden alongside the Cowan farmhouse, where they met scores of stragglers from Chalmers's brigade cowering among the outbuildings and behind the garden fence, squarely in their path. The Mississippians were too frightened to step aside, so the brigade split to keep its alignment: the Sixteenth Tennessee and three companies of the Fifty-first drifted north toward the Round Forest, while the Thirty-eighth, Eighth, and remaining companies of the Fifty-first drove west toward Cruft.

Watching the action from behind Cruft's position, John Palmer was moved by Donelson's well-dressed ranks, "advancing in solid lines and moving in admirable order. It was not easy to witness that magnificent array of Americans without emotion." Cruft may have agreed, but at the moment he was more concerned with throwing a little disorder into the Rebel ranks. To that end he sent the First Kentucky into the cotton field to meet the Tennesseans before they closed with the brigade. The Kentuckians complied, but they were too late. Planting their colors firmly in the ground beside the Cowan house, Colonel John Carter and his Thirty-eighth Tennessee opened a "murderous fire" on the First, forcing it into a precipitate retreat back to its original position.

The First Kentucky returned to find the brigade in imminent danger of collapse. A. P. Stewart's Tennesseans, rolling through the cedars in pursuit of Negley, had gained the rear of the Second Kentucky. Captain William Standart wheeled a section of his Battery B, First Ohio, to engage them, but their numbers were overwhelming. "We were now completely flanked," Cruft despaired. "Our own troops impeded our retreat. Cannons, caissons, artillery wagons, and bodies of men in wild retreat filled the road and woods to my rear, precluded everything like proper and orderly retreat." Nevertheless, the Second Kentucky held together well enough to drag off three of Standart's guns, while the Nineteenth Ohio rescued a fourth. For Standart retreat came not a moment too soon—only sixteen rounds remained in his caissons.[3]

The withdrawal of Cruft, although a setback, posed no real danger to the army. Behind Cruft were several commands still largely intact: Captain Charles Parsons remained in his first position, a slight rise near the intersection of McFadden's Lane and the turnpike, his guns trained toward the southwest; Grose lay nearby with four regiments; behind Grose, Shephard had rallied his regulars; still farther to the rear stood Milo Hascall's uncommitted brigade.

Thomas and Rosecrans responded to Cruft's withdrawal by sending the regulars back into the cedars to impede the advance of Stewart and Donelson and to afford Grose time to retire to a new position along the turnpike, perpendicular to Hazen. Thomas's instructions were simple: "Shephard, take your brigade there and stop the Rebels." The regulars hurried down the turnpike to comply. As the head of the column neared McFadden's Lane the brigade halted, formed line of battle, and disappeared into the timber. They halted after fifty yards to permit Cruft's men to clear its lines. Stewart's Butternuts were right behind, and within moments the regulars' predicament was critical. Extending only a quarter mile, the brigade front was easily outflanked by the more numerous Confederates—Donelson's Eighth Tennessee on the left, and Stewart on the right. The appearance of the Eighteenth Ohio and

Eleventh Michigan, personally led into the fray by Rousseau, eased the pressure on the regulars' right momentarily. But the weight of numbers soon told, and Shephard, thinking "it proper to order a retreat, which was probably quite long enough deferred," began to extricate his battalions. By the time the final company cleared the wood, some four hundred regulars had fallen, including Major S. D. Carpenter of the Nineteenth United States, struck by six bullets as he directed his battalion's withdrawal.

But the regulars' heavy losses were not in vain. In twenty minutes of bitter fighting they decimated Stewart's brigade so completely that "Old Straight" was forced to halt at the edge of the cedars, and Maney and Anderson followed his lead. Only Donelson's Eighth and Thirty-eighth Tennessee, joined perhaps by the Nineteenth Tennessee, dared to confront the Federals on open ground. There, near the Round Forest, they found themselves quickly and hopelessly overwhelmed.

The Round Forest indeed had become a whirlpool into which all idle Federal units were thrown. Grose fed it first, deploying the Twenty-fourth Ohio and a portion of the Thirty-sixth Indiana on Hazen's right. And when Hazen's Forty-first Ohio and Sixth Kentucky withdrew to refill their cartridge boxes, Milo Hascall detached the Third Kentucky to take their place. Ten minutes later, Hascall's adjutant returned from the front with word that the commander of the Third was dead, the regiment badly cut up.

Realizing that he was the only general officer near the Round Forest, the thirty-three-year-old New Yorker decided to assume personal responsibility for its defense. Calling upon the Twenty-sixth Ohio to follow him, Hascall rode forward to direct the fight. A brief glance at the forest convinced him that "the position . . . must be held, even if it cost the last man we had." As he explained in his report of the battle: "The line they were trying to hold was that part of our original line of battle lying immediately to the right of the railroad. This portion of our original line, about two regimental fronts, together with two fronts to the left, held by Colonel Wagner's brigade, was all of our original line of battle but what our troops had been driven from; and if they succeeded in carrying this they would have turned our left, and a total rout of our forces could not then have been avoided."

Hascall also found the Third Kentucky reduced to less than 50 percent of its original strength. Ten of the fourteen officers still alive were badly wounded; Major Daniel Collier, the acting commander, had been shot in the chest and leg, but remained with his regiment. Hascall deployed the Twenty-sixth Ohio to the right of the Kentuckians, brought up Lieutenant George Estep's Eighth Indiana Battery in support, and watched as the struggle raged for another hour: "By far the most terrible and bloody in my command," recalled Grose.[4]

Finally, a little after 12:00, the Confederates broke contact. They had come within a few yards of the turnpike, but lacked the numbers to take it. The Eighth Tennessee had come closest, and their effort cost them dearly. Colonel W. L. Moore went down in the first volley to strike his regiment as it passed the Cowan house. Assuming Moore to be dead, Lieutenant Colonel John Anderson took command and led the Tennesseans toward Cruft. Within minutes a withering fire had engulfed the regiment; in their haste to close with the enemy, the Tennesseans had outdistanced the remainder of the brigade, and now found themselves facing Cruft alone. Anderson paused only long enough to permit his men to fix bayonets, then waded into the Federals. Shattering Cruft's first line with the impetuousity of their attack, the Tennesseans were preparing to move on when their colonel rejoined them on foot, still very much alive. Anderson happily returned command to Moore, only to see him fall, shot through the heart, moments later. In the meantime, Cruft had given way completely, and the Eighth pursued until it encountered Shephard's regulars. Again the Eighth gave battle, and again the Tennesseans swept their front clear of Federals. Joined now by the Nineteenth Tennessee and one hundred men from the Fifty-first, Anderson pushed on into the cotton field. Here the slaughter was greatest. The regimental color sergeant collapsed badly wounded. He crawled forward, colors in hand, until a second bullet killed him. In Company D, eleven of twelve company-grade officers and noncommissioned officers fell. When Parsons and Estep opened a "perfect hail of grape and canister," Anderson knew the time had come to retreat. Falling back to the right of Stewart, Anderson redistributed ammunition and took stock of his command. Its losses were appalling—the heaviest suffered by a Confederate regiment in any single battle of the war. Of the four hundred forty men who went into action, forty-one were dead, another two hundred sixty wounded. In all, 68 percent of the regiment had been lost. To the credit of the Eighth, not a single man was reported missing.[5]

East of the turnpike, the story was the same. There the Sixteenth Tennessee and three companies of the Fifty-first fought two Federal brigades for control of the Round Forest. Colonel John Savage's Tennesseans initially struck the Federal line from the southeast, near the railroad. After changing direction to face the forest, Savage pushed forward in line of battle along the track—two companies to the right, eleven (including the three from the Fifty-first) to the left. Those on the left made contact first. A blistering fire from the Ninth Indiana, posted immediately to their front, brought them to a halt. As those to the right of the railroad emerged from a field of dry cornstalks, they too were engaged by the Hoosiers. Savage coaxed his men forward another fifty yards before the intensity of the Federal fire forced them to the ground.

"The space between the two lines was now an unobstructed plain of about one hundred yards," recalled Captain J. J. Womack, "we lying and shooting, they standing." By noon, the commander of the Ninth Indiana noted that the fire to his front had "grown feeble," and that "many had retired in disorder, many were killed and wounded." Indeed many were. Lieutenant Colonel L. N. Savage was dead and Captain Womack lay unconscious, a minie ball having shattered his right arm just minutes after he had watched his brother J. B. fall badly wounded. Federal bullets had so thinned the ranks of the Sixteenth that Savage could muster no more than a skirmish line from the survivors. As standing to retreat was more dangerous than remaining among the cotton rows, Savage and his men lay for three hours until Dan Adams's brigade passed by them on its way toward the Round Forest, allowing the Tennesseans to escape. Few, however, would survive; of the three hundred seventy-seven men taken into action, Savage could count only one hundred fifty at dusk.[6]

As the Tennesseans clung to the cotton field, Rosecrans advanced a regiment almost equally decimated to skirmish with them. Phil Sheridan had just that moment emerged from the cedars with what remained of Schaefer's brigade and the Thirty-sixth Illinois. Rosecrans noticed them as they searched for ammunition near the railroad. As the Ninth Indiana, occupying a critical position in the front line, was itself wavering for lack of ammunition, Rosecrans ordered Sheridan to march to its relief. Leaving the Thirty-sixth and Seventy-third Illinois behind the Round Forest in reserve, Sheridan inserted the Second Missouri alongside the Hoosiers and deployed the Fifteenth Missouri forward as skirmishers. This was too much for Savage, who ordered his men to cease firing and hold their ground from behind what cover they could find.[7]

An uncertain silence now fell over the field. Rosecrans rode away to supervise the final repulse of Cleburne, and Hascall again found himself the only general officer near the Round Forest. Well aware that the lull represented only a respite between attacks, Hascall moved swiftly to bolster the Round Forest line, relieving the Third Kentucky with the Fifty-eighth Indiana, a large regiment that more than filled the space held by the Kentuckians, and placing Estep's battery and the Ninety-seventh Ohio behind the Sixth Ohio. Hazen, meanwhile, reinforced those units within the forest with the One Hundredth Illinois, an action that Hascall heartily approved. With the lines now arranged to his satisfaction, Hascall rode rearward to consult with Rosecrans, whom he found behind Rousseau's division. The commanding general accompanied Hascall on an inspection of the Round Forest line. He approved the troop dispositions, offered a few words of encouragement to the men, and was off again to another threatened part of the field. Although it was Hascall and Hazen who truly were responsible for the successful defense of the Round Forest, here as elsewhere most soldiers in the ranks were very impressed by Rosecrans: "The commanding general was, to all appearances, as cool and composed as though the battle was not going on," wrote one.[8]

The same could not be said for Bragg, who was as removed from the struggle as Rosecrans was submerged in it. At the headquarters of the Army of Tennessee, indecision prevailed. During the critical late-morning hours, while Hardee threw the exhausted divisions of Cleburne and McCown against the Nashville Turnpike and Polk delivered his piecemeal blows against the Round Forest, Breckinridge's four brigades lay idle on the east side of the river. Precious hours slipped by, and the brigades did nothing.

Why were these units not committed to revive Hardee's flagging attack before it dissolved against the massed Union batteries along the turnpike, or at the very least sent to Polk in time to be deployed in conjunction with Chalmers and Donelson against the Federal left? Historians have long accused Bragg of a tactical apoplexy that robbed the Army of Tennessee of almost certain victory.

But while Bragg must be held accountable for the decision ultimately to deploy Breckinridge's brigades against the Round Forest, evidence suggests that he may have offered them to Hardee, had he succeeded in wresting them from Breckinridge. The record is unclear, the more so as a result of apologia submitted to Richmond by all concerned in the months following the battle. In his official report filed 23 February 1863, Bragg asserts that "as early as 10 A.M." he called on Breckinridge for one brigade to "reinforce, or act as a reserve to, Lieutenant General Hardee." Breckinridge denies receiving any such order. The first mention he makes in his report of any communication from Bragg is of a "suggestion" delivered by Colonel J. Stoddard Johnson of the general staff at 10:30 that the Kentuckian move against a body of Federals supposedly to his front. Lieutenant Colonel John Buckner, a member of Breckinridge's staff and a confidant of the general, supports his account in a letter to him of 20 May 1863, during the height of the post-battle acrimony within the army high command.

But what prompted Bragg's unusual "suggestion" that Breckinridge give battle to what proved to be a phantom force? On this Breckinridge is silent. In his report he neglects to explain why he wrote Bragg at 10:10 that "the enemy are undoubtedly advancing upon me," and that "the Lebanon road is unprotected and I have no troops to fill out my line." In the absence of an explanation, it may be assumed that Breckinridge's fears came in response to some message from Bragg—perhaps a call for troops to support the left—or to erroneous reports from Pegram's cavalry, which was screening his front.

In any event, Bragg countermanded his request for reinforcements and instead instructed the Kentuckian to launch a peremptory attack on the east bank. Either unwilling or unable to inspect the ground himself, Bragg relied on Breckinridge's interpretation of events on his front. Breckinridge acknowledged the command (or suggestion) and set his division in motion. But again he was bedeviled by chimera. Breckinridge was told—perhaps by Pegram's troopers—that a heavy Federal column was moving down the Lebanon road toward his right. "I am obeying your order," he reported to Bragg, "but . . . if I advance my whole line farther forward . . . it will take me clear away from the Lebanon road, and expose my right and that road to a heavy force of the enemy advancing from Black's."

Bragg was baffled. Nothing had prepared him for such information; he and his staff had assumed the entire Union army to be drawn up on the west bank of Stones River. Nevertheless, Bragg countermanded his order to Breckinridge, going so far as to sound out the hard-pressed Polk as to the possibility of detaching two brigades to reinforce the Kentuckian. At the same time, however, Bragg circumvented Breckinridge and sent orders directly to Pegram to ascertain precisely the threat on the east bank. Pegram found no Federals on the Lebanon road and only "a small body of sharpshooters" to Breckenridge's immediate front.

Bragg was now furious. His anger persisted long after the guns fell silent, and he scourged Breckinridge in his report of the battle. Referring to the incredible messages emanating from the east bank, Bragg commented:

> These unfortunate misapprehensions on that part of the field (which, with proper precaution, could not have existed) withheld from active operations three fine brigades until the enemy had succeeded in checking our progress, had re-established his lines, and had collected many of his broken battalions. Having now settled the question that no movement was being made against our right, and none even to be apprehended, Breckinridge was ordered to leave two brigades . . . on his side of Stone's River, and with the balance of the force to cross to the left and report to Lieutenant General Polk.

It was 1:00 P.M. when Breckinridge was handed this final, conclusive order. The brigades of brigadier generals Dan Adams and John Jackson, being nearer to the river, were started across the ford above the Murfrees farm. A short time later, Breckinridge led Palmer and Preston in column toward the crossing site.

What was Breckinridge's reaction to Pegram's conclusion that his fears had been groundless? He dismisses the affair in two sentences in his report: aside from criticizing Pegram for having reported Van Cleve's dawn crossing at McFadden's Ford but not his subsequent recall ("It is to be regretted that sufficient care was not taken by the authors of the reports to discriminate rumor from fact"), Breckinridge says nothing. His report is strangely silent with respect to his claim of a Federal threat to his right. This silence, coupled with the apparent lack of a culprit for the alleged sightings of Federals along the Lebanon road (Breckinridge chastises Pegram only for inaccurate reporting of Union activity to his front) raises an intriguing question: Did Breckinridge fabricate the report to forestall the probable mishandling of his troops by Bragg? The Kentuckian's acknowledged lack of confidence in his commanding general, compounded by a tragic incident a week earlier, suggests that this may have been the case.

The incident in question was the execution of young Asa Lewis of the Sixth Kentucky. As related earlier, Lewis had received word from home that his widowed mother desperately needed him; ironically, he had reenlisted only days earlier. Lewis's request for leave was denied. Overcome with despair, he left camp and set out for home, only to be captured by the provost marshal and returned to his command. Given his previously exemplary record, Lewis was merely reprimanded and turned over to his company. Again he left camp, and again he was captured, this time to be sentenced to death, allegedly at Bragg's insistence. The Orphan Brigade circulated a petition pleading clemency, but Bragg remained adamant; an eleventh-hour appeal by Breckinridge failed as well. At Bragg's command the division was formed to witness the execution. "The lieutenant in command of the detail . . . gave the command, 'Ready-Aim-Fire,' " remembered Johnny Green of the Ninth Kentucky, then "all was over and a gloom settled over the command." By 31 December the gloom had deepened to a state of near mutiny.[9]

It was 2:00 P.M. before Adams reported to Polk. The bishop was reluctant to commit his brigade, but orders were orders. After listening to a brief description of the terrain and enemy dispositions, Adams agreed to assault a four-gun section of the Tenth Indiana Light Artillery perched on high ground near the river that had been wreaking havoc on Butternut infantry advancing toward the Round Forest.

"Onward they came," recalled the commander of the Sixth Kentucky (Union), "the colors of five or six regiments advancing abreast in line of battle . . . on the crest of the ridge. A further view of this line was intercepted by intervening inequalities of ground and woods." These "intervening inequalities of ground and woods" conspired with the Cowan farm and its checkerboard of fences to impede Adams's advance, much as they had Chalmers and Donelson's. Unable to continue in line of battle, the Louisiana general fed his regiments through the farmyard individually. The Thirteenth and Twentieth Louisiana Consolidated snaked through the gate, reformed in the yard, and marched by the right flank off the ridge and toward the river. The Sixteenth Louisiana went next, skirting the eastern slope of the ridge on its way up the turnpike in column of companies. The Thirtieth Alabama, having moved by the left flank to avoid the farm, rejoined the Sixteenth as it neared the Round Forest.

With all units now clear of the Cowan farm, Adams once again deployed his brigade in line and moved on the irksome guns. The Louisianians never stood a chance. Although they swept the Fifteenth Missouri from the field, Hascall's artillery stopped them short of the forest. Cockerill, Estep, Parsons, and Cox converged their guns on the Butternuts as they stumbled over bodies and discarded equipment; simultaneously, Colonel George Wagner—until now merely a spectator as Rosecrans, Palmer, and Hascall had alternated in deploying and redeploying his regiments—saw a

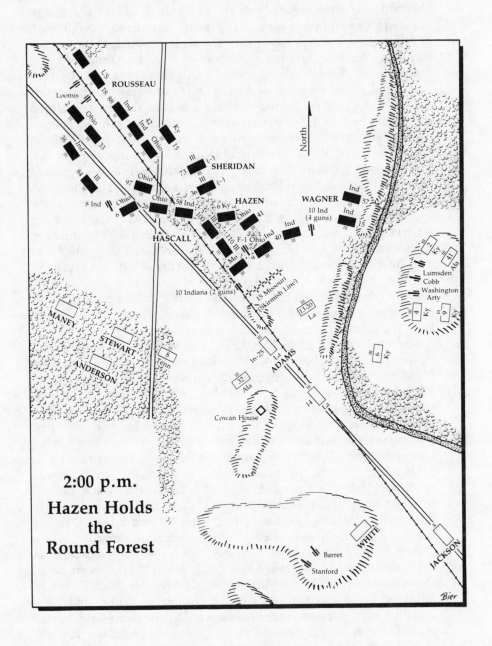

US 1
US
18 88 Ind   ROUSSEAU
Loomis   42
2   Ohio
36 Ind   33
Ohio   Ky
84   3   15
Ohio
97   Ohio   73   (−)   SHERIDAN
Ohio   Ohio   36   (−)
8 Ind   26   58 Ind   6 Ky   HAZEN   WAGNER   Ind
Ohio   Ohio   41   57
6   110   F-1 Ohio Ind   40 Ind   10 Ind   Ind
HASCALL   Mo   9   (4 guns)   15

North

10 Indiana (2 guns)   (5 Missouri
Skirmish Line)   2
Ky   41
13-20   Ala
MANEY   La   Lumsden
Cobb
STEWART   Washington
Arty
8   4   9
ANDERSON   Tenn   Ky   Ky
In-25   6 Ky
La
32   ADAMS
Ala
14
Cowan House   3

2:00 p.m.

Hazen Holds
the
Round Forest
x
WHITE
Barret
Stanford   JACKSON
Bier

chance to act independently as the right flank of the Thirteenth Louisiana passed by his front. At Wagner's command the Fifteenth and Fifty-first Indiana swept forward with fixed bayonets to take the Confederates completely by surprise, and within minutes, seventy-eight Rebels fell captive. His flank turned, Adams prudently pulled his men out of range. Thirty minutes of bitter fighting had contributed nothing to Bragg's goal of turning the Union left except four hundred twenty-six more dead and wounded.

Tragically, the slaughter was not over. As quickly as Adams cleared the field, Brigadier General John Jackson's independent brigade stepped forward. The ease with which the Federals repulsed this fourth attack was ridiculous; the accompanying slaughter was sickening, the more so for its fruitlessness. "On they came in steady column, notwithstanding the murderous fire," Gilbert Stormont observed from the ranks of the Fifty-eighth Indiana. "We could see their men falling like leaves, but the broken ranks were filled and they held their ground with a heroism worthy of a better cause. At last they had to yield, but they retired in good order, leaving their dead on the field." Two hundred ninety-one more irreplaceable veterans were cut down in two suicidal charges; lying among them were the commanders of all three regiments of the brigade.[10]

And still more killing lay ahead. The brigades of Preston and Palmer filed into Chalmers's abandoned rifle pits as the survivors of Adams's attack began streaming rearward. Breckinridge, at the head of Palmer's column, was horrified to see his Louisianians retreating in "considerable disorder" as fast as their feet could carry them. We can only imagine his wrath, directed at Polk, who had committed the brigades before their supporting lines had forded Stones River. Polk never explained his decision, an "error so palpable . . . as to render an excuse for failure necessary," in the words of an eyewitness. Although Bragg had ordained the attack, he had left its timing and execution to the bishop; certainly Polk could have waited the hour necessary to muster all four brigades, rather than commit them individually to almost certain defeat.

Darkness began to settle on the dreary, winter landscape as Palmer and Preston dressed their ranks behind the Cowan farm. Having witnessed four assaults by single brigades dissolve before the Round Forest salient, Polk elected to deploy Palmer and Preston simultaneously on line: Preston would drive across the blood-soaked cotton field pounded flat by Chalmers, Donelson, Adams, and Jackson; Palmer, on Preston's left, was instructed to approach Hazen from the west.

Hazen narrates what followed: "The battle had hushed, and the dreadful splendor of this advance can only be conceived, as all my description must fall vastly short. His right was even with my left, his left was lost in the distance. He advanced steadily, and, as it seemed, certainly to victory. I sent back all my remaining staff successively to ask for support, and braced up my own lines as perfectly as possible."

Hazen, perhaps overwrought from having withstood so many attacks, was unduly concerned. There were, by this time, more Federal units on hand than could be squeezed into the front line; moreover, Hascall had replaced three of the most jaded regiments—the Second Missouri, Fiftieth Indiana, and Twenty-sixth Ohio—with the Sixth Kentucky, Fortieth Indiana, and Twenty-third Kentucky.

Palmer and Preston's assault, when it came, was repulsed so handily that some Federals wondered whether it really represented a serious effort at taking the Round Forest. J. B. Palmer marched his Tennesseans into the cedars west of the Cowan farm correctly but, contrary to orders, they never came out. Palmer attributed his failure to emerge from the wood to Preston's inability to drive home the assault from the front—with Preston stopped so far short of his objective, Palmer saw no reason to sacrifice his command. So, after a loss of just two men killed and twenty wounded, Palmer instructed his men to bivouac for the night alongside what remained of Stewart and Coltart's brigades.

Palmer may have had a point, although it is unclear whether Preston abandoned his attack before Palmer could initiate his flanking movement or as a result of the Tennessean's inactivity. In either case, Preston was justified in desisting as he did; certainly the sight of nearly one thousand dead or wounded strewn over just four acres was enough to give the general and his men pause as they neared the Cowan farm. Any notion Preston may have had of continuing forward he abandoned as his lines became snagged in the farmyard. The Federal artillery, accustomed to a turkey shoot as each Confederate brigade struggled among the outbuildings and picket fences, opened on the hapless Butternuts. Preston watched for a moment as his command "fell into a confusion under a crashing fire" and three of four staff officers went down around him, then decided to put a halt to the charade. Grabbing the colors of the Fourth Florida, he galloped over the rows of cotton and into the wood. Raising a cheer, the Floridians followed him "with enthusiasm." Companies E, F, H, and K of the Sixtieth North Carolina heeded their example and entered the cedars after them, stopping only long enough to pluck bits of cotton from the few dried stalks left standing to stuff in their ears and dull the roar of the Union artillery. Only Company A, separated from the regiment near the farm, and the Twentieth Tennessee dared to challenge the Federal infantry. Hazen ordered his units to wait until the Butternuts were within one hundred yards, "when a single fire from my men was sufficient to disperse this portion of his line." After taking a handful of prisoners from among careless Union skirmishers, the Tennesseans scampered to the protection of a neck of wood along the river bank.

Although they repelled this final attempt to carry the Round Forest handily, the Federals had suffered. Cobb's Kentucky battery, reinforced by a section of the Washington Artillery, had torn large gaps in the Federal lines with well-directed fire from atop Wayne's Hill. In fact, one of Cobb's rounds almost robbed the Army of the Cumberland of its commander. While riding by Sheridan's reserve column on the way to the Round Forest, a solid shot flew past Rosecrans, sparing the general but decapitating his closest friend in the army, Julius Garesche. Rosecrans, his overcoat spattered with Garesche's brains, winced a moment, then regained his composure enough to turn to Sheridan and mutter something to the effect that good men must die in battle.

Good men must die, but William Preston was not going to have any unnecessary blood on his hands. Reflecting on the day's action as his men settled down for the night amid the naked oak and damp limestone outcrops, the Kentuckian had no cause to regret his decision to terminate the assault. "I lost a tenth of my command in the engagement," he wrote after the battle, "and if I had hammered away like Adams would probably have lost half." Regrettably, Bragg and Polk had been of a different mind.[11]

CHAPTER THIRTEEN

WE LAID TO REST POOR BOYS GONE

A heavy mist rolled over the battlefield. Above, a waxing moon drifted in and out of the clouds; below, the ground—churned to paste by thousands of feet—began to freeze as the temperature plummeted. The "dismal groans and cries of the wounded and dying," punctuated by the rumbling of ambulances, replaced the crash of musketry and the roar of artillery.

Those wounded left on the field who survived the night have handed down chilling tales of suffering. Joseph Teeter of the Thirty-fourth Illinois, among the first struck during McCown's dawn assault, fell on a cluster of small bushes near the Franklin road. Too weak to move, he lay facedown across the shrubbery, alternately losing and regaining consciousness, for three days until Federal ambulance stewards spotted him. Captain Womack of the Sixteenth Tennessee fared better. He lay in the cotton field where he had fallen only until dark, when his brothers crept forward to retrieve him. They carried him to a private residence in Murfreesboro, where he began a long convalescence. Corporal Hannaford of the Sixth Ohio, who had crawled away from his regiment in search of a quiet place to die, found himself still very much alive as the fighting sputtered out. Now aware that he had a chance for survival, Hannaford fashioned a signal flag from a knit sleeping cap and a stick in the hope of drawing attention to his plight. But no ambulance details came within hailing distance, and the Ohioan soon gave up in despair. As the minutes passed, the sky darkened, and the air grew colder. Hannaford realized that his chances of surviving a night in the open were slim; if the ambulance corps would not come to him, he would seek them out. Hannaford struggled to his feet, then started rearward:

> Reluctantly leaving my blanket, my haversack, and canteen, as a prize for some fortunate rebel, I wandered away back toward our lines. Across those corn and cotton fields again, now strewn with the dead and wounded—our own blue and the rebel gray mingled together—heedless alike of the piteous calls and prayers from every side for the assistance I could not give, and of the perils of shot and shell whistling past me; and at last I reached the turnpike, faint and exhausted. A little further down I came to a little, low log-cabin, with its strip of red flannel fluttering before it to indicate its present use, its two small rooms crowded hours before with the wounded and dying, and scores more sitting or lying around smoking fires on the outside. Ambulances were coming and going, freighted with their precious burden of maimed and helpless humanity; and still the wounded were accumulating constantly.
>
> I remember the almost hopeless weariness with which I sat down before the fire to wait my turn for removal, when a familiar voice called me. It was one of my own company, who had escaped this morning's ordeal of fire by a fortunate detail of a few weeks before on the "Pioneer Corps," and whose kindness to me in this hour shall have an abiding place in my remembrance. He took off my cartridge-box, of which I had in vain tried to unburden myself, cleared for me a better place by the fire, rolled up a barrel for me to rest against, and as soon as possible procured me a seat in an ambulance; then, with such feeble thanks as I had strength to give him, we were driven off.
>
> The road was blockaded with troops and confused masses of artillery, ammunition trains, and ambulances; and stragglers, singly or in fragmentary squads, skulked about everywhere. The afternoon was waning fast, when we finally reached the field-hospital of our division, which had been established the day before about five miles back from Murfreesborough. It was a motley collection of tents—hospital, Sibley, wall, bell, flies, any thing, indeed, that could be found and made to afford shelter—pitched in a promiscuous heap in a large, open meadow, sloping up from the turnpike off to the left. No one could direct us to the hospital of the Sixth Ohio, and I was little able to go farther; so a place was presently made for me among our comrades of the Ninetieth, where I found needful care and rest at last.

Others tried to follow Hannaford's example, but with considerably less success. Fellow Ohioan John Rennard of the Fifteenth, shot in the thigh while trying to cross the fence near the Smith farm, watched as the Confederates turned the house into a makeshift hospital. As the farm lay only two hundred yards away, Rennard was certain he could drag himself to it. "My feet were toward it, and I found I must get around with my head towards it," he remembered. "I drew up my sound leg, anchored my heel in a horse track, and made the effort. But I might as well have tried to crawl away with my body chained to the rock of Gibralter." Rennard collapsed, exhausted. About noon, a group of Confederates stopped to talk with him. "One of them asked if I was cold. I asked him if he did not see my teeth chattering." The sympathetic Rebel gathered some discarded blankets, placed Rennard gently upon them, and then offered the Ohioan a sip of whiskey from his canteen. Rennard thanked his Butternut benefactor and, a bit warmer now, prepared for a night on the field.[1]

There were many similar instances of kindness shown the wounded that night, as Colonel William Blake of the Ninth Indiana noted approvingly: "Before twilight I sent details to collect and bury my dead. A mutual truce was granted, in which the soldiers of both sides, without arms, gathered their fallen comrades without interruption. The fierce acerbity of the deadly strife had given place to the mutual expression of kindness and regard."

William Erb of the Nineteenth Ohio volunteered for one such detail. At midnight, he and a companion passed through their picket line. "Gliding from tree to tree, and much of the way creeping," they evaded the enemy and reached the position their regiment had occupied that afternoon. "We found no one alive. . . . Peering through the darkness, we saw our line of battle plainly marked with dead bodies." The Ohioans picked their way carefully through the line of corpses, at every turn recognizing the faces of friends: "At one place, near the right of the line, we saw two lying side by side, with another on top of the two. Then at right angles to these, was another with his head close up to his 'breastworks.' It was plain to us. The first three had been killed and the last had been mortally wounded, and, unable to get away, he had built a little barricade of his dead comrades and had lain down behind them to die."

A party of Confederates, approaching from the opposite direction, shook them back to the world of the living. Concealing themselves among the dead, they waited in silence until it became clear that the Rebels too were on a mission of mercy. Erb spoke first. "Hello, Johnny," he whispered. "Hello, Yank," came the reply. The two parties talked briefly—Erb learned that his comrade had been taken to an enemy field hospital—then returned to the work at hand. Erb and his companion passed from body to body, identifying the dead and straightening their stiffened limbs until, their work done, they bade farewell to the Confederates and returned safely to their bivouac.

Other details were less fortunate in their chance encounters with the enemy. Some, such as that of the Thirty-eighth Indiana, were captured "while in the act of giving water to the wounded" and shipped to prison camps; others, such as that of the Fifteenth United States, convinced their captors to release them by citing the informal truce that both picket lines had agreed upon.

Not all the soldiers who gave succor to the wounded were members of organized details. Many, moved by the "groans and cries of strong men stricken," felt compelled to do whatever they could to ease the suffering. John Magee of Smith's Mississippi battery, riding over the field in search of harnesses, was so overwhelmed by the panorama of agony that he dismounted to build fires for as many as he could. For some, his efforts came too late: "Many, many were chilled to death already that might have been saved could they but have had attendance. I could not repress a few falling tears."[2]

Of course, there was no guarantee that those taken to hospitals would fare any better in the long run—there were simply too many wounded and too few surgeons. Sergeant James Maxwell of the Thirty-fourth Alabama, detailed as a hospital nurse throughout the battle, recalled: "We had no leisure, night or day. The house was filled by wounded and kept filled. As fast as one would die and be carried to his grave, another was put in his place." Solon Marks, operating behind enemy lines at the General Smith plantation, frankly acknowledged the inadequacy of the care provided: "Many limbs were severed from bodies, not with the expectation of saving life, but to relieve the sufferer from an offensive mass and render his last hours more comfortable." Corporal Hannaford, resting in the hospital tent of the Ninetieth Ohio, watched in silence as the surgeon made his rounds, until at last his turn came.

"A very narrow escape, young man," the surgeon remarked after examining Hannaford's neck wound.

"A bad wound, doctor, I know; but if I do well, very well, is it possible for me to get through?"

"If you were at home, I should not hesitate to say yes; but here in an army hospital, you know, the case is different. It is more than I should like to promise."

Ira Owen of the Seventy-fourth Ohio, shot in the leg, has left perhaps the most moving description of the plight of the wounded that night. Carried to a hospital near Stewart's Creek, Owen watched as orderlies brought in a steady stream of mangled soldiers:

It was impossible to supply all the wounded with tents. Rails were hauled and thrown in piles . . . and large fires built. The wounded were brought and lain by these fires. Men were wounded in every conceivable way, some with their arms shot off, some wounded in the body, some in the head. It was heart-rending to hear their cries and groans. One poor fellow who was near me was wounded in the head. He grew delirious during the night, and would very frequently call his mother. . . . The poor fellow died before morning with no mother near, to soothe him in his dying moments, or wipe the cold sweat from off his brow. I saw the surgeons amputate limbs, then throw the quivering flesh into a pile. Every once in a while a man would stretch himself out and die. Next morning rows of men were laid out side by side for the soldiers' burial.

No one could easily forget such scenes. "The frost, the dead and dying and the dark cedars among which we bivouacked were wild enough for a banquet of ghouls," wrote William Preston, whose brigade lay opposite the Round Forest. In the forest itself, it was the same. Recalled Sergeant William Newlin of the Seventy-third Illinois:

Nine . . . were lying in cold death near us, awaiting the simple, un-ceremonious burial accorded a soldier on the field of battle. Some . . . looked as though they had just fallen asleep—eyes closed, hands at their sides, and countenances unruffled. Others appeared as if their last moments had been spent in extreme pain—eyes open, and apparently ready to jump from their sockets; hands grasping some portion of their garments and their features all distorted and changed. It was a sickening sight to look upon or contemplate, and one from which a sympathetic heart would quickly turn away.[3]

And there were the innumerable burial details, composed of men who barely had strength enough to stand, that worked deep into the night. "At 0100 by the light of the moon we dug a grave and laid to rest poor boys gone where there is no fighting," remembered James Nourse, almost with envy for the dead.

For all its horror, the soldiers could endure the proximity of the dead and the groans of the dying. Harder to accept was the absence of their evening rations. Unlike their perpetually hungry foe, the troops of the Army of the Cumberland were accustomed to regular meals. When brigade trains failed to arrive during the night, many resorted to horse meat. Others, less scrupulous, rummaged the haversacks of the dead for crackers or bacon.[4]

The Federals could thank Joe Wheeler for their empty stomachs. Under orders from Bragg to harass Rosecrans's supply lines,

Wheeler's troopers broke camp at midnight on 29 December, splashing across Stones River, then pounding north along the Lebanon road toward Jefferson. At the Jefferson Pike they turned west and rode until they neared the outskirts of town and the flickering campfires of Colonel John Starkweather's brigade, detailed to protect the army's rear. The Southerners formed line of battle at 4:00 A.M. and lay quietly in wait until dawn, when Starkweather's train appeared on the horizon—sixty-four heavily laden wagons meandering lazily into camp, guarded by fifty invalids of the Twenty-first Wisconsin. Wheeler struck while the train was still a mile outside of camp. In the melee that followed, twenty wagons were burned. Wheeler's next prey was the consolidated trains of McCook's Right Wing, parked in a field near Lavergne. Again the element of surprise was with Wheeler: charging in three columns, his men swept up four hundred prisoners, two hundred wagons, and over one thousand mules. The prisoners were paroled, the mules scattered, and the wagons burned. With two hours of sunlight remaining, Wheeler pushed his command on to Rock Springs, where they captured another brigade train. From there they descended on Nolensville, seizing a detachment of some two hundred men without firing a shot. More wagons—this time an ammunition and medical train—were put to the torch. Their appetite for plunder only whetted, Wheeler's troopers galloped on toward Franklin on the chance they might encounter more easy prey. They did. Strung out along the road were numerous Federal foraging parties heavily laden with corn, poultry, eggs, butter, and bedding—all items in short supply in the Army of Tennessee. Nightfall finally brought an end to the raiding, and Wheeler's column bivouacked five miles southeast of Nolensville. Wheeler reported his command to Bragg shortly before noon the following day, having crippled Rosecrans's supply line and prevented the brigades of Walker and Starkweather from joining the army until dusk on 31 December.[5]

The effects of Wheeler's raid reverberated down the Nashville Turnpike to the log-cabin field headquarters of the Army of the Cumberland, where Rosecrans and his lieutenants gathered at midnight to ponder the fate of the army. Twenty-four hours earlier, confident of success, Rosecrans had summoned his generals only to issue orders to them; now, his plan of battle foiled before it could be launched and his army nearly annihilated, Rosecrans was open to suggestions.

Eyewitness accounts of the gathering vary according to the feelings of the writer toward the participants. John Yaryan, who arrived with General Wood shortly after the council of war convened, asserts that Rosecrans queried each division and corps commander in turn whether the army should hold its ground or retreat. Yaryan neglects to relate most of their responses, but says that Rosecrans appeared listless and unaware of what was being said—that is, until he came to Thomas. At that moment he hesitated, as if to underscore the esteem he held for the Virginian.

"General Thomas, what have you to say?"

Slowly and silently, Thomas rose to respond. "General, I know of no better place to die than right here." Having uttered these few words, Thomas walked out of the room and into the night. This, according to Yaryan, put an end to the conference.

Yaryan's story is dramatic and inspiring: the crackling fire, throwing light and casting weird shadows across the room, a dismal rain beating mournfully against a clapboard roof, an unspoken gloom almost palpable. But it rings false. Yaryan's entire account of the battle is fraught with errors of time and place; there is no reason to suppose his narrative of the nocturnal council of war is any more accurate.

Rosecrans's own version finds Thomas and Crittenden deferring to his judgment and McCook alone advising retreat. Yet another portrays Rosecrans, despising the "counsel of the fainthearted" who would turn the army rearward, as affirming his resolve to stand and fight at any cost: "Gentleman, we have come to fight and win this battle, and we shall do it. Our supplies may run short, but we will have our trains out again tomorrow. We will keep right in, and eat corn for a week, but we will win this battle. We can and will do it."

Crittenden's account seems the most plausible, largely because of the matter-of-fact manner in which he presents it. There was some talk of retreat, Crittenden recalled, although he was uncertain who started it. As for himself, Crittenden was for staying: "I expressed the opinion that my men would be very much discouraged to have to abandon the field after their good fight of the day, during which they had uniformly held their position."

Regardless of who said what, the opinions of his lieutenants were insufficient to sway Rosecrans one way or the other, and he decided to inspect the ground to the army's rear personally before making a decision. Asking his generals to await his return, Rosecrans and McCook rode off toward Overall Creek. Years later, McCook told Crittenden that Rosecrans made the ride to find a point beyond the creek to which the army might fall back. Mc-

Cook did not say that Rosecrans necessarily intended to retreat, but his remarks imply that the general did. In any event, what Rosecrans and McCook saw ruled out retreat. All along the creek, torches flickered and danced. "They have got entirely in our rear and are forming a line of battle by torchlight," Rosecrans suggested. McCook agreed, and the two returned to headquarters. Rosecrans ended the council, telling his lieutenants to rejoin their commands and prepare "to fight or die."

Gallant words, but Rosecrans had erred. The torches he had seen were not those of enemy guides; rather, they were firebrands carried by Federal cavalrymen to ignite the campfires of infantrymen who, numbed almost senseless by the bitter cold, chose to flaunt Rosecrans's standing order prohibiting fires.[6]

There was no talk of retreat at the headquarters of the Army of Tennessee. Bragg was satisfied with the army's performance and confident that the New Year would find him in sole possession of the battlefield. "We assailed the enemy at seven o'clock this morning, and after ten hours' hard fighting have driven him from every position except the extreme left," he wired Richmond after dark. "With the exception of this point, we occupy the whole field." Aside from returning Palmer's brigade to the east bank, Bragg issued no orders of consequence during the night.

Although daybreak found the Federals still out in front in force, Bragg remained certain of Rosecrans's eventual withdrawal, his confidence fed by unusually poor intelligence from his cavalry. Joe Wheeler, off on another ride around the Union rear, wired army headquarters at 1:30 P.M. that he had seen vast numbers of wagons creaking up the Nashville Turnpike toward the capital; John Wharton, whose troopers joined Wheeler near Lavergne in the early afternoon, confirmed the general's message with a similar report of his own at 6:00 P.M.

An army in the Civil War, before it retreated, normally dispatched its wagons rearward; consequently, Bragg's conclusion that a withdrawal was imminent is understandable. But there was another explanation—that the wagons were empty, in search of provisions for the soldiers and forage for the horses, and that they would return to feed the army along Stones River. Neither Wheeler nor Wharton offered this interpretation, and Bragg appears not to have arrived at it himself until after the battle.

While the Army of Tennessee lay on its arms, Rosecrans strengthened his lines. At 3:00 A.M. of the New Year, he directed Crittenden to occupy the high ground above McFadden's Ford on the east bank. (This ground, Colonel Urquhart of Bragg's staff asserts, ultimately cost the Confederates the battle, as it set in motion the chain of events that led inexorably to Breckinridge's tragic assault the following day.) At dawn, Sam Beatty (in command of the division after a painful foot wound forced Van Cleve to leave the battle) moved to execute the order. Colonel Samuel Price crossed Stones River first, forming his brigade in line of battle eight hundred yards from the ford. Fyffe took position on Price's left, in an elevated field west of a belt of timber. Colonel Benjamin Grider of the Ninth Kentucky tucked Beatty's brigade into a hollow just below the ford, two regiments on the east bank, two on the west.[7]

As the day passed and the Federals entrenched, the feeling grew within the Army of Tennessee that victory was slowly slipping from its grasp. St. John Liddell tried to be upbeat. On the evening of the thirty-first he ran into Hardee. Liddell pointed out that they effectively commanded the turnpike and the railroad, and that one more Confederate attack in that sector would win the battle. But Hardee did not hear a word Liddell spoke. He mumbled his disgust with the results of the day's battle and rode away. Ed Porter Thompson of the Orphan Brigade recalled that many soldiers likewise had given up all hope of defeating the Yankees: "This gloomy New Year's day went by with the Confederate troops thus inactive; and even before its noon the golden opportunity . . . had passed away from General Bragg. The disposition of the troops of Rosecrans were completed . . . and as the Federal army had nothing to lose but everything to gain by waiting, it waited—but meanwhile it worked. The Confederate army waited, and hoped."

The Federals waited and worked, and as they worked their hunger sharpened. Supplies trickled in throughout the afternoon, but they were too few to make any real difference. The Seventeenth Ohio lined up to receive a half pint of beans and two spoonfuls of molasses per man; the Thirty-eighth Indiana could offer its men only a quarter pint of flour per soldier. Officers fared no better. Gates Thruston dined on a few hard grains of parched corn, John Beatty found a slice of raw pork and a few crackers in his coat pocket: "No food ever tasted sweeter," and Michael Fitch joined his colonel in a meal of steaks cut from Fred Starkweather's dead horse.[8]

But despite their hunger the Federals were encouraged as the end of another day found them still on the field. Some felt that Bragg had played out his hand and that time was now on their side; most praised the obstinacy with which Rosecrans held his ground. Beatty sensed this new optimism as darkness again settled over the battlefield: "I draw closer to the camp-fire, and, pushing the brands together, take out my little Bible, and as I open it my eyes fall on the xci Psalm: 'I will say of the Lord, He is my refuge and my fortress, my God, in Him I will trust. Surely He shall deliver thee from the snare of the fowler, and from the noisome pestilence.' Camp-fires innumerable are glimmering in the darkness. Now and then a few mounted men gallop by. Scattering shots are heard along the picket line. The gloom has lifted, and I wrap myself in my blanket and lie down contentedly for the night."[9]

CHAPTER FOURTEEN

THUNDER ON THE LEFT

THE second day of January dawned gray, cloudy, and cold, "as peculiarly dreary as the day before had been." And the Federals remained, their lines compact and well entrenched. Bragg at last accepted that only a determined assault could dislodge Rosecrans, who showed no intention of leaving without a fight. Accordingly, Bragg searched the field for a suitable place to resume the attack. Every point his army had struck during the afternoon of the thirty-first had held firm; only Rosecrans's extreme left was untried. With this in mind, Bragg directed his trusted aide, Colonel George Brent, and Captain Felix Robertson, the obsequious commander of a battery in Withers's division, to find artillery-firing positions on the east bank from which the Federal left might be enfiladed.

Brent and Robertson rode forward of Breckinridge's picket line to discover Price's brigade on the very hill they had hoped to reconnoiter. Brent reported the disturbing intelligence to Bragg, adding his belief that possession of the hill was critical: "It commanded the entire field of battle. From this point, either the enemy's or our line could be enfiladed."

Bragg agreed. He too was concerned that Federal artillery might use it to sweep Bishop Polk from the Round Forest, an eventuality that "involved consequences not to be entertained." The Yankees, then, must be driven from the east bank. And regardless of what Bragg thought of Breckinridge, his was the only division available for the task. Bragg sent orders to the Kentuckian directing him to concentrate his entire command opposite Beatty. Wharton and Pegram received instructions to protect Breckinridge's right flank, and Robertson was told to take ten guns across the river to augment the Kentuckian's artillery. Bragg allowed Breckinridge to determine the hour of the assault.

Bragg's plan shocked Breckinridge. He had conducted his own reconnaissance, and the conclusions he had drawn did not support an attack. Shortly after daybreak, Captain W. P. Bramblett, whose Company H, Fourth Kentucky, manned the picket line of the Orphan Brigade, had crawled through weeds and briars to within three hundred yards of Sam Beatty's six-regiment front line. Lieutenant Lot D. Young accompanied Bramblett. For a time they watched the troop formations and artillery batteries in silence. Finally, Bramblett remarked to Young that Rosecrans must be baiting a trap for Bragg. They snaked their way back to the picket line, and Bramblett reported his findings to Breckinridge.

Bramblett's report so troubled the Kentuckian that he rode out to the picket line to inspect the enemy's dispositions himself. Accompanied by Major W. D. Pickett of Hardee's staff, Breckinridge continued beyond the pickets toward a belt of timber along the river bank; simultaneously, his assistant adjutant general, Lieutenant Colonel John Buckner, and his chief of artillery, Major Rice Graves, made their way forward of the division's right.

Pickett had run into Breckinridge while riding along the Confederate front line with Hardee and Polk. When they met, the three generals fell immediately into an earnest discussion of the tactical significance of the ground near McFadden's Ford. All agreed that a careful reconnaissance of the position should be made at once. Hardee and Polk were about to accompany Breckinridge when a courier appeared to remind them that they were needed at their respective headquarters. Hardee left Pickett to represent him. Breckinridge, Pickett, and a retinue of staff officers then cantered north along the east bank of the river until they came upon a two-story farmhouse, appropriated by the Second Kentucky as a picket post. Although the timber and brushwood obscured their view, the pop-pop of rifle fire convinced them that there were Federal pickets to their front. Dismounting, Breckinridge and Pickett edged forward to the northern limit of the wood. Beyond stretched a cultivated field several hundred yards wide that ended abruptly at the base of a small hill. Although not occupied, the hill was of sufficient size to mask any force that might be deployed behind it. The presence of Northern pickets nearby, added to the obvious tactical significance of the terrain beyond, reinforced Breckinridge's suspicion that there was a strong Union force at hand.

Meanwhile, Buckner and Graves had seen the Federals—at least that portion of the line held by Price. Graves ordered Moses's Georgia battery to fire a few shots at Price "to develop his strength." Price did not respond, but Graves was satisfied that the Federals were out in force and notified Breckinridge accordingly.

At noon, Bragg summoned Breckinridge to army headquarters. Beneath a sweeping sycamore at the river's edge, the two generals conferred. Major Pickett, who was present throughout the meeting, came away with the impression that "General Bragg had already determined to make the attack, as he at once commenced explaining the order of attack." Breckinridge listened, and as he listened his anger grew. After Bragg finished, the Kentuckian picked up a stick and illustrated his objections in the dirt. Sketching the boomerang-shaped rise north of McFadden's Ford and west of Fyffe's position, as well as the lower elevation he was to carry, Breckinridge pointed out that the disparity in altitude meant that, in falling back, the Federals would occupy a position that actually dominated his division's objective. Bragg was unmoved. No one, least of all the argumentative Kentuckian, was going to change Bragg's mind for him. Bragg now fixed the hour of the assault at 4:00 P.M., one hour before dark. As it was already 2:30, Bragg suggested that Breckinridge return to his command at once.

Breckinridge rode away in disgust. According to one account, he paused to confide in William Preston his doubts: "General Preston, this attack is made against my judgement, and by the special orders of General Bragg. If it should result in disaster, and I be among the slain, I want you to . . . tell the people that I believed this attack to be very unwise, and tried to prevent it." Preston makes no mention of the encounter in a lengthy letter of 26 January 1863 to his nephew, William Preston Johnston, in which he airs much of the Army of Tennessee's dirty laundry, so the episode may be the fabrication of one of Bragg's detractors. On the other hand, Preston was an outspoken member of the anti-Bragg clique, so it is conceivable that Breckinridge would choose to confide in him.

In fairness to Bragg, Major Pickett recalled nothing "invidious or critical" in his instructions to Breckinridge. Pickett agreed with Bragg's conclusion that the Kentuckian's division was the least cut up and thus most able to make an attack and that an assault launched so near dark, if successful, would preclude a Federal counterattack.[1]

Breckinridge's return brought his troops to life. Skirmishers moved forward, staff officers crisscrossed the lines carrying orders—everywhere were the unmistakable signs "of a general waking up." Before long, the Orphans were filing off Wayne's Hill by the right flank to join the remainder of the division.

Sam Beatty and his brigade commanders watched this flurry of activity closely. The Ohioan suspected trouble long before any Confederate action suggested it and during the morning had requested that Grose's brigade be sent over to reinforce his left. Palmer complied. Grose deployed behind Fyffe, placing the Twenty-fourth Ohio and the Thirty-sixth Indiana behind log breastworks and the Sixth Ohio and the Eighty-fourth Illinois to their rear. Grose's remaining regiment, the Twenty-third Kentucky, advanced to support Fyffe's second line. Beatty also brought the Third Wisconsin Artillery across the river, and they unlimbered in front of Price.

By noon, reports from his front line confirmed Beatty's suspicions. Price notified him that he had counted fifteen regiments and an undetermined number of guns passing across his front; a few minutes later, Confederate skirmishers opened on Price and Fyffe, leading Beatty to feed Grider's Seventy-ninth Indiana into the front line. At 1:00 P.M. Confederate artillery joined in with a barrage that continued intermittently for two hours.

Crittenden was keeping Rosecrans apprised of these ominous developments. Apparently having learned from the destruction of the Right Wing not to place undue confidence in his lieutenants (Thomas excepted), Rosecrans moved at once to shore up the left. He pulled Negley's division from the far right and placed it in reserve behind McFadden's Ford. Morton's Pioneer Brigade formed on Negley's left a short time later. Artillery followed. Captain George Swallow's Seventh Indiana Battery, Cockerill's Battery F, First Ohio, and Parson's eight guns unlimbered on a gentle slope overlooking the ford. By 3:00 P.M., there were four brigades—those of Miller, Stanley, Morton, and Cruft—and eighteen guns within supporting distance of Beatty.[2]

Actually, for a time it appeared as if any Confederate effort would be directed once again against the Nashville Turnpike—Nashville and Chattanooga Railroad salient. Before dawn, Bishop Polk concentrated five batteries below the Round Forest. The rumble of limbers and caissons escaped the Federals' notice, and the opening salvo at 8:00 A.M. caught them by surprise. Harker's infantrymen, sandwiched between the Confederate artillery and their own startled gunners, fell immediately to the ground and largely escaped harm. But the artillerymen and battery horses were forced to stand by their pieces and return the fire. Harnessed to caissons

and limbers, the horses were an easy mark. Lieutenant George Estep lost so many that, when he tried to withdraw his guns to a less
exposed position, he had to leave two pieces behind for want of
teams to pull them.

Captain Cullen Bradley faced an additional, wholly unexpected,
threat to the integrity of his command. Captain Stokes, responding
to an order to advance his battery to what today is the southeast-
ern edge of the national cemetery and engage Polk's artillery, mistook Bradley's gunners for his target. His four James Rifles
unleashed a volley of grape into the backs of the unsuspecting
Ohioans, wounding five. For Bradley, anger quickly overcame
amazement, and he spurred his horse toward the Chicagoans.
Again they fired. Bradley's mount was hit, and animal and rider
tumbled. Regaining his balance, Bradley sprinted the last hundred
yards, reached the battery just as its gunners were ramming home
a third charge, and "by the use of very vigorous English" convinced them to cease fire.

Fortunately for the Bluecoats, the barrage lasted just thirty minutes. Polk never explained why he ordered it, but his artillery
must have welcomed the opportunity to inflict some damage on
the Federals after their comparative inactivity on Wednesday.[3]

Back on the east bank, events moved toward a violent climax.
Shortly after 1:00 P.M., Pegram and his troopers trotted into position on Breckinridge's right. At Wharton's suggestion, the brigade
dismounted and formed a skirmish line.

The infantry, meanwhile, was still struggling into line. What began as an annoying drizzle had by noon turned into a numbing,
driving sleet that slapped and blinded the soldiers as they tried to
dress ranks and even alignment. It was 3:00 before Colonel Randall Gibson, successor to the wounded Dan Adams, had his brigade up and ready behind the Orphans. William Preston was not
even notified of the impeding assault until 2:30; as his command
was then below the Round Forest on the west bank, it is unlikely
that he was in position much before the signal gun sounded at
4:00. When Preston finally did fall in behind Brigadier General
Gideon Pillow's brigade, he was disturbed by the spacing between
the two waves. Three hundred yards customarily separated
regiment- or brigade-sized lines, or waves, in an attack. This spacing insured that the trailing line would be safe from enemy bullets
that might sail over the first line, yet near enough to provide effective support. But Preston had been instructed to follow Pillow at a
distance of only one hundred fifty yards. This spacing may not

have troubled Gibson, whose brigade lay a similar distance behind Hanson, but it alarmed Preston. Even before the attack began, he saw clearly that balls passing over Pillow's line would plough through his ranks and that his men would be unable to reply or maneuver.

And then there was the presence of Pillow himself. Opportunely or inopportunely, depending on one's opinion of the man, the Tennessean had arrived on the field just an hour earlier. Ambitious, deceitful, mendacious, and—of cardinal importance to the soldiers he was about to lead—incompetent, Pillow was perhaps the last person Breckinridge would have chosen to command a brigade in his division. But the unsavory Tennessee lawyer had parlayed friendships within the government into a brigadier general's commission. A friend and neighbor of President James K. Polk, he had obtained a commission by similar means during the War with Mexico. Pillow accomplished little during that war, except to alienate Winfield Scott, who regarded him as insubordinate. Pillow was doing little better in the Civil War. During the Fort Henry and Fort Donelson campaigns, his vacillation and bungling had contributed substantially to the loss of both posts; in the bargain, he had made a lasting enemy of Leonidas Polk, with whom Pillow differed over the appropriate strategy to pursue in Middle Tennessee. Nonetheless, or perhaps because of these differences, he was a favorite of Bragg. The nearly friendless general was only too pleased to assign Pillow to brigade command on his arrival at headquarters. Whatever his other shortcomings, Pillow was not one to forget a favor: in the months that followed, he testified on behalf of his beleaguered commander, distorting the truth just enough to implicate Breckinridge in the failure of the attack.

So Breckinridge was stuck with Pillow. To complicate matters, the brigade that the Tennessean rode imperiously forward to command had been assigned to the front line. But the hour of the assault was drawing near, and so no changes were made.

Other personalities clashed as the seconds ticked away. While awaiting the arrival of Preston's four regiments from the west bank, Breckinridge and Captain Robertson fell into an impassioned argument over the proper disposition of divisional and attached artillery batteries. Robertson understood that the attack was to be launched by infantry alone; on the contrary, replied Breckinridge, it would be made by a combination of arms. In asserting his point, the Kentuckian ordered Robertson to insert his batteries between the two waves of infantry. Robertson demurred. Breckinridge then asked him to form behind the second wave and advance with it. Robertson refused: "I . . . repeated the general's [Bragg's] orders to me, viz, to wait until the infantry had crowned the crest, and then to rush up and occupy it." Breckinridge relented, allowing Robertson to commit his guns as he saw fit; his own batteries, however, would move behind and simultaneously with the second wave. Robertson agreed that the two batteries under his control would occupy the hill near McFadden's Ford as soon as the infantry cleared it.

The minutes passed slowly. "The short time seemed long as with strained nerves," recalled H. B. Clay of Pegram's brigade. "We listened for the signal gun." With nothing better to do, Ed Porter Thompson of the Orphan Brigade contemplated the ground over which he would be charging: "[It] was an uncleared space, covered, for the most part, with sassafras and other brushwood, and with briars, and a little ahead was another open flat of ground, descending from the bushes, for some distance, then ascending to the line upon which the enemy lay. The general character of the ground along the whole division was undulating and broken by thickets, forest trees and patches of briars."[4]

A little after 3:00, skirmishers threw down the fences to their front. A few minutes before 4:00, the men of the Sixth Kentucky descried the fleshy form of Brigadier General Roger Hanson galloping toward them. Hanson drew up in front of the regiment, accosted its colonel, and—in a stentorian voice that everyone could hear—yelled out: "Colonel, the order is to load, fix bayonets and march through this brushwood. Then charge at double quick to within a hundred yards of the enemy, deliver fire, and go at him with the bayonet." Hanson relayed the order with more enthusiasm than he felt. When Breckinridge first explained Bragg's plan to him, the thirty-five-year-old Kentuckian had exploded in rage. The order was tantamount to murder, Hanson asserted; to forestall its execution, he would commit murder himself, and Breckinridge and Preston had to restrain him from shooting Bragg.

Of course the men in ranks knew none of this. Snapping to attention at Colonel Joseph Lewis's command, the troops of the Sixth loaded their rifles and waited. At precisely 4:00 P.M., a single cannon boomed, and "the line seemed to leap forward."

The Kentuckians were immediately under fire. "There was nothing to prevent the enemy from observing neatly all of our movements and preparations," Breckinridge wrote. Just after stepping off, Lot D. Young recalled seeing little white puffs of smoke rise from

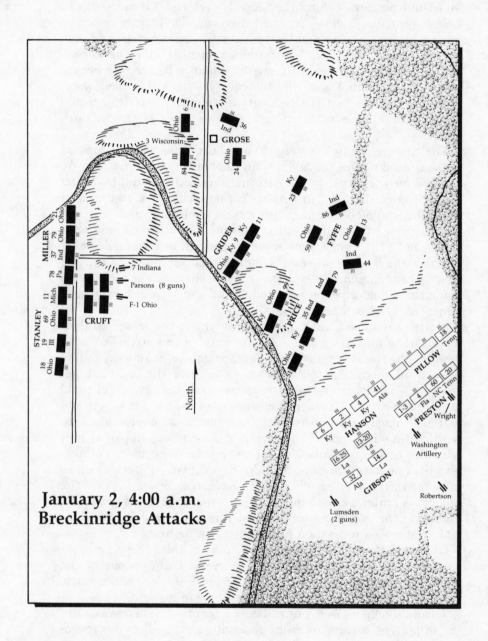

GROSE

6 Ohio

Ind 36

3 Wisconsin

84 Ohio

24 Ohio

Ky 23

Ind 86

Ohio 59

FYFFE

Ohio 13

Ind 44

MILLER

21 Ohio

79 Ohio

37 Ind

78 Pa

STANLEY

11 Mich

69 Ohio

19 Ohio

18 Ohio

7 Indiana

Parsons (8 guns)

F-1 Ohio

CRUFT

GRIDER

Ky 9 Ky 11

Ohio 79

Ind 79

Ohio 99

PRICE

35 Ind

Ky 8

Ohio 51

18 Tenn

PILLOW

20 Tenn

1-3 Fla

4 Fla

60 NC

PRESTON

Wright

41 Ala

4 Ky

2 Ky

HANSON

6 Ky

13-20 La

14 La

16-25 La

GIBSON

32 Ala

Washington
Artillery

Robertson

Lumsden
(2 guns)

North

January 2, 4:00 a.m.
Breckinridge Attacks

the Union batteries above McFadden's Ford, followed by "bursting shells that completely drowned the voice of man . . . plunging and tearing through our columns." As they marched through the brushwood, Young saw a shell fall in the midst of Company E, just a few yards away: "When I recovered from the shock the sight I witnessed was appalling. Some eighteen or twenty men hurled in every direction."

Despite the telltale activity of his skirmishers an hour earlier, Breckinridge's attack, launched with only forty-four minutes of daylight remaining, surprised most Federals. Given the hour, "we now supposed that the attack which we had all day expected would be postponed until daylight the next day," Colonel Benjamin Grider conceded. Sam Beatty was down by McFadden's Ford with Colonel Fyffe when the Rebel signal gun sounded. A messenger followed with news of the advance, and the two colonels hurried back to their commands. William Erb of the Nineteenth Ohio was about to enjoy his first meal in three days when the call came to fall in. Earlier that afternoon, while resting in a meadow, Erb's attention had been drawn to a spot where a Rebel shell had struck the sod and ricocheted away. The Ohioan decided to look for it. He traced its path to an old barn where, to his delight, he discovered a "fine, fat laying hen" and a brood of eggs. Sweeping the eggs into his forage cap and the hen under his arm, Erb retreated to his regiment amid the cries of hundreds of half-starved soldiers that he "drop that chicken." A kettle was requisitioned, the bird boiled, and Erb and his messmates began dividing up the meat when the picket line released a volley. "We instantly knew the cause as well as the probable effect," remembered Erb. The bird returned to the kettle, and the Bluecoats ran to grab their stacked rifles.

Hanson's Kentuckians were the first to close with the enemy. Aside from a turgid pond, swollen by the heavy rains, that forced the Sixth Kentucky to trail the Second momentarily, the Orphan Brigade encountered no serious obstacles during the first nine hundred yards of its advance; not even the hail of shot and shell had disrupted its "perfect line of battle." Only one hundred yards now separated them from Price's front line, which remained strangely silent. But the Federals simply were waiting for targets too close to miss. At ninety yards the Thirty-fifth Indiana opened fire, and the Fourth Kentucky wavered. At sixty yards Colonel Richard McClain ordered the men of the Fifty-first Ohio to their feet. Rising from behind a small declivity, the Ohioans stunned the Butternuts with their first volley, and the Second Kentucky shivered. Under orders to fire just one volley and then close with the bayonet, the Kentuckians kept coming, and Price's front line collapsed. As so often happened, retreating troops from frontline regiments threw those of the second line into confusion, and the Twenty-first Kentucky and Ninety-ninth Ohio managed only a few ragged volleys before Price waved them rearward.

The Orphans had carried the hill at the price of their brigade commander's life. Only minutes earlier, Breckinridge had watched his Orphans, their portly brigadier general in front, raise a cheer and disappear over a rise and into a meadow. Despite his disdain for Bragg's plan, Breckinridge could not contain the admiration he felt for his favorite subordinate. "Look at old Hanson," he yelled as the Kentuckians marched out of sight. Accompanied by his staff and Major Pickett, who had attached himself to the party to see the attack through, Breckinridge followed the brigade across the briar-laced field. They were within a few yards of Price's abandoned breastworks when they spotted Hanson, lying alone against a fence. A shell fragment had gashed his leg and sliced open the femoral artery. Breckinridge tried vainly to stop the bleeding, and his staff summoned an ambulance. Pickett never forgot the scene: "It was a sight indelibly impressed on my memory—the dying hero, his distinguished friend and commander kneeling by his side holding back the lifeblood. . . . All this under the fiercest fire of artillery that can be conceived made it ever memorable. The scene passed almost as quick as it takes to write it. General Hanson was promptly moved by the ambulance. Breckinridge was soon as alert and clear-headed as ever."

Doctor John Scott, surgeon of the Second Kentucky, applied a tourniquet as the ambulance bounced toward Murfreesboro, and Captain Stephen Chipley maintained pressure above the artery. But the Kentuckian knew the wound was mortal. "Hanson did not utter a groan or speak a complaining word," recalled Scott. "When I had done the little it was possible to do there, he asked me to leave him . . . and go to the help of his wounded men.[5]

Gideon Pillow's behavior on the field was as craven as Hanson's was heroic. Breckinridge found the Kentuckian dying alongside a fence; he found Pillow cowering behind a tree, very much alive and apparently willing to do whatever was necessary to remain that way. The language Breckinridge used to order him forward can only be imagined.

Pillow's brigade was fighting well, despite—or perhaps because of—their commander's absence. Colonel Palmer, relegated to command of the Eighteenth Tennessee with the arrival of Pillow, found that the line of defending Federals overlapped his regiment on the right; but, as his Tennesseans already were engaged with the Seventy-ninth Indiana, there was nothing he could do to silence the fire that the Forty-fourth Indiana was pouring into his flank. Lieutenant Colonel F. M. Lavender, following Palmer with the Twentieth Tennessee, ran into the same oblique fire. Screened in front by the Eighteenth, Lavender was able to swing his unit by the right flank until it faced the troublesome Hoosiers. Lavender ordered his men to take cover and return the fire. As regimental historian William McMurray later wrote, "the slaughter was terrible." At that moment, Wright rushed forward with his Tennessee battery. He had fired only a few rounds into the Forty-fourth Indiana and Thirteenth Ohio, which lay on the extreme left of Beatty's front line, when they broke contact and fell back. The Thirteenth attempted a stand three hundred yards to the rear, but Wright continued the duel from behind the fence it had abandoned, and Colonel Jarvis reluctantly withdrew his regiment across the river.

Despite this initial success, the Confederate attack was beginning to unravel, particularly in front of the Seventy-ninth Indiana. There Pillow's left regiments had taken cover soon after striking the Hoosier's line. They were trading volleys with the Bluecoats and apparently getting the better of the exchange, when Preston's supporting line stumbled upon them. At first, the Floridians tried to stand and fire over the heads of their prone countrymen. It was a mistake. This unexpected "fire in the rear greatly alarmed my line," wrote Pillow, echoing the sentiments of his regimental commanders, "and . . . my officers expressed the opinion that my men suffered severely from this fire." Preston's men eventually joined the Tennesseans on the ground, but this was no better: now there was "one line of four deep . . . exposing both lines to a most destructive fire." Colonel William Miller of the First and Third Florida Consolidated recognized the dilemma, but was unable to correct it. "The combination of movements caused an intermingling of regiments, which led to no little confusion, separating commands, and, again, the men from their commanders." Despite the confusion, the weight of numbers told, and after forty minutes the Seventy-ninth Indiana joined the remainder of its brigade in flight across the river.[6]

Farther to the left, Randall Gibson was having similar problems. Gibson had left the front for a moment to redirect the Thirteenth and Twentieth Louisiana Consolidated, on a collision course with the river. In his absence, the confusion mounted. As Stones River meanders toward McFadden's Ford it curls westward, then loops abruptly to the north. At that point a nearby belt of timber and parallel high ground channeled any unit approaching from the southeast; consequently, the brigades of Hanson, now led by Colonel Trabue, and Pillow intermingled badly as they neared the river. "The peculiar nature of the ground and the direction of the river and the eagerness of the troops caused the lines of General Pillow's brigade and this brigade to lap on the crest of the hill," explained Trabue. Ed Thompson was more direct: "In the madness of pursuit all order and discipline were forgotten."

That madness was contagious, infecting even the regimental mascots. Gervis Grainger, hugging the ground with his comrades as their regiment prepared to charge Price's second line, watched as Frank, their canine companion, leapt after a rabbit. A few of the Kentuckians raised a cheer of encouragement, then more, until the entire line was yelling wildly. Believing they were about to be charged, the Federals unleashed their first volley, which passed harmlessly over the heads of the Kentuckians but which caused the rabbit to double back toward the Sixth Kentucky. As he darted through the ranks, with Frank close behind, one soldier reflected aloud: "Run, cottontail, run! Had I no more reputation to sustain than you, I would run too!"[7]

Meanwhile, Sam Beatty was beginning to see that, unless the Confederate advance were arrested, his first engagement as a division commander would be remembered as a rout. So he turned to Colonel Grider, whose three remaining regiments were resting in the ravine near McFadden's Ford, and ordered him to counterattack. Grider turned in the saddle and galloped back to his command.

Actually, Beatty already had sent a staff officer directly to the commander of the Nineteenth Ohio, the nearsighted Charles Manderson, with the same instructions. As this was "contrary to rule and custom," Manderson contemplated ignoring them; but, "presuming the occasion to be an emergency requiring such a deviation," he thought better of it and obeyed. In one of the few recorded instances of hand-to-hand combat during the battle, the Nineteenth bested the Fourth Kentucky. At the same time, Grider appeared with the Ninth and Eleventh Kentucky (Union), which cleared their fronts with just four or five volleys.

Grider was elated. "Colonel, we have them checked," he told Beatty. "Give us artillery and we will whip them." Beatty promised it, and Grider felt confident; that is, until he looked to the right and saw Manderson's regiment coming apart. Grider called to Manderson as he rode by: "Major, the Ninth is still standing: let us rally the Nineteenth and sustain her." "We are flanked on our right," Manderson answered. "We had better fall back and rally at the foot of the hill, if we can." Grider accepted Manderson at his word, and the Ninth and Eleventh Kentucky joined the rearward tide.

Manderson may have been premature. The units he had spotted beyond his right were merely fragments of the Second and Sixth Kentucky that, having been crowded against the river bank, splashed across without orders and scampered up the east bank. Gervis Grainger was among them. He and several others from Company I crossed together, then scattered. Grainger darted behind a large sycamore and opened fire on a handful of Federals clustered in a cabin sixty yards away. Looking back for a moment, he saw only a dense cloud of smoke where his regiment had been.[8]

It was 4:45 P.M. The sun had set, the temperature was falling, and the sleet continued to slap at the soldiers. In the gathering darkness, Breckinridge's men fixed their gaze on flashes of cannon fire from across the river and pushed on.

There was little on the east bank to stop them. In spite of Beatty's best efforts, Price's shattered regiments had swarmed past him toward the river. "Their flight was down the river, whither we pursued them for nearly half a mile, dealing fire and death in their backs. . . . In the rout hundreds of them fell . . . with their faces . . . upon the field," observed Palmer. And with Fyffe down (his horse having thrown, then dragged him), his brigade swarmed rearward through Grose's lines.

Preston was right behind. The commanders of the Twenty-third Ohio and the Twenty-fourth Kentucky, not expecting an attack from the southeast after Pillow deviated toward the river, were as surprised to see Preston as he was to be leading the attack. After only the feeblest attempt to hold their positions, both regiments fled toward Grose's line. Sergeant Louis Simmons of the Eighty-fourth Illinois watched their disordered approach and Preston's determined pursuit: "Out of the woods into the open fields in our front . . . they came, in the greatest possible confusion. The whole division was in full retreat, and apparently taking one of those terrible stampedes which any troops will, when routed and pressed by the enemy. Each man seemed to be looking out only for himself, and making every possible effort to get out of danger. Out of the

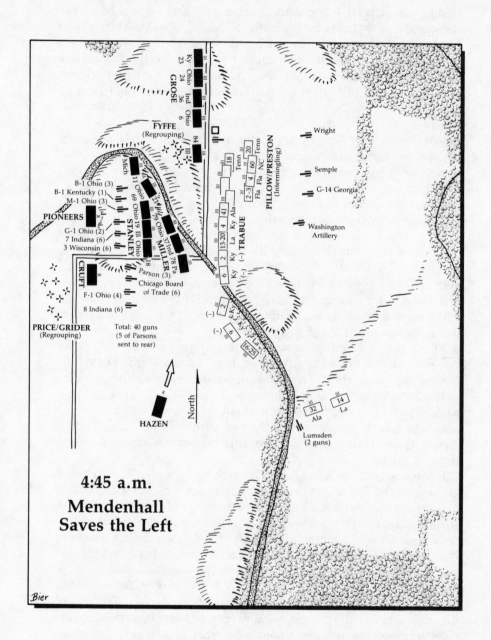

Ky Ohio Ind Ohio
23 24 36 6

GROSE

FYFFE
(Regrouping)

84

Wright

Semple

PILLOW/PRESTON
(Intermingling)

G-14 Georgia

18
Tenn

60 Tenn
4
Fla Fla NC
2-3

Washington
Artillery

Mich

11 Ohio

41
4
La Ky Ala

B-1 Ohio (3)
B-1 Kentucky (1)
M-1 Ohio (3)

69 Ohio 19 Ill

21 Ky

13 20 4
Ky

(–) TRABUE

PIONEERS

STANLEY

79 Ohio 97 Ind 78 Pa

MILLER

6 2 (–)

G-1 Ohio (2)
7 Indiana (6)
3 Wisconsin (6)

28

CRUFT

Parson (3)

Chicago Board
of Trade (6)

(–) 2

F-1 Ohio (4)

8 Indiana (6)

(–) 6

Ky

PRICE/GRIDER
(Regrouping)

16 25

Total: 40 guns
(5 of Parsons
sent to rear)

North

32
Ala

14
La

x

HAZEN

Lumsden
(2 guns)

4:45 a.m.

**Mendenhall
Saves the Left**

Bier

woods, pursuing them came the brigades of the enemy in most splendid lines of battle, their colors flying and apparently secure of an easy and complete victory."

Simmons's Eighty-fourth Illinois, the Sixth Ohio, and the Thirty-sixth Indiana rose in unison from behind their breastworks to engage the Floridians, now within three hundred yards. They halted, and a brisk exchange followed.

Just as he had been on the thirty-first, Rosecrans was in the thick of the fight now, scraping together idle units with which to bolster the flagging left. The general was in only slightly firmer control of his emotions than he had been on Wednesday. "Old Rosy came galloping down the pike where we lay, the sweat pouring down his face, and sent for Colonel Carlin," Colonel Hans Heg wrote his wife after the battle. Heg quotes Rosecrans's impassioned command: "I beg you for the sake of the country and for my own sake to go at them with all your might. Go at them with a whoop and a yell!" Carlin saluted and led his command toward the river.[9]

While Rosecrans begged Carlin to save the country and his career, Captain John Mendenhall, Crittenden's chief of artillery, was less dramatically but more effectively striving to concentrate all available guns to meet Breckinridge's assault. His efforts were decisive. By the time Breckinridge's infantry crested the hill above McFadden's Ford that was their objective, Mendenhall had collected forty-five pieces, enough to blow the Butternuts back to their line of departure.

Although Mendenhall gathered the guns at Crittenden's request, his success most certainly exceeded the general's expectations. Mendenhall and Crittenden had been riding along the Nashville Turnpike when Breckinridge struck Beatty. Riding to the sound of the guns, they drew rein alongside the Seventh Indiana Artillery in time to witness the rout of Price and the abortive counterattack of Grider. "Now, Mendenhall, you must cover my men with your cannon," Crittenden ordered.

Mendenhall obeyed. The Seventh Indiana already had opened fire, so Mendenhall left them where they were and called on Parsons to bring his four three-inch ordnance rifles alongside the Hoosiers. Riding up the turnpike, he found Lieutenant Estep, who had pulled out of the duel with Polk's artillery that morning. Estep went into action beside Battery F, First Ohio. Next, Mendenhall sought out Morton, whose Pioneer Brigade was resting in reserve. Morton committed the Chicago Board of Trade Battery and also advanced his brigade. As Battery B, Twenty-sixth Pennsylvania Artillery, lay near the ford, Mendenhall permitted its commander to remain where he was, ordering him merely to change front to the left and open fire. Battery B, First Ohio, laying in the field where Rains's assault had been shattered two days earlier, moved to cover the ford itself. Returning to supervise the deployment of his collected guns, Mendenhall ran across the Sixth Ohio Artillery on the railroad. Captain Bradley had his pieces trained on the enemy, and Mendenhall left him with orders to commence firing at the first opportunity.

Mendenhall deployed his guns perfectly, arraying them hub to hub on a slope at least ten feet higher than the highest point on the east bank, so that their crews would have unobstructed fields of fire.

Breckinridge's Confederates crested the hill above the ford, and Mendenhall's guns roared their greeting. The destruction was terrific. "So it was here, if a soldier ever saw the lightning and heard the thunder bolts of a tornado, at the same time the heavens opened and the stars of destruction were sweeping everything from the face of the earth, if he was in this charge he saw it," wrote the historian of the Twentieth Tennessee. Lieutenant Colonel Buckner of Breckinridge's staff agreed, writing simply: "A more terrific fire of artillery I have never been under than in this position." Ed Thompson's recollection of the last moments of the attack are particularly poignant: "The very earth trembled as with an exploding mine, and a mass of iron hail was hurled upon them. The artillery bellowed forth such thunder that the men were stunned and could not distinguish sounds. There were falling timbers, crashing arms, the whirring of missiles in every direction, the bursting of the dreadful shell, the groans of the wounded, the shouts of the officers, mingled in one horrid din that beggars description." As the initial shock of the barrage wore off, the men regained their composure—the "composure of despair," recalled Thompson. First individually, then by squads, finally by entire regiments, the Confederates recoiled. "Some rushed back precipitately, while others walked away with deliberation, and some even slowly and doggedly, as though they scorned the danger or had become indifferent to life."[10]

The suddenness and completeness of the Confederate collapse surprised the Federals. They "cannot be said to have been checked in their advance—from a rapid advance they broke at once into a rapid retreat," remembered Crittenden. But their surprise in no way prevented those troops gathered along the west bank, among them Stanley's and Miller's brigades, from spontaneously splashing across the river in pursuit. The Seventy-eighth Pennsylvania crossed first. Walking behind his Nineteenth Illinois as it lay among the limestone outcrops near the bank, Colonel Joseph Scott noticed the Pennsylvanians wading across beyond his right; drawing his sword, he yelled, "Follow me!" and sprinted down the bank, his regiment trailing after him. Colonel Miller decided against recalling those already across. Instead he supported them with the remainder of the brigade, and into the waist-deep waters went the Twenty-first and Seventy-fourth Ohio and several companies of the Thirty-seventh Indiana. Miller himself was already on the east bank, exhorting his men as they fired into the backs of the fleeing Confederates, when a courier from General Palmer brought a startling message: He, Miller, was not to cross; the enemy had gained his right rear. Before Miller could react, a second rider arrived with a peremptory order cancelling the one just received. Miller shrugged: "Having no inclination to turn back, I ordered the troops forward."

Palmer's strange orders emerged from the continued presence of fragments of the Second and Sixth Kentucky, joined now by the Sixteenth and Twenty-fifth Louisiana Consolidated, in the belt of timber along the west bank, beyond Miller's right. Determined to dislodge them, Palmer called upon Cruft, whose brigade lay behind Mendenhall's guns, to provide him with two regiments. They arrived, and Palmer led them forward with fixed bayonets to sweep the bank clean of Butternuts.

Gervis Grainger was still absorbed in his private war with the Yankees in the cabin when Palmer approached. A Union brass band blaring to his right drew his attention to the larger struggle around him. Glancing "in the direction I had left our men, not one was to be seen. Our army had retreated, leaving me alone to fight the Federal forces single-handed." Not quite, but one can imagine Grainger's fear. The Kentuckian leveled his rifle for one final, defiant shot (which he claims dropped a Federal color sergeant), then jumped from the bank and into the river. Bullets peppered the water around him, but Grainger reached the east side and began running. He tried to grab a riderless horse, but a shell fragment carried away its head. Continuing on foot, he passed four men carrying a wounded soldier on a litter. Another shell struck the litter, killing two bearers and their charge. The remaining two joined Grainger, and together they sprinted toward the rear, not stopping until they reached the belt of timber behind which the attack was first organized.[11]

By the time Grainger reached the east bank, most of his comrades had succumbed to panic. Hundreds surrendered. Corporal Joseph Johnston of the Nineteenth Illinois wrote his mother that many, overcome with fear, simply fell to their knees and begged mercy, claiming to be conscripts compelled to fight in the Confederate army. Private Nourse of the Chicago Board of Trade Battery, bouncing across the field on a limber, swore that the enemy "fled faster than our men had done before, throwing away everything that impeded their flight, and muskets and equipment covered the ground."

Captain Robertson told Bragg substantially the same story: "I have never seen troops so completely broken in my military experience. In more than one instance I found it necessary to cock my revolver and level it in order to bring men to a realizing sense of their duty." Major Pickett took exception to Robertson's remarks. No troops had ever displayed greater valor, he replied: given the circumstances, retreat was the only alternative to slaughter—and the retreat was orderly. Others, aware that Robertson penned his report as Bragg wished it to read, also dismissed the captain's remarks as invective. But more than one troop commander attested to the veracity of Robertson's account. Colonel Joseph Lewis in his report admitted the impossibility of restoring order to his Sixth Kentucky once Mendenhall's guns were trained on them; Preston had only slightly better luck with his troops and those of Pillow. Grabbing the colors of the first fleeing standard-bearer he encountered, Preston used his free hand to beat everyone within reach with his sabre, until he had gathered a corporal's guard around him. Finding that he had snatched the colors of the Forty-fifth Tennessee, one of Pillow's regiments, he called for its colonel, gave him the standard, and together they restored a semblance of order to the unit. "My persuasions were not very effective, but the blows were, and finally by an appearance that I was going to take them to a place of safety, I got a good many together and left them with their colonel." Preston then turned his attention to his own brigade, which he rallied only after it reached the safety of the woods.

Breckinridge's artillery was wholly unprepared for this sudden turn of events. Lieutenant W. C. D. Vaughan had led his Washington Artillery dutifully forward to occupy the ground abandoned by Price and Fyffe. From there he opened on Mendenhall's massed batteries. The results were predictable: Vaughan expended all his ammunition in dismounting just one Napoleon twelve-pounder belonging to Parson's battery. The Washington Artillery delivered its final volley as Pillow's shattered regiments streamed past. By the time Vaughan limbered the last of his four guns, the Federals were a mere fifty yards away.

Wright's Tennessee battery was less fortunate. Wright scarcely had deployed his guns when Breckinridge's retreating infantry poured through his position. Nevertheless, Wright held his ground, covering the withdrawal until the Yankees were within seventy-five yards and a bullet killed him. At that point, Major Graves stepped in. He barked the order, "Limber to the rear," but just as the pieces were fastened he countermanded the command and directed the battery to unlimber and ram the guns with double charges of canister. They fired, a cloud of smoke swallowed the Federals, and Graves repeated the order to limber up. It came too late. Lieutenant John Mebane, the senior section commander, could only write: "Had our battery gone to the rear when the other batteries of the division did, we would have saved our guns; but being under the immediate supervision of the chief of artillery, we did not move without orders from him."[12]

As Confederate resistance dissolved, more Northern units joined in the pursuit. Grider grabbed the colors of the Ninth Kentucky (Union) and led his brigade in on Miller's left. Hazen crossed the river with his brigade at about the same time. Leaving three of his four regiments near the ford in reserve, he took the Twenty-third Kentucky, Thirty-sixth Indiana, and Twenty-fourth Ohio of Grose's brigade and, forming them in column, advanced beside Grider.

The counterattacking Federals were now closing on the woods from which Breckinridge had launched his attack only an hour earlier, just forty-two minutes earlier by Ed Thompson's calculation. For a time, it appeared as if Miller, Stanley, Grider, and Hazen might roll on into Murfreesboro. But Wharton's troopers galloped over from the right and dismounted across the field, and the Washington Artillery and Semple's Alabama battery (minus one gun lost to Grider's Ninth Kentucky) rallied on Robertson's battery, which had never advanced. Although it was a scratch line, it was enough to halt the Federals who, in the gathering twilight, assumed they had struck a much larger force. Stanley pulled his men out of the briar-laced sward, where they were badly exposed, and back behind a hill north of the woods. Miller did the same, although he attributed the halt more to "the disorder which follows such success" than to the Confederates' patchwork defense. Grose's troops and Hazen's single regiment stopped earlier, a mere five hundred yards from their original position. Grider appears to have followed the example of Miller and Stanley.

Although Wharton's troopers undoubtedly contributed to the success of the covering action, they had been invisible during the attack. Neither Wharton nor Pegram had advanced to protect the right flank of the infantry. Pillow told Bragg that they had remained on the ridge beyond his right, watching as Hazen turned his flank but doing nothing. Brent wrote in his journal that "the cavalry on the right were ordered to cooperate, but they were mere spectators." Nonetheless, it is unlikely that their participation would have made any real difference in the outcome of the assault.[13]

Deeply shaken by the disaster that had befallen his division, Breckinridge raged "like a wounded lion" as he passed the remnants of each command. But it was the sight of his beloved Orphan Brigade that reduced him to tears. Nearly one-third of the twelve hundred engaged had failed to return: thirteen of twenty-three officers in the Fourth Kentucky had fallen; in the Second Kentucky, four standard-bearers had been killed carrying the colors thirty feet. Riding among the survivors, Breckinridge cried again and again: "My poor Orphans! My poor Orphans!"[14]

Bragg's initial response, considerably less emotional, was to dispatch Patton Anderson to cover the withdrawal and to forestall any further Federal advance. Anderson's column arrived well after dark. Being unfamiliar with the ground, Anderson asked Brent to guide him into position. Brent conducted him to the open wood north of Wayne's Hill. After throwing forward a strong skirmish line, Anderson faced his columns to the front and deployed. A little before 9:00 P.M., Breckinridge appeared and ordered him to withdraw his line three hundred yards to the next belt of timber. Anderson complied, but soon discovered that he was alone. Apparently, Breckinridge had implied that he would support the Tennessean on both flanks; in reality, the Kentuckian had withdrawn his command another seven hundred yards. At 10:45 P.M., with the nearest friendly infantry eight hundred yards away, Anderson dispatched E. T. Sykes with a message to Withers that the brigade hung in the air. Withers passed this on to Bragg, who immediately called Breckinridge and Sykes to headquarters.

An aide-de-damp led Sykes through the sleet and darkness to the Murphy house, a fine mansion in the center of town. From there, Sykes was ushered into an elegantly furnished parlor, where he found Bragg with his corps and division commanders. Mudstained and weary, Sykes felt uneasy in "this galaxy of generals." Bragg questioned him and, satisfied with the accuracy of his report, upbraided Breckinridge, who Sykes said acknowledged his error. Turning next to Hardee, he ordered McCown and Cleburne withdrawn from the west side of the river and formed behind the Kentuckian. Apparently the gathering closed amicably, although the bickering between Anderson and Breckinridge bode ill for the Army of Tennessee's command cohesion.[15]

Anderson's anxiety was wasted, as the Federals on the east bank had no intention of attacking. To the contrary, Rosecrans and Crittenden's primary concern was that Bragg might renew his attack. During the night, Rosecrans ordered Davis to relieve Miller and Stanley, and Crittenden added Milo Hascall's division for good measure.

While their generals tried to outguess Bragg, the soldiers of the Army of the Cumberland looked to their own comfort. With the enemy checked, William Erb and his messmates retraced their steps to the location of their abandoned supper. "By this time my chicken had been fought over twice by each army," recalled Erb. "The cracker-box had been pierced by a score of bullets; but, when I lifted it off the kettle, my chicken . . . was still there, untouched and yet warm." The little band sat down to a "glorious dinner."

Jacob Adams of the Twenty-first Ohio went hungry, but he did find shelter. His regiment returned to the west bank late in the night to bivouac near a house long since abandoned by its owners. Rather than pass another sleepless night in the cold and rain, Adams entered the house and lay down among a group of recumbent soldiers. "They did not protest in the least," Adams noted. He thought this peculiar, but was too tired to let it trouble him. When he awoke at dawn, after a sound sleep, he saw why they had been so accommodating: his bunkmates were corpses.

Alfred Hunter of the Eighty-second Indiana found neither food nor a dry place to sleep. West of the Nashville Turnpike, the sleet had let up at dusk. Taking advantage of the break in the storm, Hunter and his brother built a fire on an outcrop large enough to accommodate them both. After the blaze had dried the surface, they swept it clean and lay down for what they thought would be a warm, dry slumber. But the sleet returned with a vengeance, and Hunter found himself standing and cursing until dawn.

Despite the persistent rain and cold, the mood of the army was improving. The optimism Beatty had noted the night before was more general now, thanks largely to the sound thrashing handed Breckinridge. As Beatty observed, ambling among the campfires of his brigade:

There is more cheerful conversation among the men. They discuss the battle, the officers, and each other, and give us now and then a snatch of song. Officers come over from adjoining brigades, hoping to find a little whiskey, but learn, with apparent resignation and well-feigned composure, that the canteens have long been empty, that even the private flask, which officers carry with the photographs of their sweethearts, in a side pocket next to their hearts, are destitute of even the flavor of this article of prime necessity. My much-esteemed colleague of the court-martial, Colonel Hobart, stumbles up in the thick darkness to pay his respects. The sentinel, mistaking him for a private, tells him, with an oath, that this is neither the time nor place for stragglers, and orders him back to his regiment; and so the night wears on, and fifty thousand men lay upon their guns again.[16]

CHAPTER FIFTEEN

THIS ARMY SHOULD BE PROMPTLY PUT IN RETREAT

BEN CHEATHAM and Jones Withers left the commanders' meeting at the Murphy mansion deeply disturbed. Both had serious misgivings about remaining longer before Murfreesboro, misgivings that Bragg's unwillingness to rule out another attack and the transfer of Cleburne and McCown to the east bank (leaving Cheatham and Withers alone on the west side of Stones River with seven decimated brigades) only sharpened. And so they talked deep into the night.

As they talked, Cheatham and Withers found themselves in agreement on several points: that confidence in Bragg was wanting, that the troops were exhausted, and that to continue the battle was to invite disaster. Accordingly, they drafted an unorthodox letter to Bragg in which they spelled out their conviction that the army "should be promptly put in retreat." Rather than challenge Bragg's fitness to command directly, they cast doubt on the ability of his lieutenants, asserting that only three reliable divisions remained and that, among even these, there were a number of brigades in which the soldiers lacked confidence in their commanders. In short, they wrote, "we do fear great disaster from the condition of things now existing, and think it should be averted if possible." Cheatham and Withers delivered their recommendation to Polk, who forwarded it with his endorsement to army headquarters by staff courier.

Bragg was awakened at 2:00 A.M. After glancing briefly at the note from his bed, he snapped a reply to Polk's messenger: "Say to General Polk we shall hold our own at every hazard."

This was not what Polk had hoped to hear. Perhaps regretting that he had not consulted with Hardee before endorsing the note,

Polk wrote him at 3:00 to apprise him of its contents, his own endorsement, and Bragg's laconic reply. Hardee's response was no more encouraging. He told Lieutenant Richmond of Polk's staff that Bragg's reply had effectively closed the subject.[1]

That might have ended the issue, had Bragg not called Hardee and Polk to headquarters at 10:00 A.M. the following morning a changed man. Rosecrans had been reinforced, he told them, so that his army now exceeded their own by over two to one. Moreover, he asserted, the continued rain meant that Stones River would soon be a raging torrent, unfordable and capable of cutting the army in two. Perhaps, concluded Bragg, it would be wiser to withdraw than to face defeat in detail by a numerically superior enemy. Hardee and Polk agreed. At noon, Bragg issued orders for a movement of the army's trains and for the preparation of the troops for a night march.[2]

What had led to Bragg's change of heart? St. John Liddell offered the best explanation. Ducking into the Murphy house to escape a cold rain that fell the night of the third, the ubiquitous Liddell was surprised to find himself in Bragg's headquarters. Liddell did not hesitate, but immediately sought out Bragg to learn his intentions. Liddell found Bragg "thoughtful and hesitating." Bragg told Liddell that the army was too tired to fight on. Liddell, still confident of victory, disagreed emphatically. Bragg switched his line of argument: Rosecrans had been heavily reinforced, he explained. Surprised, Liddell asked who had told him this. "Wheeler," Bragg replied.

"It can't be so, for I have just come from the extreme left. I could have clearly seen the reinforcements approach, and I have seen none. Where is Rosecrans to get them from?" Liddell asked.

His logic was lost on Bragg. "It must be so. Wheeler seems assured of the fact," Bragg sighed.

Liddell launched into an impassioned monologue: "General, don't regard his reinforcements. Even could I believe such to be the case, everything depends on your success here. If you will throw your army between Rosecrans and Nashville, you will cut off all reinforcements. They will withdraw at the sight of your forces. Then I would fight Rosecrans to the last. I would rather bury my bones here than give up this field and our previous successes. Great results will follow this complete victory. You have Rosecrans in a close place. You have only to push him to extremities."

To this Bragg revealed his deepest doubt: "General, I know that you will fight it out, but others will not."

"Give the order, General, and every man will obey you," answered Liddell.

"No, it has now become a matter of imperative necessity to withdraw. It must be done at once," Bragg insisted.

Liddell returned to his brigade, convinced Bragg was wrong to rely so much on Wheeler's report of reinforcements. (Liddell, of course, was correct. Rosecrans had received no appreciable reinforcements.)

The Louisiana Brigadier could not mask his disappointment: "When I went back to my command, some of the men familiarly called out to me, 'What's up now, General?' I answered impatiently, 'Ask General Bragg.' They saw the hidden meaning and said, 'Well, boys, retreat again. All our hard fighting thrown away, as usual.'"

The Confederate retreat began at 10:00 P.M. Breckinridge led the way through mud nine inches deep down the Nashville Turnpike. Withers followed an hour later. At 11:30 Bragg and his staff left Murfreesboro, bound for Shelbyville on the Duck River, ostensibly the objective of the withdrawal. Cheatham abandoned his position at 1:00 A.M., and Cleburne and McCown cleared Murfreesboro at dawn.

The retreat was a nightmare of suffering. It rained incessantly, the temperature hovered about freezing, and rations were short. The Sixth Kentucky received food only after it had marched eighteen miles on 4 January, and then was issued simply six ounces of flour. "We had no cooking utensils and nothing but this flour," Squire Bush wrote disgustedly in his diary. "Our rations gave out at breakfast," remembered Johnny Green. "The roads are terrific. Time and time again we had to march through liquid much which came way above our knees."

Gervis Grainger's plight during the withdrawal was typical. Grainger had forded Stones River under fire twice on 2 January, stood on the skirmish line in the same wet clothes until 2:00 A.M. the following morning, passed the day without food, crossed the river again after dark, and marched eight miles before dawn. By the time his regiment halted at noon, Grainger was spent. He fell asleep on a log, only to awaken sick and chilled. Too weak to keep up with the regiment, Grainger was given permission to march at will. He found a horse and rode until he collapsed with pneumonia. A passing ambulance carried Grainger to Wartrace, and from there he was taken by train to Chattanooga, where he eventually recovered.

Compounding the misery of the soldiers was the lack of a clearly defined destination. Bragg initially directed a concentration along the Duck River, near Shelbyville. But on 5 January, just as the army made camp outside of town, he shifted the line of defense to the Elk River. As crossing sites had not been reconnoitered in advance, Bragg dispatched his chief engineer, S. W. Steeler, to report on the fords near Estell Mill, meanwhile halting the army near Tullahoma. Steele replied through Polk that only one of the two fords was adequate; the others would require repairs by sappers and miners. Again Bragg vacillated. Two days later, he returned to the Duck River as the objective of the withdrawal. Polk would occupy Shelbyville, and Hardee would make camp south of the river at Tullahoma. Colonel Brent, normally an apologist for the general, was shaken by Bragg's irresolution. While he praised Bragg's desire to hold as much of Tennessee as possible, he wished the general had settled on the Duck River line before leaving Murfreesboro. "The movement so far to the rear has had a bad effect on the troops and the public mind," he admitted. "Spirits bad. Matters look gloomy."

Spirits were bad indeed. Most of Bragg's lieutenants, believing as he did that Rosecrans had been reinforced, approved of the retreat. But the common soldier, knowing only that he had fought well and had bested Billy Yank more often than not, was confused and angry. "I can't see for my life why Bragg left Murfreesboro after whipping them so badly," one private wrote his family from Tullahoma. "We have completely demoralized the Yankee army. There is no doubt but that the Yankees were badly whipped. General Bragg has . . . lost the confidence of the army and many think that there was no reason for the retreat from Murfreesboro, and that he will in consequence be removed," another confided to his wife, adding that "the retreat has caused much alarm in this section, and many persons are preparing to leave with their Negroes."[3]

The Army of the Cumberland had been hurt badly, so badly that Rosecrans never seriously contemplated a pursuit. Joe Wheeler, left behind to cover the withdrawal, was surprised to find the "enemy pickets . . . in the same position that they were when we changed our lines." Not until late in the afternoon of 4 January did Rosecrans make his first tentative forward movement, edging Stanley's brigade along the railroad and turnpike toward town as far as the north bank of Stones River. As Stanley encountered nothing more than a handful of cavalry, Rosecrans advanced a battalion of Pioneers to rebuild the demolished trestle over the river.

Rosecrans was more confident the next day. At dawn, he directed Negley to occupy Murfreesboro with Stanley's brigade. While Morton continued work on the trestle, Negley crossed downstream and entered the town. There was no sign of Bragg's army. Wheeler had disappeared during the night to a new delaying position three miles below Murfreesboro astride the Manchester Pike. The way to Murfreesboro clear, Negley hastened to cross the remainder of his division. By 9:00 A.M. Miller had joined Stanley in Murfreesboro, and Federal cavalry was feeling its way toward Shelbyville and Manchester. A handful of Rebel stragglers surrendered to the troopers who, after a brief clash with Wheeler, were content to return to Murfreesboro.[4]

Meanwhile, on the battlefield, the disagreeable task of interring the hundreds of still-unburied dead went on. In many cases, identification was impossible; bloated and discolored after five days on the field, numerous Federal corpses were found almost naked, their coats, shoes, blouses, and trousers stripped off by poorly clad Confederates.

But as distasteful as the duty was, many soldiers, anxious to learn the fate of missing comrades, volunteered to assist the burial details. A few found friends and relatives, given up for dead, still alive. One infantryman from the Thirty-fourth Illinois discovered his brother resting on the second floor of a Murfreesboro residence. Some considerate troops from the Second Arkansas had carried the wounded Illinoisan to the rear, where he was loaded into a wagon and taken into town. There he passed three days with no medical care and only a canteen of water and an ear of corn. When his brother removed his trousers for him, they were so stiff with blood that, placed on the floor, they stood "as readily as two pieces of stovepipe would have done."

Most were less fortunate than the brother of the wounded Illinoisan. Hoping to find his friend and former neighbor William Nash among the wounded, John Russell of the Twenty-first Illinois obtained permission from his brigade commander to accompany a burial detail. But Nash was dead. A bullet had cut through his chest during the retreat of 31 December, killing him instantly. Gathering up the body, Russell carried it into a wood a short distance from where the burial detail was rolling the regimental dead into a common grave. There he buried it. Russell scratched his friend's name and unit on a board, drove it into the frozen ground, and returned to his bivouac to write the dead man's family.

Not searching for anyone in particular but merely curious, Thomas Dornblaser of the Seventh Pennsylvania Cavalry visited the Confederate hospitals in Murfreesboro. Riding into town, the Pennsylvanian found most homes and all the churches filled with wounded. Dornblaser wandered into one such makeshift hospital, only to be momentarily driven back by the stench of open wounds. But his curiosity overcame his revulsion. "We sat down beside a poor fellow, shot through from breast to back," Dornblaser recalled, noting every detail of the man's suffering with a morbid exactness. "A minie ball made a ghastly wound in his breast and lungs, from which the air was escaping at every breath. He was fully conscious that he had less than twenty-four hours to live."

Conditions were little better in the Federal field hospitals. By 5 January, Corporal Hannaford felt well enough to sit and study his surroundings. All around him men were dying. In the cot opposite him, a soldier writhed as blood gushed from his nose, mouth, and a hole in his throat. Less fortunate than Hannaford, he had been struck in the carotid artery. While a surgeon was summoned, a nurse held the man upright to prevent him from drowning in his own blood; "but his endeavors, I saw, were hopeless. In less than five minutes the nurse was supporting only a drooping corpse." The scene impressed Hannaford deeply. For days he replayed the soldier's final moments in his mind; "wounded in much the same spot, how soon might not the end of earth come so to me?"

One wonders how Hannaford and others like him would have felt, had they known that no such agony or nightmares troubled their leaders. Whiskey, the demigod of the officer corps, inured them to the suffering. Returning from a ride over the battlefield, John Beatty ran across Rousseau, McCook, and Crittenden, all of whom had been drinking heavily. Crittenden was the most drunk. As the party rode toward Rousseau's tent, where more liquor awaited them, the Left Wing commander, "in a voice far from melodious," entertained all who cared to listen with a rendition of "Mary Had a Little Lamb." "Evidently the lion had left the chieftain's heart, and the lamb had entered and taken possession," quipped Beatty.[5]

Perhaps the Ohioan was too hard on his superiors. Although what they had accomplished fell considerably short of a decisive victory, they at least had avoided defeat at a time when the Union could scarcely have borne another setback.

December had been nothing short of diastrous for the Lincoln administration and those loyal to the government and its war policy. Earlier that month two major Union offensives, launched in concert, had met with disaster. On the heights above Fredericksburg, in northern Virginia, another Federal commander went down before Robert E. Lee as Major General Ambrose Burnside lost over twelve thousand men in a series of brutal and fruitless assaults. And in Mississippi, major generals U. S. Grant and William T. Sherman floundered in the bayous and back country above Vicksburg as what was to have been a two-pronged thrust against the Mississippi River citadel degenerated into a comedy of errors. Confederate cavalry under Earl Van Dorn descended on the massive Federal supply depot at Holly Springs, destroying everything in sight and compelling Grant to abort his advance. Sherman continued downriver, only to come to grief against Rebel entrenchments along Chickasaw Bayou. Finally, in faraway Texas, John Magruder assembled a two-boat flotilla of "cottonclads" and recaptured Galveston in a surprise attack on New Year's Day, ridding the Lone Star State of Federals.

The repeated humbling of Union arms, culminating in the defeats of December 1862, deepened Northern war weariness, particularly in the Northwest, home to most of the soldiers of the Army of the Cumberland. For a time, Republican governors Oliver P. Morton of Indiana and Richard Yates of Illinois actually feared open insurrection in their states. On 3 January 1863, before news of Breckinridge's repulse reached the Northern press, Morton wired Secretary of War Stanton from the statehouse in Indianapolis: "I am advised that it is contemplated when the Legislature meets in this state to pass a joint resolution acknowledging the Southern Confederacy, and urging the states of the Northwest to dissolve all constitutional relations with the New England states." Morton added that "the same thing is on foot in Illinois."

The causes of disillusionment in the Northwest ran deeper than battlefield setbacks, although victories might allow the Republicans to contain it. As Allan Nevins has pointed out, the Democrats had "a historic ascendancy" in Ohio, Indiana, and Illinois, of which the election of Republican governors in 1860 represented an anomalous interruption: when the Democrats swept the legislative elections in 1862, they were simply regaining their traditional hold over these states. In addition to being antiwar Democrats, many residents of Illinois and Indiana's southern counties had only recently emigrated from slave-holding states. They had left behind their slaves, if they had them, but not their emotional attachment to the South. As the war ground on and abolitionists strove to convert it into an antislavery crusade, the transplanted grew restless. Antiwar rallies were common. The New Year opened with pro-administration Republican assemblymen and state governors confronting antiwar Democrats in the legislatures of Illinois and Indiana. Should the Democrats succeed in passing legislation aimed at reducing their states' contributions to the war effort, a second rebellion—potentially fatal to what remained of the Union—might erupt in the Northwest.

Then news of Rosecrans's victory, won largely by troops from the Northwest, exploded in the headlines of the Union press. "Rosecrans Wins a Complete Victory; the Enemy in Full Retreat," announced the *Chicago Tribune* on 6 January as the first reports came in from the field. Stones River was "the thrilling sound, the prophet's word, which delivers their own names to fame and history forever," the battlefield correspondent of the Louisville *Journal* wrote, adding that Rosecrans's name, "already famous, has now become immortal. Of all our commanding generals, he is the only one that knows how to fight a battle." M. S. Furay of the Cincinnati *Gazette* echoed the praise of Rosecrans's "splended generalship," as did the ubiquitous W. D. Bickham of the *Gazette's* crosstown rival, the Cincinnati *Commercial*, telling his readers that the Ohioan had "won a high place in the confidence and affections of his countrymen."

The overstated claims of the *Chicago Tribune* and other pro-administration dailies were effective. Pro-war mass meetings were held throughout the Northwest surpassing antiwar gatherings in militancy. Regiments held similar meetings in Murfreesboro and addressed indignant letters to wavering homefolk. Public sentiment shifted from the antiwar Democrats, who in turn backed down in the statehouses. The General Assembly of Ohio offered a vote of thanks to Rosecrans for his "glorious victory." The General Assembly of Indiana passed a similar resolution two weeks later.

None were more grateful for the defeat of Bragg than members of the beleaguered Lincoln administration. A month earlier, Secretary of War Stanton had upbraided Rosecrans for his endless requests for more rifles, more horses, more everything; now he assured the Ohioan that "there is nothing you can ask within my power to grant to yourself or your heroic command that will not be cheerfully given." President Lincoln agreed. "God bless you, and all with you. Please tender to all, and accept for yourself, the nation's gratitude for your and their skill, endurance, and dauntless courage." Time and subsequent reverses would not diminish Lincoln's sense of gratitude. Eight months later, on the verge of Rosecrans's thrashing at Chickamauga, the president wrote him of his continued belief in the importance of Stones River to the Union cause: "I can never forget, whilst I remember anything, that about the end of last year and the beginning of this, you gave us a hard-earned victory, which, had there been a defeat instead, the nation could scarcely have lived over."[6]

CHAPTER SIXTEEN

BRAGG'S ARMY? HE'S GOT NONE

"No cheer salutes him as he passes. . . . No terror of his discipline or executions is felt by the brave soldiery he leads. We obey but do not tremble, and enter action without hope of honor or renown and retreat with sullen indifference and discontent." So wrote William Preston of Bragg and of the Army of Tennessee as it trudged toward Shelbyville and Tullahoma, and the grumbling grew louder with each passing mile.

Outside the army, disappointment over the results of Stones River was as great as that following Perryville. And as with the Kentucky campaign, criticism of Bragg's handling of the Murfreesboro campaign by the Southern press was severe and unrelenting. Some of this Bragg brought on himself. In dispatches written from the battlefield on the night of 31 December, he had assured the Southern public that victory was all but guaranteed. The press accepted Bragg's assurances at face value: the Augusta *Chronicle* told its readers that the gains of the thirty-first were so decisive as to be irreversible, and the normally critical Chattanooga *Rebel* announced that Stones River would place Bragg in a new light. When the truth became known, the press railed at the apparent deception. The Augusta *Chronicle* suggested that Bragg had lied to the public in his dispatches. The Chattanooga *Rebel* went further. In a series of scathing editorials, the *Rebel* asserted that Bragg had lost the confidence of the army and of its generals. It stated categorically that Bragg had ordered the retreat from Murfreesboro against the advice of his lieutenants and added that he soon would be relieved of command.[1]

The *Rebel* editorials were more than Bragg could bear. Already troubled by rumors that he was about to be replaced by Beauregard or Kirby Smith, he assembled his staff on 10 January and asked them if he had lost the confidence of the army and ought to resign. Yes, they replied, he had lost the army's confidence; all things considered, he should resign.

Bragg would not resign, but neither would he let the matter rest. He was determined to uncover and, if possible, crush whatever opposition to his leadership might exist within the high command of the Army of Tennessee.

Ironically, it was Bragg himself who finally released the latent hostility of his generals. On 11 January, he sent Hardee, Breckinridge, Cleburne, and Cheatham what was perhaps the most incredible document addressed by a commander to his lieutenants during the war. It was a circular letter, in which Bragg solicited their views on the propriety of the retreat from Murfreesboro and (although there was doubt among its recipients as to whether the intent of the note was to raise this second issue) Bragg's fitness for continued command of the Army of Tennessee. A similar letter was mailed to Polk, then on leave at his home in North Carolina. Having in effect placed his fate in the hands of his subordinates, Bragg awaited their reply, naively confident that such discontent as might exist was limited to a handful of corps and division staff officers and to those few "who have felt the sting of discipline."

Bragg miscalculated. At first, Hardee and his division commanders were not sure just what issue they were being asked to address. All but one sentence of the circular letter dealt with the advisability of the retreat; it was on this sentence, however, that the generals ultimately focused. Bragg had concluded the letter with a reference to Kirby Smith's recall to Richmond—he went, "it is supposed, with a view to supersede me"—and had assured his lieutenants that "I shall retire without regret if I find that I have lost the good opinion of my generals, upon whom I have ever relied as upon a foundation of rock."

But the rock was fissured. Yes, Hardee replied, he had concurred with Bragg's decision to abandon Murfreesboro, but had not advised it. Then came an admission for which Bragg was wholly unprepared. "I have conferred with Major General Breckinridge and Major General Cleburne . . . and I feel that frankness compels me to say that the general officers, whose judgment you have invoked, are unanimous in the opinion that a change in the command of this army is necessary. In this opinion I concur."

Breckinridge's reply followed. While Hardee admitted only to having concurred with Bragg's decision to retreat, the Kentuckian actually acknowledged having played a leading role in advising it. Aside from this, however, he was in agreement with his corps commander: For the sake of the army, Bragg should resign. Breckinridge then took the matter a step further. He showed the circular letter to his brigade commanders, whom he told Bragg were in agreement that the general should yield command of the army. Three days later, Cleburne responded. The Irishman recommended only that Bragg resign, evading the issue of the withdrawal from Murfreesboro altogether.

To Bragg, these replies could have but one meaning: A conspiracy to supplant him existed in Hardee's corps, with Breckinridge at the center and Hardee the heir apparent to the army command.

Despite these convictions, Bragg initially was too stunned and humiliated to retaliate. Instead, he prepared for what he thought would be his imminent dismissal. To a note from Davis in which the president apologized for his inability to reinforce the Army of Tennessee, which "would enable them to crown the recent victory," Bragg replied by explaining his reasons for abandoning Murfreesboro and, perhaps to save face, offering to resign so that Davis might be spared the political costs of standing by him. With the responses to his circular letter before him, Bragg warned Davis that "influences will be brought to bear, both political and military," in favor of his removal. Bragg was careful, however, to understate the extent of such feelings within his army, claiming that they were limited to a few "new men under new officers."[2]

Davis responded much as he had after Perryville, although this time he ordered Joseph Johnston to Tullahoma with absolute authority to take any action necessary to restore the Army of Tennessee, to include assuming command, rather than go himself. Referring to the circular letter, Davis mused: "Why General Bragg should have elected that tribunal and have invited judgment upon him is to me unexplained. It manifests, however, a condition of things which seems to me to require your presence."

Johnston went reluctantly. In spite of a distaste for his present duties as theater commander, Johnston had no desire to fill Bragg's shoes. He was unwilling—or so he told Davis—to "deprive an officer, in whom you have confidence, of the command for which you have selected him."

So Johnston, averse to taking the field in the troubled West, downplayed the discord within the Army of Tennessee. He limited his conversations on the subject to Bragg, Polk, Hardee, and Governor Isham Harris of Tennessee, a frequent guest at headquarters and a man with whom Bragg's disaffected lieutenants felt they could speak freely. Either Hardee, Polk, and Harris were less than candid with him or, more likely, Johnston heard only that which he wanted to hear, because he came away convinced that any disaffection or want of confidence in Bragg that might exist stemmed largely from the Kentucky campaign and was actually on the wane. He sensed nothing of this among the troops, who were "well clothed, healthy, and in good spirits." There was no indication, he assured Davis, that the men considered themselves any less able to beat the Yankees in battle than they had before Stones River.

As for Polk, the Army of Tennessee's master of intrigue was on unusually good behavior during most of Johnston's visit. Noting his anger at the responses of Hardee, Breckinridge, and Cleburne, Polk had asked Bragg to clarify his letter of 11 January: Did he really mean to invoke the judgment of his subordinates regarding his fitness to command? Certainly not, Bragg replied. His enemies within the army had "grossly and intentionally misrepresented" the intent of his letter in order to injure him; he simply had wished to record his lieutenants' views of the retreat from Murfreesboro.

Polk was delighted. By compelling his silence, Bragg allowed Polk to reap the benefits of a change of commanders without having to implicate himself in what inevitably would be seen as an unseemly effort to discredit a superior officer. And so Polk ignored the circular letter and parried Johnston's questions, arguing that his recent leave of absence prevented him from commenting on the present state of affairs within the army.

Polk's ploy may have succeeded, had Johnston been inclined to remove Bragg. But because he was not, Polk had to act, and act fast. In a final conversation with Johnston just prior to his departure, Polk played his hand: Bragg had lost the confidence of the army, or at least of Polk's corps, and should be replaced immediately, preferably by Johnston himself. Simultaneously, Polk took the issue directly to Davis. Forwarding to him copies of Cheatham and Withers's note of 3 January, his endorsement, Bragg's circular letter, his note requesting an explanation of the letter, and Bragg's reply, Polk bluntly advised the president to replace Bragg with Johnston, the sooner the better, as "the state of this army demands immediate attention, and . . . could find relief in no way so readily as by the appointment of General Joseph E. Johnston."

Polk had erred again. Davis simply reiterated his decision to leave the matter in Johnston's hands.

But Johnston would have none of it. After his conversation with Polk, he presented Davis with his own recommendation. It was true that many of Bragg's generals lacked confidence in him, but morale within the army was improving. And, although Hardee and Polk had suggested that he supersede Bragg, "the interests of the service require that General Bragg should not be removed." Besides, Johnston added, his sense of personal honor would not permit him to replace one whose departure he in any way had helped orchestrate. Davis told Johnston that no one thought his honor tarnished and that, in any event, such considerations should not prevent him from taking any action that might be in the best interest of the army and of the nation. But Johnston remained unmoved. Replying to Davis on 2 March, he came out strongly for Bragg's retention, citing both the improved state of the army—the feelings of certain generals to the contrary notwithstanding—and the likelihood of an early Federal offensive, which made familiarity with the area of operations, and by implication continuity in command, absolutely imperative. Polk tried again in late March to convince Davis to remove Bragg, but the president once more deferred to Johnston's judgment, and by mid-April the matter was closed.[3]

Now it was Bragg's turn. Having been sustained, he took the offensive against his defamers. "He hopes to crush out the officers here, after invoking our opinions," wrote William Preston, an outspoken member of the anti-Bragg clique. Bragg was "down on the political generals" (a reference to Breckinridge, Preston, and Palmer) and intended to "wipe 'em out." Nevertheless, Preston regretted nothing: "I have always shown him respect, but was heartfully willing to give him my opinion that we have no confidence in him. I have used no means to pull Bragg down, but when the facts warrant me in commending the chalice to his own lips, I do not feel any compunction or pity for his situation."

Hardee and Polk were too powerful to confront directly, so Bragg went after their subordinates. Cheatham was the first to feel his wrath—and with reason. There can be no denying that he was dilatory in attacking on 31 December, and little doubt that he was drunk. Distressed at the sight of the Tennessean's brigades going individually into action instead of simultaneously and in conjunction with his own attack, it was Hardee who first brought

Cheatham's drunken condition to Bragg's attention. Bragg referred the matter to Polk, who admitted that others had told him the same. (Years later, Bragg wrote friend and former staff officer E. T. Sykes that "in the battle of Murfreesboro, Cheatham was so drunk on the field all the first day, that a staff officer had to hold him on his horse.")

The Tennessean's drunkenness was an open secret in the officer corps. The subject came up during a visit paid Liddell at Wartrace by the army chaplain, the Reverend Doctor Charles Quintard. Quintard alluded to the drunken state of some officers at Stones River. Liddell quipped that Cheatham in particular seemed to have been on his "high horse" during the battle. "Yes, I am sorry to say, he was on his low horse too," Quintard replied. "How so, doctor?" Liddell asked, knowing full well the answer. "Why, he fell, he went under," said Quintard.

Cheatham's condition was apparent to his troops as well. In a letter to the state librarian of Tennessee years after the war, Private John Johnston of the Sixth Tennessee recalled Cheatham's behavior as he led—or tried to lead—his men forward: "While his troops were standing in line waiting for orders to move, General Cheatham rode out in front and in attempting to make an appeal to his 'Tennesseans,' rolled off his horse and fell to the ground as limp and helpless as a bag of meal—to the great humiliation and mortification of his troops. This was told to me by a personal friend, a lieutenant in Company K, Sixth Tennessee Infantry, who was present and witnessed it."

Cheatham's losing battle with the bottle predated Stones River and continued to the war's end. Writing his father as early as January 1862, a captain in the Second Tennessee complained that "Frank Cheatham drinks too much to rely upon." And at Spring Hill, Tennessee, during the Franklin campaign, John Bell Hood missed an opportunity to crush the scattered army of John Schofield in detail, allegedly because Cheatham was off drinking and seducing women when he should have been directing his troops.

Because of Cheatham's popularity among Tennessee units and influence in the state, as well as a previously distinguished combat record, Bragg did not try to dismiss him. Instead, he convinced Polk to censure him and, in his official report of the battle, Bragg failed to commend him, as was customary. Cheatham returned Bragg's contempt, telling Governor Harris that he would not fight so long as Bragg commanded the Army of Tennessee.[4]

Having fewer friends in high places, John McCown was an easier target than Cheatham. Bragg blamed McCown for delaying the attack on the morning of 31 December by as much as two hours; McCown, in turn, criticized Bragg in public; Bragg countered by having him court-martialed.

The most damaging evidence at McCown's March 1863 court-martial came from Gideon Pillow, who eagerly responded to a request from Major William Clare of the general staff that he "reduce to writing the substance of vituperative language used in (his) presence by Major General McCown at Shelbyville." McCown had visited his headquarters in late January, wrote Pillow. After they exchanged pleasantries, McCown sat down and launched into a denunciation of Bragg, whom he accused of placing artillery behind his division at Stones River in order to disgrace it and of subsequently robbing it of two of its finest regiments. But no matter, McCown concluded, his division had done the "only good fighting" at Stones River, and if Bragg sacked him, no matter either, as "he had four acres of land in East Tennessee" and "could go there and make potatoes." At this point Pillow's narrative becomes suspect. Obviously angered at having been relieved of troop command and put out to pasture to raise conscripts for the western armies, Pillow perhaps saw in his testimony a chance at taking McCown's division and regaining Bragg's favor, which he had lost when he joined Breckinridge, Preston, and Trabue in expressing their lack of confidence in him. As Pillow assured Major Clare:

> I was anxious to conciliate his feeling and said to (McCown), General, you have no right to complain. In the Mexican War, I was a major general and you were a lieutenant. In the beginning of this war, I was a major general commanding the whole Army of Tennessee and I assisted to have you appointed a lieutenant colonel of artillery. Now I am a brigadier general without any command at all, and you a major general with a fine division. . . . Yet you have not heard me complain, although I am now put on a most distasteful service—totally repugnant to my feelings. If you are as good a patriot as I am, you will cease abusing the general commanding.

But Pillow's self-serving testimony was not the only evidence against McCown. While in Columbus, Kentucky, McCown broadened his target to include the civilian leadership of the Confederacy, which he told several junior officers was a "damned stinking cotton oligarchy . . . gotten up for the benefit of Isham G. Harris and Jeff Davis and their damned corrupt cliques." Exit John McCown, suspended from duty for six months.[5]

Bragg's skirmishes with Cheatham and McCown were mere sidelights to a longer, more bitter, yet ultimately inconclusive duel with Breckinridge—a duel of words that threatened from time to time to erupt into a duel of pistols.

Bragg shot first. In his official report he blasted the Kentuckian for failing to dispatch reinforcements across the river quickly on 31 December and for poor direction of the attack of 2 January, which Bragg implied would have succeeded had Breckinridge done his job better. To substantiate his accusations, Bragg extracted testimony from selected field commanders and staff officers. On 16 February, he requested Captain Felix Robertson to render a special report directly to army headquarters concerning the role played by artillery in the 2 January attack. Bragg's note was worded in such a way as to leave no doubt that he was less than satisfied with Breckinridge's handling of the charge and that he hoped to gather evidence to support his feeling. Robertson got the message. His original report, addressed to Breckinridge, had been simply a terse account of the movements of his guns; his revised report, however, clearly blamed the Kentuckian for the failure of the attack, at least from the standpoint of the artillery. Bragg was pleased. Similar accounts followed from Colonel Brent and Gideon Pillow, although one wonders how much of the attack Pillow could have witnessed from behind a tree.

Breckinridge was handicapped in responding to these charges by Bragg's unwillingness to share the contents of his report before he submitted it to the Department of War. When Breckinridge finally did read the report in Richmond newspapers in late March, he immediately wrote the Inspector General of the Confederacy, Samuel Cooper, requesting a court of inquiry be convened to investigate all charges raised against his division by the commanding general. Bragg endorsed Breckinridge's request with a comment that the Kentuckian's own report of the battle was "both full of errors and misstatements."

A month passed with no response from Richmond. Breckinridge again begged Cooper to convene a court of inquiry. The press was largely behind him. The Knoxville *Register* considered the criticism of Cheatham, McCown, and Breckinridge undignified and unjust: "My impression is that they made only venial mistakes, and that heroism displayed is a sufficient shield against even the official criticism of General Bragg," wrote the *Register*'s Richmond correspondent. The Richmond *Examiner* agreed, adding that simple justice demanded the publication of the reports of the censured generals, which Bragg had delayed.[6]

Breckinridge never did get his court of inquiry, and his bitterness smoldered until late May, when he was transferred to Mississippi. Hardee followed Breckinridge to Mississippi in July, and for a time it appeared that the anti-Bragg forces had been subdued.

Bragg's victory, however, was more apparent than real. The discord was merely dormant, awaiting a new battlefield setback to release it. The damage done the high command of the Army of Tennessee and Confederate fortunes in the West was permanent. The dissension sown by the twin defeats of Perryville and Stones River had all but wrecked the army from within. Bragg, Polk, Cheatham, and—until their transfers—Hardee and Breckinridge were so absorbed with their internecine feud that they neglected what should have been the sole object of their attention, the defense of what remained of Confederate Tennessee against Rosecrans and the Army of the Cumberland. From late January until the end of June, the Army of Tennessee lay idle along the Duck River line while its commanders sparred with one another. No plan of strategy was developed, no strong defensive line established. The results were predictable. When Rosecrans advanced from Murfreesboro in late June, Bragg conceded Middle Tennessee without having fired scarcely a shot in its defense. A paralyzed Army of Tennessee fell back on Chattanooga, and Tennessee was lost. The ghost of Stones River continued to haunt the army. At a time when the high command should have been united in an effort to deny Rosecrans the Confederate heartland, the anti-Bragg faction was renewing its efforts to unseat the commanding general.

By September, the clique had been revitalized by the addition of three new and powerful members. Daniel Harvey Hill had joined the army in July to replace Hardee. In September, Kentuckian Simon Buckner assumed command of the new Third Corps, and James Longstreet arrived from the Army of Northern Virginia at the head of two divisions.

Hill was much like Bragg, easily affronted and quick to criticize others; that the two should come into conflict was inevitable. But while Hill's opposition to Bragg grew out of personal contact, Buckner and Longstreet were prejudiced against the commanding general before they arrived by their understanding of Stones River. Buckner was angered by Bragg's treatment of Kentuckians and by his anti-Kentucky invective after Perryville and Stones River. The slaughter of 2 January only deepened his hostility toward Bragg. Buckner thus was a natural successor to Breckinridge as leader of the implacably anti-Bragg Kentucky faction. In Virginia, Longstreet had heard and fully accepted the anti-Bragg interpretation of Stones

River. Echoing Polk and Hardee, he told Lee as he prepared to leave for the West that the Army of Tennessee utterly lacked confidence in Bragg and that, as a consequence, Bragg could not be expected to "do a great deal for us." And if the presence of three such formidable opponents was not enough to cripple Bragg, Joseph Johnston returned Breckinridge to the Army of Tennessee in August.

The anti-Bragg group was thus nearing its apogee as the army entered the battle of Chickamauga in late September. Arrayed against Bragg, ready to exploit his slightest failing, was virtually the entire high command of his army. Bragg did not disappoint them. His performance throughout Chickamauga was that of a man who had lost all faith in himself. Bragg neglected to issue the specific orders needed to ensure a coordinated attack against the Army of the Cumberland on the first day of battle, and his plan to envelop the Federal left was doomed from the outset. That night, after the army had dissipated its strength in a series of uncoordinated assaults, Bragg decided upon a complete reorganization of the army in the face of the enemy. He created two wings, placing Longstreet in command of the left and Polk the right. D. H. Hill was relegated to corps command. Bragg's stated reason for these changes was to avoid trouble in the high command. The shadow of Stones River loomed dark.

The Confederate victory at Chickamauga did nothing to silence Bragg's critics within the army. Bragg had failed to follow up the victory with a pursuit of Rosecrans. To compensate for this and other shortcomings during the battle, Bragg already was conniving to fix blame on his subordinates. On 22 September and again on 25 September, he sent Polk sharply worded notes demanding an explanation for Polk's failure to launch an early morning attack as ordered on 20 September. And, unknown to the group, Bragg had sent two letters to Davis similarly critical of Polk.

Polk could see the handwriting on the wall. He was determined not to repeat Breckinridge's mistake after Stones River of allowing Bragg to deliver the first and ultimately decisive blow. Hill, Buckner, and Longstreet supported Polk. On 26 September, they met secretly to plot what amounted to mutiny. All present agreed to begin a letter-writing campaign to unseat Bragg.

Events moved rapidly to a climactic release of pressures that had been building since Stones River. On 29 September, Bragg removed Polk. The public outcry caused Davis to hurry west. On 10 October, the anti-Bragg group attempted a countermove. In Bragg's presence, all four corps commanders—Longstreet, Hill, Buckner, and

Cheatham (commanding in Polk's absence)—told Davis emphatically that Bragg must go.

Again Bragg's opponents had miscalculated. Confronted with this open display of insubordination and near mutiny, Davis sided with Bragg. Together, they broke up the anti-Bragg bloc. On 15 October, Davis authorized the removal of Hill. Eight days later, Polk was exiled to the Department of Mississippi. Buckner lost his corps and was reduced to division command. And on 5 November, Longstreet was detached with seventeen thousand men on independent service against Burnside in East Tennessee.

With the demotion or exile of their leaders, the subordinate members of the anti-Bragg group were an easy mark. William Preston, who had felt no "compunction or pity" for Bragg's predicament after Stones River, was reduced in rank to brigadier general. Cheatham saw his division of twenty-two Tennessee regiments, the core of Polk's support within the army, broken up until only six remained. Breckinridge's division was likewise reorganized, and each of his brigades reassigned.

In the final analysis, this reshuffling accomplished nothing. As at Tullahoma after Stones River, Bragg's preoccupation with the enemy within caused him to neglect the Federal army. With each passing day, the enemy at Chattanooga grew stronger. By the time Bragg realized the weakness of his own line, it was too late. This time, however, the price of neglect was much higher. Not only were sixty-seven hundred irreplaceable veterans lost in the battles around Chattanooga, but control of the gateway to the Deep South passed forever to the Union. On 1 December, Bragg resigned as commander of the Army of Tennessee, but not before blaming the defeat on cowardice within the army and on Breckinridge's alleged drunkenness.[7]

The chaos of Chickamauga and the ignominy of Chattanooga were still months in the future as winter gave way to spring in 1863. Reflecting on what had happened since Stones River, Bragg may have been satisfied with himself: he had retained his command; McCown was gone, at least for the time being; Hardee, Breckinridge, Cheatham, and Polk were chastised; and Johnston had lauded the fine condition of the army. But the soldiers knew otherwise. Riding with Colonel Urquhart near Tullahoma, Bragg encountered a straggling Tennessean. Noticing his Butternut clothing, the general asked offhandedly if he belonged to Bragg's army. "Bragg's army? He's got none; he shot half of them in Kentucky, and the other got killed up at Murfreesboro."[8] The general rode on.

THE OPPOSING FORCES IN THE STONES RIVER CAMPAIGN

The following list was assembled from *War of the Rebellion: A Compilation of the Official Records of the Union and Confederate Armies*. With respect to officer casualties, (k) signifies killed, (mw) mortally wounded, (w) wounded, and (c) captured.

Army of the Cumberland
(Fourteenth Army Corps)
Maj. Gen. William S. Rosecrans, Commanding

Artillery
Col. James Barnett

Provost Guard
10th Ohio Infantry

General Escort
Anderson Troop, Pennsylvania Cavalry

RIGHT WING
Maj. Gen. Alexander McD. McCook

First Division
Brig. Gen. Jefferson C. Davis

Escort
36th Illinois Cavalry, Company B   2d Kentucky Cavalry, Company G

First Brigade
Col. P. Sidney Post
59th Illinois   75th Illinois
74th Illinois   22d Indiana

Second Brigade
Col. William P. Carlin
21st Illinois   101st Ohio
38th Illinois   15th Wisconsin

Third Brigade
Col. William E. Woodruff
25th Illinois   81st Indiana
35th Illinois

Artillery[1]
2d Minnesota Battery   8th Wisconsin Battery
5th Wisconsin Battery

Second Division
Brig. Gen. Richard W. Johnson

First Brigade
Brig. Gen. August Willich (c)
Col. William Wallace
Col. William H. Gibson
89th Illinois   15th Ohio
32d Indiana   49th Ohio
39th Indiana

Second Brigade
Brig. Gen. Edward N. Kirk (mw)
Col. Joseph B. Dodge
34th Illinois   30th Indiana
79th Indiana   77th Pennsylvania
29th Indiana

Third Brigade
Col. Philemon P. Baldwin
6th Indiana   1st Ohio
5th Kentucky   93rd Ohio

1. The Second Minnesota was attached to the Second Brigade, Fifth Wisconsin to the First Brigade, and Eighth Wisconsin to the Third Brigade.

Artillery[2]
5th Indiana Battery   1st Ohio, Battery E
1st Ohio, Battery A

Cavalry
3d Indiana, Companies G, H, I, and K

Third Division
Brig. Gen. Philip H. Sheridan

Escort
2d Kentucky Cavalry, Company L

First Brigade
Brig. Gen. Joshua W. Sill (k)
Col. Nicholas Greusel

Second Brigade
Col. Frederick Schaefer (k)
Lieut. Col. Bernard Laiboldt
44th Illinois   2d Missouri
73d Illinois   15th Missouri

Third Brigade
Col. George W. Roberts (k)
Col. Luther P. Bradley
22d Illinois   42d Illinois
27th Illinois   51st Illinois

Artillery[3]
1st Illinois, Battery C   1st Missouri, Battery G
4th Indiana Battery

CENTER
Maj. Gen. George H. Thomas

Provost Guard
9th Michigan Infantry

First Division
Maj. Gen. Lovell H. Rousseau

---

2.   The Fifth Indiana was attached to the Third Brigade, Battery A to the First
Brigade, and Battery E to the Second Brigade.
3.   Battery C was attached to the Third Brigade, Fourth Indiana to the First Brigade, and Battery G to the Second Brigade.

First Brigade
Col. Benjamin F. Scribner
38th Indiana 94th Ohio
2d Ohio   10th Wisconsin
33d Ohio

Second Brigade
Col. John Beatty
42d Indiana   15th Kentucky
88th Indiana   3d Ohio

Third Brigade
Col. John C. Starkweather
24th Illinois   1st Wisconsin
79th Pennsylvania   21st Wisconsin

Fourth Brigade
Lieut. Col. Oliver L. Shephard
15th United States, 1st Battalion
16th United States, 1st Battalion and Company B, 2d Battalion
18th United States, 1st Battalion and Companies A and D, 3d Battalion
18th United States, 2d Battalion and Companies B, C, E, and F,
3d Battalion
19th United States, 1st Battalion

Artillery[4]
Kentucky, Battery A   5th United States, Battery H
1st Michigan, Battery A

Cavalry
2d Kentucky (six companies)

Second Division
Brig. Gen. James S. Negley

First Brigade
Brig. Gen. James G. Spears
1st Tennessee   5th Tennessee
2d Tennessee   6th Tennessee
3d Tennessee

---

4. Battery A, Kentucky was attached to the Third Brigade, Battery A, First Michigan to the Second Brigade, and Battery H, Fifth United States to the Fourth Brigade.

Second Brigade
Col. Timothy R. Stanley
19th Illinois   18th Ohio
11th Michigan   69th Ohio

Third Brigade
Col. John F. Miller
37th Illinois   74th Ohio
21st Ohio   78th Pennsylvania

Artillery
Kentucky, Battery B   1st Ohio, Battery M[5]
1st Ohio, Battery G

Third Division[6]
Brig. Gen. Speed S. Fry

Escort
2d Kentucky Cavalry, Company B

First Brigade
Col. Moses B. Walker
82d Indiana   31st Ohio
12th Kentucky 38th Ohio
17th Ohio

Second Brigade
Col. John M. Harlan
10th Indiana   10th Kentucky
74th Indiana   14th Ohio
4th Kentucky

Third Brigade
Brig. Gen. James B. Steedman
87th Indiana   9th Ohio
2d Minnesota 35th Ohio

Artillery
1st Michigan, Battery D   4th United States, Battery I
1st Ohio, Battery C

5. Attached to Second Brigade.
6. The First Brigade (except the Twelfth Kentucky) and First Michigan, Battery D, were the only troops of this division engaged in the battle of Stones River. All commanders are given as they stood 31 December 1862.

Fourth Division
Brig. Gen. Robert B. Mitchell[7]

First Brigade
Brig. Gen. James D. Morgan
10th Illinois   10th Michigan
16th Illinois   14th Michigan
60th Illinois

Second Brigade
Col. Daniel McCook
85th Illinois   125th Illinois
86th Illinois   52d Ohio

Cavalry
2d Indiana, Company A   3d Tennessee
5th Kentucky

Artillery
2d Illinois, Battery I   10th Wisconsin Battery

Unattached Infantry
8th Kansas (five companies)   1st Middle (10th) Tennessee

Artillery Reserve
11th Indiana Battery   1st Michigan, Battery E
12th Indiana Battery

Fifth Division[8]
Brig. Gen. Joseph J. Reynolds

First Brigade
Col. Albert S. Hall
80th Illinois   101st Indiana
123d Illinois   105th Ohio

Second Brigade
Col. Abram O. Miller
98th Illinois   72d Indiana
17th Indiana   75th Indiana

Artillery
18th Indiana Battery   19th Indiana Battery

7. The Fourteenth Michigan, Eighty-fifth Illinois, a detachment from the Third Tennessee Cavalry, and two sections of the Tenth Wisconsin Artillery participated in the battle of Stones River (2 and 3 January) under the command of Brig. Gen. Spears. These were the only elements of the Fourth Division to take part in the campaign.

8. Not engaged at Stones River. Commanders given as they stood 31 December 1862.

LEFT WING
Maj. Gen. Thomas L. Crittenden

First Division
Brig. Gen. Thomas J. Wood (w)
Brig. Gen. Milo S. Hascall

First Brigade
Brig. Gen. Milo S. Hascall
Col. George P. Buell
100th Illinois   3d Kentucky
58th Indiana   26th Ohio

Second Brigade
Col. George D. Wagner
15th Indiana   57th Indiana
40th Indiana   97th Ohio

Third Brigade
Col. Charles G. Harker
51st Indiana   64th Ohio
73d Indiana   65th Ohio
13th Michigan

Artillery[9]
8th Indiana Battery   6th Ohio Battery
10th Indiana Battery

Second Division
Brig. Gen. John M. Palmer

First Brigade
Brig. Gen. Charles Cruft
31st Indiana   2d Kentucky
1st Kentucky   90th Ohio

Second Brigade
Col. William B. Hazen
110th Illinois   6th Kentucky
9th Indiana   41st Ohio

Third Brigade
Col. William Grose
84th Illinois   6th Ohio
36th Indiana   24th Ohio
23d Kentucky

9.   The Eighth Indiana Battery was attached to the First Brigade, the Tenth Battery to the Second Brigade, and the Sixth Battery to the Third Brigade.

Artillery
1st Ohio, Battery B   4th United States, Batteries H and M
1st Ohio, Battery F

Third Division
Brig. Gen. Horatio P. Van Cleve (w)
Col. Samuel Beatty

First Brigade
Col. Samuel Beatty
Col. Benjamin C. Grider
79th Indiana   11th Kentucky
9th Kentucky   19th Ohio

Second Brigade
Col. James P. Fyffe
44th Indiana   13th Ohio
86th Indiana   59th Ohio

Third Brigade
Col. Samuel W. Price
35th Indiana   51st Ohio
8th Kentucky   99th Ohio
21st Kentucky

Artillery
7th Indiana Battery   3d Wisconsin Battery
Pennsylvania, Battery B (26th)

CAVALRY
Brig. Gen. David S. Stanley

Cavalry Division
Col. John Kennett

First Brigade
Col. Robert H. G. Minty
2d Indiana   4th Michigan
3d Kentucky   7th Pennsylvania

Second Brigade
Col. Lewis Zahm
1st Ohio   4th Ohio
3d Ohio

Artillery
1st Ohio, Battery D (section)

Reserve Cavalry[10]
15th Pennsylvania   2d Tennessee
1st Middle (5th) Tennessee

Unattached
4th U.S. Cavalry

MISCELLANEOUS

Pioneer Brigade
Capt. James St. C. Morton
1st Battalion   2d Battalion   3d Battalion
Illinois Light Artillery, Stokes' Battery

Engineers and Mechanics
1st Michigan

Post of Gallatin, Tenn.[11]
Brig. Gen. Eleazer A. Paine

Ward's Brigade
Brig. Gen. William T. Ward
102d Illinois   70th Indiana
105th Illinois   79th Ohio
Indiana Light Artillery, 13th Battery

Cavalry
1st Kentucky   11th Kentucky
7th Kentucky

Army of Tennessee
Gen. Braxton Bragg, Commanding

POLK'S CORPS
Lieut. Gen. Leonidas Polk

First Division
Maj. Gen. B. F. Cheatham

First Brigade
Brig. Gen. Daniel S. Donelson
8th Tennessee   51st Tennessee
16th Tennessee   84th Tennessee
38th Tennessee   Carnes' (Tennessee) Battery

10. Under the immediate command of General Stanley, Chief of Cavalry.
11. Not engaged at Stones River. Commanders given as they stood 31 December 1862.

Second Brigade[12]
Brig. Gen. Alexander P. Stewart

4th Tennessee	31st Tennessee
5th Tennessee	33d Tennessee
19th Tennessee	Mississippi Battery
24th Tennessee	

Third Brigade[13]
Brig. Gen. George Maney

1st Tennessee	9th Tennessee
27th Tennessee	Tennessee Sharpshooters
4th Tennessee (Provisional Army)	Smith's (Mississippi) Battery
6th Tennessee	

Fourth (Preston Smith's) Brigade
Col. A. J. Vaughan, Jr.

12th Tennessee	154th Tennessee
13th Tennessee	9th Texas
29th Tennessee	Allin's (Tennessee) Sharpshooters
47th Tennessee	Tennessee Battery

Second Division
Maj. Gen. Jones M. Withers

First (Deas') Brigade
Col. J. Q. Loomis (w)
Col. J. G. Coltart

19th Alabama	39th Alabama
22d Alabama	17th Alabama Battalion Sharpshooters
25th Alabama	1st Louisiana (Regulars)
26th Alabama	Robertson's Battery

Second Brigade
Brig. Gen. James R. Chalmers (w)
Col. T. W. White

7th Mississippi	9th Mississippi Battalion Sharpshooters
9th Mississippi	Blythe's (Mississippi) Regiment
10th Mississippi	Garrity's (Alabama) Battery
41st Mississippi	

12. The Fourth and Fifth Tennessee were consolidated under the command of Col. O. F. Strahl during the Stones River campaign, the Thirty-first and Thirty-third Tennessee under Col. E. E. Tansil.

13. The First and Twenty-seventh Tennessee were consolidated under the command of Col. H. R. Field during the Stones River campaign, the Sixth and Ninth Tennessee under Col. C. S. Hurt.

Third (Walthall's) Brigade
Brig. Gen. J. Patton Anderson

45th Alabama	30th Mississippi
24th Mississippi	39th North Carolina[14]
27th Mississippi	Missouri Battery
29th Mississippi	

Fourth (Anderson's) Brigade[15]
Col. A. M. Manigault

24th Alabama	10th South Carolina
28th Alabama	19th South Carolina
34th Alabama	Alabama Battery

HARDEE'S CORPS
Lieut. Gen. William J. Hardee

First Division
Maj. Gen. John C. Breckinridge

First Brigade[16]
Brig. Gen. Daniel W. Adams (w)
Col. Randall L. Gibson

32d Alabama	25th Louisiana
13th Louisiana	14th Louisiana Battalion
20th Louisiana	Washington Artillery (5th Battery)
16th Louisiana	

Second Brigade
Col. J. B. Palmer
Brig. Gen. Gideon J. Pillow

18th Tennessee	32d Tennessee
26th Tennessee	45th Tennessee
28th Tennessee	Moses' (Georgia) Battery

Third Brigade[17]
Brig. Gen. William Preston

1st Florida	60th North Carolina
3d Florida	20th Tennessee
4th Florida	Tennessee Battery

14. Joined brigade 31 December; transferred 2 January to Manigault's brigade.

15. The Tenth and Nineteenth South Carolina were consolidated under the command of Col. A. J. Lythgoe during the Stones River campaign.

16. The Thirteenth and Twentieth Louisiana were consolidated under the command of Col. R. L. Gibson during the Stones River campaign, the Sixteenth and Twenty-fifth Louisiana under Col. S. W. Fisk.

17. The First and Third Florida were consolidated under the command of Col. William Miller during the Stones River campaign.

Fourth Brigade
Brig. Gen. R. W. Hanson (mw)
Col. R. P. Trabue

41st Alabama	6th Kentucky
2d Kentucky	9th Kentucky
4th Kentucky	Kentucky Battery

Jackson's Brigade[18]
Brig. Gen. John K. Jackson

5th Georgia	8th Mississippi
2d Georgia Battalion Sharpshooters	Pritchard's (Georgia) Battery
5th Mississippi	Lumsden's (Alabama) Battery

Second Division
Maj. Gen. P. R. Cleburne

First Brigade
Brig. Gen. L. E. Polk

1st Arkansas	2d Tennessee
13th Arkansas	5th Tennessee
15th Arkansas	Helena Artillery
5th Confederate	

Second Brigade[19]
Brig. Gen. St. John R. Liddell

2d Arkansas	7th Arkansas
5th Arkansas	8th Arkansas
6th Arkansas	Swett's (Mississippi) Battery

Third Brigade
Brig. Gen. Bushrod R. Johnson

17th Tennessee	37th Tennessee
23d Tennessee	44th Tennessee
25th Tennessee	Jefferson Artillery

Fourth Brigade
Brig. Gen. S. A. M. Wood

16th Alabama	45th Mississippi
33d Alabama	15th Mississippi Battalion Sharpshooters
3d Confederate	Alabama Battery

18. Temporarily assigned to Breckinridge's division.
19. The Sixth and Seventh Arkansas were consolidated under the command of Col. S. G. Smith during the Stones River campaign.

McCown's Division[20]
Maj. Gen. J. P. McCown

First Brigade[21]
Brig. Gen. M. D. Ector
10th Texas Cavalry   15th Texas Cavalry
11th Texas Cavalry   Texas Battery
14th Texas Cavalry

Second Brigade
Brig. Gen. James E. Rains (k)
Col. R. B. Vance
3d Georgia Battalion   11th Tennessee
9th Georgia Battalion   Eufaula Light Artillery
29th North Carolina

Third Brigade[22]
Brig. Gen. Evander McNair[23]
Col. R. W. Harper
1st Arkansas Mounted Rifles   30th Arkansas
2d Arkansas Mounted Rifles   4th Arkansas Battalion
4th Arkansas   Arkansas Battery

CAVALRY[24]
Brig. Gen. Joseph Wheeler

Wheeler's Brigade
Brig. Gen. Joseph Wheeler
1st Alabama   1st Tennessee
3d Alabama   Tennessee Battalion
51st Alabama   Tennessee Battalion
8th Confederate   Arkansas Battery

Buford's Brigade
Brig. Gen. A. Buford
3d Kentucky   6th Kentucky
5th Kentucky

20. Of Smith's corps, serving with Hardee.
21. The regiments of the First Brigade served as infantry during the Stones River campaign.
22. The First and Second Arkansas Mounted Rifles fought as infantry during the Stones River campaign.
23. McNair took ill during the fighting on the morning of 31 December and turned over brigade command to Harper.
24. Forrest and Morgan's commands on detached service.

Pegram's Brigade[25]

1st Georgia   1st Louisiana

Wharton's Brigade

Brig. Gen. John A. Wharton

14th Alabama Battalion	Tennessee Battalion
1st Confederate	8th Texas
3d Confederate	Murray's (Tennessee) Regiment
2d Georgia	Escort Company
2d Tennessee	McCown's Escort Company
4th Tennessee	White's (Tennessee) Battery

Artillery[26]

Baxter's (Tennessee) Battery   Gibson's (Georgia) Battery
Byrne's (Kentucky) Battery

25. Probably incomplete.
26. Only Byrne's Battery was engaged in the Stones River campaign.

NOTES

ABBREVIATIONS

ADAH	Alabama Department of Archives
B and G	*Blue and Grey* magazine
CHS	Chicago Historical Society
CV	*Confederate Veteran* magazine
CWM	College of William and Mary
CWTI Coll.	*Civil War Times Illustrated* Collection
DU	Duke University
ISHL	Illinois State Historical Library
LSU	Louisiana State University
MOLLUS	Military Order of the Loyal Legion of the United States
NA	National Archives
NYHS	New-York Historical Society
OR	*War of the Rebellion: A Compilation of the Official Records of the Union and Confederate Armies* (All references are to Series 1)
SHSP	*Southern Historical Society Papers*
THQ	*Tennessee Historical Quarterly*
TSLA	Tennessee State Library and Archives
TU	Tulane University
UNC	University of North Carolina
US	University of the South
USAMHI	U.S. Army Military History Institute
WRHS	Western Reserve Historical Society

Stones River also has been referred to as Stone's River or Stone River, particularly in early works on the battle.

CHAPTER ONE / SUMMER OF HOPE, AUTUMN OF DESPAIR

1. Joseph Wheeler, "Bragg's Invasion of Kentucky," in *Battles and Leaders of the Civil War*, ed. Clarence Buell and Robert Johnson, 4 vols. (New York: Thomas Yoseloff, 1956), 3:19; Don C. Seitz, *Braxton Bragg, General of the Confederacy* (Columbia, S. C.: The State Company, 1924), 206; Stanley Horn, *The Army of Tennessee* (Norman: University of Oklahoma Press, 1941), 190; James Phelan to Braxton Bragg, 4 December 1862, William P. Palmer Collection of Braxton Bragg Papers, WRHS.

2. David Urquhart, "Bragg's Advance and Retreat," in *Battles and Leaders* 3:600; E. T. Sykes, "A Cursory Sketch of General Bragg's Campaigns. Paper Number 2," *SHSP* 11 (1883): 468.

3. Wheeler, "Bragg's Invasion," 3:23.

4. Richard Taylor, *Destruction and Reconstruction: Personal Experiences of the Late War* (New York: D. Appleton, 1879), 100.

5. Sir Arthur Freemantle, *Three Months in the Southern States: April-June, 1863* (New York: J. Bradburn, 1864), 145; Taylor, *Destruction and Reconstruction*, 100–101; A. J. Foard to Braxton Bragg, 31 January 1863, Palmer Collection of Bragg Papers; L. H. Stout, *Reminiscences of General Braxton Bragg* (Hattiesburg, Miss.: The Book Farm, 1942), 7–13; John S. Wise, *The End of an Era* (Boston: Houghton, Mifflin, 1902), 175; Seitz, *Braxton Bragg*, 174; Freemantle, *Three Months in the Southern States*, 145.

6. James Fry, *Operations of the Army under Buell from June 10th to October 30th, 1862, and the "Buell Commission"* (New York: D. Van Nostrand, 1884), 43–50; Wheeler, "Bragg's Invasion" 3:9–10.

7. Urquhart, "Bragg's Advance and Retreat" 3:601; Fry, *Army under Buell*, 49–50.

8. Wheeler, "Bragg's Invasion," 3:13.

9. Ibid., 13–14.

10. Fry, *Army under Buell*, 60–62; Wheeler, "Bragg's Invasion," 3:16–19; Sykes, "Bragg's Campaigns," 470–71; Urquhart, "Bragg's Advance and Retreat," 3:603; Seitz, *Braxton Bragg*, 207; John Lindsley, *The Military Annals of Tennessee. Confederate. First Series: Embracing a Review of Military Operations, with Regimental Histories and Memorial Rolls* (Nashville: J. M. Lindsley, 1886), 535, 814.

11. Horn, *Army of Tennessee*, 190; George C. Brent journal, 2 November 1862, Palmer Collection of Bragg Papers; Urquhart, "Bragg's Advance and Retreat," 3:603.

12. Horn, *Army of Tennessee*, 190.

13. Freemantle, *Three Months in the Southern States*, 139; Samuel R. Watkins, *"Co. Aytch," Maury Grays, First Tennessee Regiment; or, a Side Show of the Big Show* (Chattanooga: Times Printing Company, 1900), 154; Ezra Warner, *Generals in Gray: Lives of the Confederate Commanders* (Baton Rouge: Louisiana State University Press, 1964), 243.

14. Special Order Number 29, Headquarters Department Number 2, 4 November 1862, Leonidas Polk Papers, US; William Polk, *Leonidas Polk,*

Bishop and General, 2 vols. (New York: Longmans, Green, 1893), 2:158, 168; Horn, *Army of Tennessee*, 190; Joseph H. Parks, *General Edmund Kirby Smith, C. S. A.* (Baton Rouge: Louisiana State University Press, 1954), 136, 242–45; Kirby Smith to his wife, 8 November 1862, Kirby Smith Papers, UNC.

CHAPTER TWO / THE ROSECRANS TOUCH

1. Fry, *Army under Buell*, 83–87, 93–96; Henry M. Cist, *The Army of the Cumberland* (New York: Scribner's, 1882), 75–76; Henry J. Aten, *History of the Eighty-fifth Regiment, Illinois Volunteer Infantry* (Hiawatha, Kans.: Comp. and Pub. under the Auspices of the Regimental Association, 1901), 43.

2. Edward Ferguson, "The Army of the Cumberland under Buell," *War Papers Read before the Commandery of the State of Wisconsin, MOLLUS*, 3 vols. (Milwaukee: Burdick, Armitage and Allen, 1891), 1: 432–33; Ephraim A. Otis, "The Murfreesboro Campaign," *Papers of the Military Historical Society of Massachusetts*, Vol. 7, *Campaigns in Kentucky and Tennessee Including the Battle of Chickamauga, 1862–1864* (Boston: By the Society, 1908), 253; *OR*, 20, pt. 2, 91; J. Warren Keifer, *Slavery and Four Years of War, a Political History of Slavery in the United States, Together with a Narrative of the Campaigns and Battles of the Civil War in Which the Author Took Part, 1861–1865*, 2 vols. (New York: G. P. Putnam, 1900), 1:295–96.

3. Frederick H. Dyer, *A Compendium of the War of the Rebellion, Comp. and Arranged from Official Records of the Federal and Confederate Armies, Reports of the Adjutant Generals of the Several States, the Army Registers, and Other Reliable Documents and Sources*, 3 vols. (1911; reprint, New York: Thomas Yoseloff, 1959), 1:425, 438–39; William Bickham, *Rosecrans' Campaign with the Fourteenth Army Corps, or the Army of the Cumberland: a Narrative of Personal Observations . . . with Official Reports of the Battle of Stone River* (Cincinnati: Moore, Wilstach, Keys, 1863), 18; *OR*, 20, pt. 2, 311.

4. William Ross Hartpence, *History of the Fifty-first Indiana Veteran Volunteer Infantry. A Narrative of Its Organization, Marches, Battles and Other Experiences in Camp and Prison; from 1861 to 1866. With Revised Roster* (Harrison, O.: By the Author, 1894), 93; Hans Christian Heg, *The Civil War Letters of Colonel Hans Christian Heg*, ed. Theodore C. Blegen (Northfield, Minn.: Norwegian-American Historical Association, 1936), 152; John Beatty, *The Citizen Soldier; or, Memoirs of a Volunteer* (Cincinnati: Wilstach, Baldwin, 1879), 235.

5. Whitelaw Reid, *Ohio in the War: Her Statesmen, Her Generals, and Soldiers*, 2 vols. (Cincinnati: Moore, Wilstach and Baldwin, 1868), 1:311–27; Michael Fitch, *Echoes of the Civil War As I Hear Them* (New York: R. F. Fenno, 1905), 12–15, 39.

6. William Shanks, *Personal Recollections of Distinguished Generals* (New York: Harper, 1866), 260–61; Thomas L. Crittenden, "The Union

Left at Stone's River," in *Battles and Leaders*, 3:633; Keifer, *Slavery and Four Years of War*, 1:308; James Henry Haynie, *The Nineteenth Illinois; a Memoir of a Volunteer Infantry Famous in the Civil War of Fifty Years Ago for Its Drill, Bravery, and Distinguished Services* (Chicago: M. A. Donohue, 1912), 179; Bickham, *Rosecrans' Campaign*, 28–29, 143.

7. Beatty, *Citizen Soldier*, 255–57.

8. Bickham, *Rosecrans' Campaign*, 28–29, 53–54.

9. Ibid., 12–13, 47; OR, 20, pt. 2, 91.

10. Bickham, *Rosecrans' Campaign*, 36–38; OR, 20, pt. 2, 20–22; Haynie, *Nineteenth Illinois*, 179.

11. Bickham, *Rosecrans' Campaign*, 47; OR, 20, pt. 2, 55–60, 108; Aten, *Eighty-fifth Illinois*, 54; David Lathrop, *The History of the Fifty-Ninth Regiment Illinois Volunteers, or a Three Years' Campaign through Missouri, Arkansas, Mississippi, Tennessee and Kentucky, with a Description of the Country, Towns, Skirmishes and Battles . . . Embellished with Twenty-four Lithographed Portraits of the Officers of the Regiment* (Indianapolis: Hall and Hutchinson, 1865), 178–79; Levi Wagner manuscript reminiscences, CWTI Coll., USAMHI; Dyer, *Compendium*, 3:1073.

12. Bickham, *Rosecrans' Campaign*, 29–30.

13. Ibid., 24; OR, 20, pt. 2, 9, 27, 31, 58.

14. Dyer, *Compendium* 1:438; OR, 20, pt. 1, 175–82; pt. 2, 283–85.

15. Bickham, *Rosecrans' Campaign*, 31–32.

16. Shanks, *Distinguished Generals*, 61–77.

17. Beatty, *Citizen Soldier*, 236.

18. Reid, *Ohio in the War*, 1:806; William Sumner Dodge, *History of the Old Second Division, Army of the Cumberland* (Chicago: Church and Goodman, 1864), 239–40; Alexander Stevenson, *The Battle of Stone's River near Murfreesboro', Tenn. December 30, 1862, to January 3, 1863* (Boston: J. R. Osgood, 1884), 31; Shanks, *Distinguished Generals*, 249; Lathrop, *Fifty-Ninth Illinois*, 192; Beatty, *Citizen Soldier*, 235–36; Horace Greeley, *The American Conflict: A History of the Great Rebellion in the United States of America, 1860–1865*, 2 vols. (Hartford: O. D. Case, 1879), 2:245.

19. Beatty, *Citizen Soldier*, 235–36; Bickham, *Rosecrans' Campaign*, 40–41; Shanks, *Distinguished Generals*, 249.

20. Ezra Warner, *Generals in Blue; Lives of the Union Commanders* (Baton Rouge: Louisiana State University Press, 1964), 470–71; Joseph G. Vale, *Minty and the Cavalry: A History of Cavalry Campaigns in the Western Armies* (Harrisburg, Pa.: E. K. Meyers, 1886), 107–8; Bickham, *Rosecrans' Campaign*, 76–81; Henry V. Freeman, "Some Battle Recollections of Stone's River," in *Military Essays and Recollections; Papers Read before the Commandery of the State of Illinois, MOLLUS*, 4 vols. (Chicago: The Dial Press, 1891–99), 3:228.

21. OR, 20, pt. 2, 60, 64, 102, 117, 123–24; Bickham, *Rosecrans' Campaign*, 74–75, 88–90, 120; Beatty, *Citizen Soldier*, 188; Herman Hattaway and Archer Jones, *How the North Won; A Military History of the Civil War* (Urbana: University of Illinois Press, 1983), 300–314.

CHAPTER THREE / A HASTY ADVANCE

1. Brent journal, 2 November 1862, Palmer Collection of Bragg Papers; Thomas L. Connelly, *Autumn of Glory: The Army of Tennessee, 1862–1865* (Baton Rouge: Louisiana State University Press, 1971), 16–17; *OR,* 20, pt. 2, 386–87; Edmund Kirby Smith to Braxton Bragg, 23 October 1862, Palmer Collection of Bragg Papers; Lindsley, *Military Annals of Tennessee,* 814–15, 818.

2. E. W. Cole to John C. Breckinridge, 30 October 1862; B. F. Cheatham to Breckinridge, 4 November 1862; Bragg to Breckinridge, 5 November 1862, all in John C. Breckinridge Papers, CHS; Gervis Grainger, *Four Years with the Boys in Gray* (Dayton: Press of Morningside Bookshop, 1972), 13; Urquhart, "Bragg's Advance and Retreat," 3:603.

3. Folding map of Tennessee, in Stevenson, *Stone's River; OR,* 20, pt. 2, 398–99; C. C. Henderson, *The Story of Murfreesboro* (Murfreesboro, 1929), 1–2; Fitch, *Echoes of the Civil War,* 109.

4. *OR,* 20, pt. 2, 388, 402, 417–19; Brent journal, 20 November 1862, Palmer Collection of Bragg Papers; Warner, *Generals in Gray,* 342–43; William C. Davis, *Breckinridge: Statesman, Soldier, Symbol* (Baton Rouge: Louisiana State University Press, 1974), 321–28; Edwin Porter Thompson, *History of the Orphan Brigade* (Louisville, Ky.: L. N. Thompson, 1898), 358–61; Grady McWhiney and Perry D. Jamieson, *Attack and Die: Civil War Military Tactics and the Southern Heritage* (University: University of Alabama Press, 1982), 49–52; Freemantle, *Three Months in the Southern States,* 138–39, 152–53; William J. Hardee, "Biographical Sketch of Major General Patrick H. Cleburne," *SHSP* 31 (1903): 152–54, 161–62; Seitz, *Braxton Bragg,* 79; "Autobiography of General Patton Anderson," *SHSP* 24 (1896): 67–68; Connelly, *Autumn of Glory,* 26–28.

5. Seitz, *Braxton Bragg,* 211–15; Special Orders Number 275, 14 November 1862, Joseph E. Johnston Papers, CWM; Joseph Johnston, *Narrative of Military Operations, Directed during the Late War between the States* (New York: D. Appleton, 1874), 150–51; *OR,* 20, pt. 2, 436–37, 441, 444.

6. Urquhart, "Bragg's Advance and Retreat," 3:604; Polk, *Leonidas Polk,* 2:169; Brent journal, 12–14, 16 December 1862, Palmer Collection of Bragg Papers; J. J. Womack, *The Civil War Diary of Captain J. J. Womack, Company E, 16th Tennessee Volunteers* (McMinnville, Tenn.: Womack, 1961), 75; James R. Maxwell, *Autobiography of James Robert Maxwell of Tuscaloosa, Alabama* (New York: Greenberg, 1926), 157; Jefferson Davis, *Jefferson Davis, Constitutionalist, His Letters, Papers, and Speeches,* ed. Dunbar Rowland, 10 vols. (Jackson: Printed for the Mississippi Department of Archives and History, 1923) 5:433–34; *OR,* 20, pt. 2, 150.

7. Connelly, *Autumn of Glory,* 32; *OR,* 20, pt. 2, 447–48.

CHAPTER FOUR / WE LIVED LIKE LORDS

1. Brent journal, 22 November, 20–21 December 1862, Palmer Collection of Bragg Papers; *OR,* 20, pt. 1, 415, 437; Thompson, *Orphan Brigade,* 152–53, 159.

2. Louise Wright, *A Southern Girl in '61; the War-Time Memories of a Confederate Senator's Daughter* (New York: Doubleday, Page, 1905), 105; J. E. Robuck, *My Own Personal Experience and Observation as a Soldier in the Confederate Army during the Civil War, 1861–1865; Also during the Period of Reconstruction* (Birmingham: By the Author, 1911), 42–43; Womack, *Diary*, 76; Thompson, *Orphan Brigade*, 168; Grainger, *Four Years*, 13; Lot D. Young, *Reminiscences of a Soldier of the Orphan Brigade* (Louisville: Courier-Journal Job Printing Company, 1918), 40; Henderson, *Murfreesboro*, 1–7, 59.

3. Urquhart, "Bragg's Advance and Retreat," 3:604; Horn, *Army of Tennessee*, 195; Polk, *Leonidas Polk*, 2:169.

4. Womack, *Diary*, 76; Brent journal, 17–21 December 1862, Palmer Collection of Bragg Papers; Charles Roberts, "At Murfreesboro Just Before the Battle," *CV* 6, no. 12 (December 1908): 632; John Magee diary, 25 December 1862, DU; Maxwell, *Autobiography*, 158–59; Johnny Williams Green, *Johnny Green of the Orphan Brigade: The Journal of a Confederate Soldier*, ed. A. D. Kirwan (Lexington: University of Kentucky Press, 1956), 58–59; Leonidas Polk to his wife, 25 December 1862, Polk Papers; Allan Nevins, *The War for the Union* (New York: Scribner's, 1959–71), 2:407.

5. Beatty, *Citizen Soldier*, 197; Heg, *Civil War Letters*, 158; Charles F. Manderson, *The Twin Seven-Shooters* (New York: F. Tennyson Neely, 1902), 9–10.

6. Bickham, *Rosecrans' Campaign*, 125, 138–39; *OR*, 20, pt. 1, 189–90, 617; pt. 2, 183, 192; Richard W. Johnson, *A Soldier's Reminiscences in Peace and War* (Philadelphia: J. R. Lippincott, 1886), 204; Bickham, "The Preliminaries of the Battle," *New York Times*, Friday, 9 January 1863.

7. Ebenezer Hannaford, *The Story of a Regiment: A History of the Campaigns, and Associations in the Field, of the Sixth Regiment Ohio Volunteer Infantry* (Cincinnati: By the Author, 1868), 809; *OR*, 20, pt. 2, 224, 228–29.

8. Brent journal, 25 December 1862, Palmer Collection of Bragg Papers; *OR*, 20, pt. 1, 663; Braxton Bragg's official report (draft) of the Battle of Murfreesboro, Palmer Collection of Bragg Papers.

CHAPTER FIVE / TO MURFREESBORO

1. Ebenezer Hannaford, "In the Ranks at Stone River," *Harper's Magazine* 27 (1863): 810; Bickham, *Rosecrans' Campaign*, 147–49; *OR*, 20, pt. 1, 253; Henry Eby, *Observations of an Illinois Boy in Battle, Camp and Prisons—1861–1865* (Mendota, Ill: By the Author, 1910), 68–70.

2. Company K, Fifteenth Illinois is referred to in the official report of Brigadier General Jefferson Davis as Company B Cavalry, Thirty-sixth Illinois Infantry. On 25 December 1862, the company was assigned to the Fifteenth Illinois Cavalry as Company K, although it still served as Davis's escort during the Stones River campaign. Dyer, *Compendium*, 3:1034.

3. Edwin Bearss, "Cavalry Operations in the Battle of Stones River. Part 1: Cavalry Operations during the Union Approach," *THQ* 19 (1960): 27–30; P. Sidney Post diary, Post Papers, Knox College.

4. Eby, *Illinois Boy*, 66; Will Carson to his parents, 7 January 1863, CWTI Coll.; Bearss, "Cavalry Operations, Part 1," 30–31.

5. Bearss, "Cavalry Operations, Part 1," 31.

6. *OR*, 20, pt. 1, 446, 705; Bearss, "Cavalry Operations, Part 1," 31.

7. Hannaford, "In the Ranks," 810; Horace Newton Fisher, *The Personal Experiences of Colonel Horace Newton Fisher in the Civil War; a Staff Officer's Story* (Boston, N.P.: 1960), 51; William H. Newlin, *A History of the Seventy-Third Regiment of Illinois Infantry Volunteers, Its Services and Experiences in Camp, on the March, on the Picket and Skirmish Lines, and in Many Battles of the War* (Springfield, Ill.: The Regimental Reunion Association, 1890), 119.

8. Bickham, *Rosecrans' Campaign*, 160–63; *OR*, 20, pt. 1, 253.

9. Wheeler to Bragg, 2:00 P. M., 26 December 1862; Stewart's Creek Telegraph Operator to Bragg, 26 December 1862; Wheeler to Brent, 9:30 P. M., 26 December 1862; Bragg's report of Murfreesboro; Brent journal, 26 December 1862; Hardee to Brent, 4:00 A. M., 27 December 1862, all in Palmer Collection of Bragg Papers.

10. Wheeler, "Battle of Murfreesboro," undated manuscript in Joseph Wheeler Papers, CHS; W. D. Pickett, "Reminiscences of Murfreesboro," *CV* 16, no. 9 (September 1908): 450; William J. Hardee's official report (draft) of the Battle of Murfreesboro, Hardee Papers, ADAH.

11. Bickham, *Rosecrans' Campaign*, 164; *OR*, 20, pt. 1, 253, 295, 318, 372, 636, 896; "Triune in the Civil War," undated manuscript in John Leland Jordan Papers, TSLA; Bearss, "Cavalry Operations, Part 1," 36–37; Fisher, *Staff Officer's Story*, 51; Beatty, *Citizen Soldier*, 199.

12. *OR*, 20, pt. 1, 372, and pt. 2, 247; Beatty, *Citizen Soldier*, 198; Will Carson to his parents, 7 January 1863, CWTI Coll.; Mead Holmes, *A Soldier of the Cumberland: Memoir of Mead Holmes, jr., Sergeant of Company K, 21st Regiment Wisconsin Volunteers* (Boston: American Tract Society, 1864), 128.

13. *OR*, 20, pt. 1, 447, 458–59, 575, 705; Hannaford, "In the Ranks," 810; Smyrna Telegraph Operator to Bragg, 27 December 1862, Palmer Collection of Bragg Papers; John Du Bose, *General Joseph Wheeler and the Army of Tennessee* (New York: Neale, 1912), 139.

14. *OR*, 20, pt. 1, 534; Wheeler to Brent, 4:40 P. M., 27 December 1862, and Brent journal, 27 December 1862, both in Palmer Collection of Bragg Papers.

15. *OR*, 20, pt. 1, 672–73, and pt. 2, 463–64.

16. Hardee's report of Murfreesboro, Hardee Papers, ADAH.

17. Brent journal, 27 December 1862, Palmer Collection of Bragg Papers; *OR*, 20, pt. 1, 753.

18. Lathrop, *Fifty-Ninth Illinois*, 191; Hannaford, "In the Ranks," 810; Bickham, *Rosecrans' Campaign*, 173–74.

19. Thomas Wright, *History of the Eighth Regiment Kentucky Vol. Inf., during Its Three Years Campaigns, Embracing Organization, Marches, Skirmishes, and Battles of the Command, with Much of the History of the Old Reliable Third Brigade, Commanded by Hon. Stanley Matthews, and Containing Many Interesting and Amusing Incidents of Army Life* (St. Joseph, Mo.: St. Joseph Steam Printing Co., 1880), 123; Bickham, *Rosecrans' Campaign*, 164–65, 173–74; Heg, *Civil War Letters*, 161; Fisher, *Staff Officer's Story*, 51–52; *OR*, 20, pt. 1, 635; pt. 2, 255–58.

CHAPTER SIX / THE LINES WERE FORMING

1. Bickham, *Rosecrans' Campaign*, 175–77; Hannaford, "In the Ranks," 811; Wheeler to Brent, 1:30 P. M., 29 December 1862, Palmer Collection of Bragg Papers.

2. Hannaford, "In the Ranks," 811; Bickham, *Rosecrans' Campaign*, 177; Warner, *Generals in Blue*, 358, 569; Beatty, *Citizen Soldier*, 235–36; Shanks, *Distinguished Generals*, 295; *OR*, 20, pt. 1, 448, 459.

3. Hartpence, *Fifty-First Indiana*, 104–6; *OR*, 20, pt. 1, 448, 501, 507, 836–37; Warner, *Generals in Blue*, 207; John A. Buckner to Breckinridge, 20 May 1863, John C. Breckinridge Papers, NYHS; Otis, "Murfreesboro Campaign," 302.

4. Buckner to Breckinridge, 20 May 1863, Breckinridge Papers, NYHS.

5. *OR*, 20, pt. 1, 254, 295, 635; pt. 2, 265–69.

6. John W. Lavender, *The War Memoirs of Captain John W. Lavender, C. S. A. They Never Came Back; the Story of Co. F. Fourth Arks. Infantry, C. S. A., Originally Known as the Montgomery Hunters, as Told by Their Commanding Officer*, ed. Ted. R. Worley (Pine Bluff, Ark.: W. M. Hackett and D. R. Perdue, 1956), 37–38.

7. Bragg's report of Murfreesboro, and Brent journal, 28–29 December 1862, both in Palmer Collection of Bragg Papers; *OR*, 20, pt. 1, 705; Wheeler, "Battle of Murfreesboro," Wheeler Papers.

8. *OR*, 20, pt. 1, 254.

9. Lewis W. Day, *Story of the One Hundred and First Ohio Infantry. A Memorial Volume* (Cleveland: W. M. Bayne, 1894), 80–81; Bickham, *Rosecrans' Campaign*, 181–86; James C. Howlett diary, 30 December 1862, ISHL.

10. *OR*, 20, pt. 1, 372, 407.

11. Ibid., 576.

12. James A. Barnes, *The Eighty-Sixth Regiment, Indiana Volunteer Infantry. A Narrative of Its Service in the Civil War of 1861–1865* (Crawfordsville, Ind.: The Journal Company, 1895), 98; Hannaford, "In the Ranks," 811–12.

13. Urquhart, "Bragg's Advance and Retreat," 3:606; Brent journal, 30 December 1862, Palmer Collection of Bragg Papers.

14. Wheeler, "Battle of Murfreesboro," Wheeler Papers; *OR*, 20, pt. 1, 787.

15. Washington Lafayett Gammage, *The Camp, the Bivouac, and the Battlefield; being a History of the Fourth Arkansas Regiment, from Its First Organization down to the Present Date: Its Campaigns and Its Battles, with an Occasional Reference to the Current Events of the Times, including Biographical Sketches of Its Field Officers and Others of the "Old Brigade." The Whole Interspersed Here and There with Descriptions of Scenery, Incidents of Camp Life, Etc.* (Little Rock: Arkansas Southern Press, 1958), 63; *OR*, 20, pt. 1, 773, 919–23, 931.

16. *OR*, 20, pt. 1, 773, 844.

17. Ibid., 773, 754, 966; Bragg's report of Murfreesboro, Brent journal, 30 December 1862, both in Palmer Collection of Bragg Papers.

18. Gates P. Thruston, *Personal Recollections of the Battle in the Rear at Stone's River* (Nashville, n. d.), 5–6; *OR*, 20 pt. 1, 192, 255, 277, 381; Bickham, *Rosecrans' Campaign*, 198–200; Charles Briant, *History of the Sixth Regiment Indiana Volunteer Infantry. Of Both the Three Months' and Three Years' Services* (Indianapolis: W. B. Burford, 1891), 176.

19. Bickham, *Rosecrans' Campaign*, 202; Alexis Cope, *The Fifteenth Ohio Volunteers and Its Campaigns, War of 1861–5* (Columbus: The Author, 1916), 234.

20. Barnes, *Eighty-Sixth Indiana*, 99; William Sumner Dodge, *A Waif of the War; or, the History of the Seventy-Fifth Illinois Infantry* (Chicago: Church and Goodman, 1866), 63; Joseph Gibson, *History of the Seventy-Eighth Pennsylvania Volunteer Infantry* (Pittsburg: Pittsburg Print. Co., 1905), 51; Wagner reminiscences, CWTI Coll.

21. *OR*, 20, pt. 1, 373, 460; Bickham, *Rosecrans' Campaign*, 196.

22. *OR*, 20 pt. 1, 255, 278; Johnson, *Soldier's Reminiscences*, 210; Day, *One Hundred and First Ohio*, 82; Solon Marks, "Experiences at the Battle of Stone River," *Wisconsin MOLLUS* 2:390.

23. Stevenson, *Stone's River*, 29–30; *OR*, 20, pt. 1, 348; Philip Henry Sheridan, *Personal Memoirs of P. H. Sheridan*, 2 vols. (New York: Charles L. Webster, 1888), 1:220–22; James H. Woodward, "General A. McD. McCook at Stone River," *A Paper Read before the California Commandery of MOLLUS at Los Angeles, Cal., Feb. 22, 1892* (Los Angeles: Times-Mirror, 1892), 11–12.

24. *OR*, 20, pt. 1, 313–14; Edwin W. Payne, *History of the Thirty-Fourth Regiment of Illinois Infantry, September 7, 1861–July 12, 1865* (Clinton, Ia.: Allen, 1902), 43; Sheridan, *Memoirs* 1:222.

CHAPTER SEVEN / BOYS, THIS IS FUN

1. *OR*, 20, pt. 1, 304, 309, 319; *History of Battery A, First Regiment Ohio Vol. Light Artillery* (Milwaukee: Daily Wisconsin Printing House, 1865), 61.

2. Woodward, "McCook at Stone River," 13; Marks, "Experiences at Stone River," 390; *OR*, 20, pt. 1, 300; Reid, *Ohio in the War* 1:868–69.

3. Johnson, *Soldier's Reminiscences*, 213; A. H. Heiner, "The Battle of

Murfreesboro Again," *CV* 12, no. 3 (March 1904): 118; *OR*, 20, pt. 1, 300, 320–22, 325–29, 331–36, 774, 912, 926, 931, 944, 949, 956; Lavender, *They Never Came Back*, 38–40; Gammage, *Camp, Bivouac, and Battlefield*, 63; Freemantle, *Three Months in the Southern States*, 75; Warner, *Generals in Gray*, 81–82; Payne, *Thirty-Fourth Illinois*, 44–45, 57; Thomas M. Eddy, *The Patriotism of Illinois. A Record of the Civil and Military History of the State in the War for the Union*, 2 vols. (Chicago: Clarke, 1865–66), 2:354; Warner, *Generals in Blue*, 271.

4. Robert Stewart, "The Battle of Stone River, As Seen By One Who Was There," *B and G* 5 (1895): 12; Cope, *Fifteenth Ohio*, 234, 246; *OR*, 20, pt. 1, 304, 312–14, 941–42; Battery A, First Ohio, 61–63; James M. Cole to "Friend James," 19 January 1863, ISHL.

5. Cope, *Fifteenth Ohio*, 235–37; *OR*, 20, pt. 1, 316, 325–26.

6. *OR*, 20, pt. 1, 193, 774, 853, 927, 938; Warner, *Generals in Gray*, 243–44; Watkins, *"Co. Aytch," Maury Grays*, 154–55.

7. Dyer, *Compendium*, 3:1078; *OR*, 20, pt. 1, 264, 270–73, 877; Lathrop, *Fifty-Ninth Illinois*, 188; George W. Herr, *Episodes of the Civil War, Nine Campaigns in Nine States; Fremont in Missouri—Curtis in Missouri and Arkansas—Halleck's Seige of Corinth—Buell in Kentucky—Rosecrans in Kentucky and Tennessee—Grant at the Battle of Chattanooga—Sherman from Chattanooga to Atlanta—Thomas in Tennessee and North Carolina—Stanley in Texas* (San Francisco: Bancroft, 1890), 125–26.

8. Dodge, *Seventy-Fifth Illinois*, 64–66; *Society of the Seventy-Fourth Illinois Volunteer Infantry. Reunion Proceedings and History of the Regiment* (Rockford, Ill.: W. P. Lamb, 1903), 12–14.

9. *OR*, 20, pt. 1, 320, 343, 944; Wagner reminiscences, CWTI Coll.; Johnson, *Soldier's Reminiscences*, 213; Samuel P. Timmons to his father, 17 February 1863, John Wesley Timmons Papers, DU.

10. John M. Berry, "Reminiscences from Missouri," *CV* 8, no. 2 (February 1900): 73; Freemantle, *Three Months in the Southern States*, 155; Wagner reminiscences, CWTI Coll.; St. John R. Liddell to his wife, 12 January 1863, Liddell Papers, LSU; *OR*, 20, pt. 1, 321, 856–68, 945; Robert Dacus, *Reminiscences of Company "H" First Arkansas Mounted Rifles* (Dayton: Press of Morningside, 1972), 22.

11. W. E. Bevens, *Reminiscences of a Private. Company "C" First Arkansas Regiment Infantry. May, 1861 to April, 1865* (N. P., 1912?), 36; *OR*, 20, pt. 1, 280–85, 853, 898; Day, *One Hundred and First Ohio*, 84–87; Heg, *Civil War Letters*, 165–66; Jay Butler, *Letters Home* (Binghamton, N. Y.: Privately printed, 1930), 52.

CHAPTER EIGHT / MATTERS LOOKED PRETTY BLUE NOW

1. Marks, "Experiences at Stone River," 390–93.

2. Charles Doolittle to Mollie Post, 6 February 1863, Post Papers, Knox College; *OR*, 20, pt. 1, 270, 281–85, 330, 337, 341–43, 346, 854, 893, 901;

Samuel P. Timmons to his father, 18 February 1863, Timmons Papers; Day, *One Hundred First Ohio*, 87; G. A. Williams, "Blow Your Horn, Jake," *CV* 5, no. 5 (May 1897): 226; Berry, "Reminiscences from Missouri," 73; St. John Liddell, *Liddell's Record*, ed. Nathaniel C. Hughes (Dayton, Ohio: Morningside, 1985), 109.

3. *OR*, 20, pt. 1, 306, 913, 945, 952; Bearss, "Cavalry Operations in the Battle of Stones River (Concluded)," *THQ* 19 (1960): 119–20.

4. *OR*, 20, pt. 1, 203, 306, 622, 636–37, 967–68; Thruston, *Battle in the Rear*, 8–16; Dyer, *Compendium*, 3:1637; William L. Curry, *Four Years in the Saddle. History of the First Regiment, Ohio Volunteer Cavalry. War of the Rebellion, 1861–1865* (Columbus: Champlin, 1898), 83–84; Thomas Crofts, *History of the Service of the Third Ohio Veteran Volunteer Cavalry in the War for the Preservation of the Union from 1861–1865* (Toledo: Columbus, Stoneman Press, 1910), 60; James H. Wiswell to his father, 8 January 1863, Wiswell Papers, DU.

CHAPTER NINE / THE REBELS WERE FALLING
LIKE LEAVES OF AUTUMN

1. *OR*, 20, pt. 1, 664; Warner, *Generals in Gray*, 77; Freemantle, *Three Months in the Southern States*, 146.

2. John Mitchell, *In Memoriam: Twenty-fourth Wisconsin Infantry* (Milwaukee, 1906), 27; *OR*, 20, pt. 1, 290, 293, 348, 364–66; Newlin, *Seventy-third Illinois*, 126–27; Francis T. Sherman to Richard Yates, 13 January 1863, ISHL; Captain Taylor Beatty's unpublished report of the Battle of Murfreesboro, Palmer Collection of Bragg Papers; Stevenson, *Stone's River*, 50; A. H. Brown, "Reminiscences of a Private Soldier," *CV* 18, no. 10 (October 1910): 449.

3. Warner, *Generals in Gray*, 316; Brown, "Reminiscences of a Private Soldier," 449; *OR*, 20, pt. 1, 288–89, 293, 687, 748–50; Thomas B. Van Horne, *History of the Army of the Cumberland: Its Organization, Campaigns, and Battles*, 2 vols. (Cincinnati: R. Clarke, 1875), 1:233.

4. Sherman to Yates, 13 January 1863; Day Elmore to his family, 8 January 1863, CHS; Bickham, *Rosecrans' Campaign*, 363; *OR*, 20, pt. 1, 359, 361–62, 706.

5. *OR*, 20, pt. 1, 348, 354–55, 366, 370, 706, 734–38; Stevenson, *Stone's River*, 55–57; Warner, *Generals in Gray*, 210–11.

6. *OR*, 20, pt. 1, 706, 734–35, 738, 740.

7. Newlin, *Seventy-third Illinois*, 127; *OR*, 20, pt. 1, 354–56, 362, 364, 370; Stevenson, *Stone's River*, 59–60.

8. Magee diary, 31 December 1862; *OR*, 20, pt. 1, 735–40; Watkins, *"Co. Aytch,"* Maury Grays, 93–94; Clement Evans, ed., *Confederate Military History: A Library of Confederate States History* (Atlanta: Confederate Publishing Company, 1899), vol. 3, *Tennessee*, 69; Stevenson, *Stone's River*, 62.

9. Lyman Bennett and William Haigh, *History of the Thirty-sixth Reg-*

iment Illinois Volunteers, during the War of the Rebellion (Aurora, Ill.: Knickerbocker and Hodder, 1876), 344; *OR,* 20, pt. 1, 228, 288–89, 366; Sheridan, *Memoirs* 1:228; Newlin, *Seventy-third Illinois,* 129–30, 171–72.

10. *OR,* 20, pt. 1, 368, 845, 899, 901; Stevenson, *Stone's River,* 60.

11. Evans, ed., *Confederate Military History,* 3:149; *OR,* 20, pt. 1, 846, 854, 879, 891.

12. *OR,* 20, pt. 1, 689, 764; C. Irvine Walker, "Visit to the Battlefield of Murfreesboro," *CV* 15, no. 6 (June 1907): 263; Stevenson, *Stone's River,* 63; Lieutenant Colonel J. J. Scales's unpublished report of the Battle of Murfreesboro, Palmer Collection of Bragg Papers; Robuck, *Personal Experience and Observation,* 44–45.

CHAPTER TEN / ROSECRANS RALLIES THE RIGHT

1. John Lee Yaryan, "Stone River," *War Papers, Read before the Indiana Commandery, MOLLUS* (Indianapolis: By the Commandery, 1898), 1:168; *OR,* 20, pt. 1, 467, 574, 607; Manderson, *Twin Seven-Shooters,* 12–13.

2. Bickham, *Rosecrans' Campaign,* 365–66; Yaryan, "Stone River," 1:169; *OR,* 20, pt. 1, 193; *Seventy-fourth Illinois,* 15–16; Crittenden, "Union Left," 3:633.

3. *OR,* 20, pt. 1, 193, 449, 467, 574, 607, 652–53; Barnes, *Eighty-sixth Indiana,* 107; Asbury L. Kerwood, *Annals of the Fifty-Seventh Regiment Indiana Volunteers. Marches, Battles, and Incidents of Army Life, by a Member of the Regiment* (Dayton, O.: W. J. Shuey, 1868), 155–56; Gilbert Stormont, *History of the Fifty-Eighth Regiment of Indiana Volunteer Infantry, Its Organization, Campaigns and Battles, from 1861 to 1865* (Princeton, Ind.: Press of Clarion, 1895), 115; *History of the Seventy-Ninth Regiment Indiana Volunteer Infantry in the Civil War of Eighteen Sixty-One in the United States* (Indianapolis: Hollenbeck, 1899), 60; Charles Bennett, *Historical Sketches of the Ninth Michigan Infantry (General Thomas' Headquarters Guards) with an Account of the Battle of Murfreesboro, Tennessee, Sunday, July 13, 1862* (Coldwater, Mich.: Daily Courier, 1913), 28; Stevenson, *Stone's River,* 75.

4. *OR,* 20, pt. 1, 377–78, 383, 394; Spillard F. Horrall, *History of the Forty-Second Indiana Volunteer Infantry, Its Organization, Campaigns and Battles* (Indianapolis: W. B. Burford, 1893), 165–68.

5. Robuck, *Personal Experience and Observation,* 44–45; *OR,* 20, pt. 1, 349, 370, 707, 735, 756, 764, 846; Stevenson, *Stone's River,* 67–70; Watkins, "*Co. Aytch,*" *Maury Grays,* 93–94; Shanks, *Distinguished Generals,* 150–51; Bickham, *Rosecrans' Campaign,* 239.

6. *OR,* 20, pt. 1, 378, 394, 399–400, 913, 938–39, 942; Shanks, *Distinguished Generals,* 198–200, 234; Bickham, *Rosecrans' Campaign,* 43; Dodge, *Seventy-fifth Illinois,* 290–91; Will Carson to his parents, 7 January 1863, CWTI Coll.; Alfred Pirtle, "Stone River Sketches," *Sketches of War History 1861–1865, Papers Read Before Ohio Commandery, MOLLUS,* 6 vols. (Cincinnati: By the Commandery, 1888–1908), 6:98–100; Fre-

derick Phisterer, *The Regular Brigade of the Fourteenth Army Corps, the Army of the Cumberland, in the Battle of Stone River, or Murfreesboro, Tennessee* (N.p., n.d.), 5–6; *Record of the Ninety-fourth Ohio Volunteer Infantry in the War of the Rebellion* (Cincinnati: Valley Press, 189-), 28.

7. *OR*, 20, pt. 1, 378, 383, 707, 745, 776, 854, 899; Benjamin Scribner, *How Soldiers were Made; or, the War As I Saw It under Buell, Rosecrans, Thomas, Grant and Sherman* (Chicago: Donohue and Henneberry, 1887), 78–79; Pirtle, "Stone River Sketches," 99–100; Beatty, *Citizen Soldier*, 201–3; Horrall, *Forty-Second Indiana*, 165–68; Stevenson, *Stone's River*, 78–80; Louis Philippe Albert d'Orleans, *History of the Civil War in America*, 4 vols. (Philadelphia: Porter and Coates, 1875–88), 2:518–26.

8. Hannaford, *Sixth Ohio*, 394–95; *OR*, 20, pt. 1, 394, 560, 567, 571–72, 938–39; Hannaford, "In the Ranks," 813–14.

9. Louis A. Simmons, *The History of the 84th Reg't Ill. Vols.* (Macomb, Ill.: Hampton Brothers, 1866), 28–30; Pirtle, "Stone River Sketches," 100; *OR*, 20, pt. 1, 378, 388, 405, 565, 569–72, 735, 777, 899, 938–42.

10. *OR*, 20, pt. 1, 847–48, 858, 884, 927.

11. Warner, *Generals in Gray*, 293; Haynie, *Nineteenth Illinois*, 186–87; *OR*, 20, pt. 1, 407, 421, 425–26, 725, 756; Ira Gillaspie, *From Michigan to Murfreesboro: The Diary of Ira Gillaspie of the Eleventh Michigan Infantry* (Mount Pleasant: Central Michigan University Press, 1965), 43.

12. Gibson, *Seventy-Eighth Pennsylvania*, 53; *OR*, 20, pt. 1, 407–10, 421, 426, 432, 437, 729, 764–65; Warner, *Generals in Blue*, 108; George Puntenney, *History of the Thirty-Seventh Regiment of Indiana Infantry Volunteers, Its Organization, Campaigns, and Battles, Sept. '61–Oct. '64* (Rushville, Ind.: Jacksonian Book and Job Dept., 1896), 34; Joseph S. Johnston to his mother, 14 January 1863, CHS; Jacob Adams, *Diary of Jacob Adams, Private in Company F, 21st O. V. I.* (Columbus, Ohio: F. J. Heer, 1930), 19; Silas S. Canfield, *History of the 21st Regiment Ohio Volunteer Infantry, in the War of the Rebellion* (Toledo: Vrooman, Anderson and Bateman, 1893).

CHAPTER ELEVEN / OUR BOYS WERE FORCED BACK
IN CONFUSION

1. *OR*, 20, pt. 1, 243–48, 574, 580, 584, 589, 592, 594, 927–28, 932, 935; Daniel W. Howe, *Civil War Times, 1861–1865* (Indianapolis: The Bowen-Merrill Company, 1902), 114–15; James Dobson, *A Historical Sketch of Company K of the 79th Regiment Indiana Volunteers* (Plainfield, Ind.: Progress Print, 1894), 6–8; Manderson, *Twin Seven-Shooters*, 16; Freeman, "Recollections of Stone's River," 235–36; *Seventy-Fourth Illinois*, 15–16; Robert L. Kimberly, *The Forty-First Ohio Veteran Volunteer Infantry in the War of the Rebellion* (Cleveland: W. R. Smellie, 1897), 40–41.

2. Captain C. A. Sheafe, "Personal Recollection of Battle of Stones River," *Rutherford Courier*, n. d., in Ruth White Cook Confederate Scrapbook, TSLA; John Rerick, *The Forty-Fourth Indiana Volunteer Infantry*,

History of Its Service in the War of the Rebellion and a Personal Record of Its Members (Lagrange, Ind.: The Author, 1880), 79–80; Barnes, *Eighty-Sixth Indiana*, 102; *OR*, 20, pt. 1, 502, 597–98, 601–6, 848, 858, 861, 879, 893–94.

3. William Erb, *The Valley of Death, the Battles of Stones River: Extract from the Battles of the Nineteenth Ohio* (Washington, D. C.: Judd and Detweiler, 1893), 22–23; *OR*, 20, pt. 1, 502, 507, 510–11, 517, 554, 584, 594, 879, 884; Manderson, *Twin Seven-Shooters*, 16–17; Hartpence, *Fifty-First Indiana*, 106.

4. *OR*, 20, pt. 1, 503, 508, 511, 589, 594, 598, 605, 777, 848, 861–69, 879, 881, 884–85, 891–94; Liddell, *Liddell's Record*, 109, 112–13; Hartpence, *Fifty-First Indiana*, 108; George Blakemore to Lu, 15 January 1863, Blakemore Letters, Ray D. Smith Civil War Collection, Knox College.

CHAPTER TWELVE / WHIRLWIND IN THE ROUND FOREST

1. Warner, *Generals in Blue*, 225–26; William B. Hazen, *A Narrative of Military Service* (Boston: Ticknor, 1885), 71; *OR*, 20, pt. 1, 516–17, 529, 543–44, 558; Kerwood, *Fifty-Seventh Indiana*, 155–56; Kimberly, *Forty-First Ohio*, 40; Eddy, *Patriotism of Illinois*, 2:361.

2. Major Jo Thompson's unpublished report of the Battle of Murfreesboro, Palmer Collection of Bragg Papers; J. N. Thompson, "The Gallant Old Forty-Fourth Mississippi," *CV* 28, no. 10 (November 1920): 407; *OR*, 20, pt. 1, 529, 533, 537–38, 689–90; C. A. Sheafe, "Personal Recollections of the Battle of Stones River," undated article in *The Rutherford Courier*, Ruth White Cook Confederate Scrapbook, TSLA; John Smith, *A History of the Thirty-First Regiment of Indiana Volunteer Infantry in the War of the Rebellion* (Cincinnati: Western Methodist Book Concern, 1900), 48–49; John B. Guthrie to his aunt, 10 January 1863, Guthrie Papers, DU.

3. *OR*, 20, pt. 1, 537–38, 545, 558, 711–12, 715, 720, 725; Warner, *Generals in Gray*, 74; Evans, *Confederate Military History; Tennessee*, 3:68; John M. Palmer, *Personal Recollections of John M. Palmer: The Story of An Earnest Life* (Cincinnati: R. Clarke, 1901), 145; Guthrie to his aunt, 10 January 1863; Stevenson, *Stone's River*, 108.

4. *OR*, 20, pt. 1, 395, 401, 405, 421, 429, 560–61, 565, 570–72, 689–90, 707, 715, 717–18, 735, 756, 765; Hannaford, *Sixth Ohio*, 396–98; Simmons, *84th Ill.*, 29–31; Phisterer, *Regular Brigade*, 9–10; Will Carson to his parents, 7 January 1863; Gillaspie, *Michigan to Murfreesboro*, 43–44; Bickham, *Rosecrans' Campaign*, 267–68.

5. *OR*, 20, pt. 1, 467–68, 476, 481, 488–89, 565, 561, 569, 572, 707, 709, 712, 715; Stormont, *Fifty-Eighth Indiana*, 116–17; Warner, *Generals in Blue*, 214; Hannaford, *Sixth Ohio*, 598; Stevenson, *Stone's River*, 107.

6. Womack, *Diary*, 78; *OR*, 20, pt. 1, 552–56, 712, 717, 720.

7. *OR*, 20, pt. 1, 350, 366, 717.

8. Stormont, *Fifty-Eighth Indiana*, 116–17; *OR*, 20, pt. 1, 350, 366–67, 468–69, 481–83, 488–89, 545, 551, 553, 556; Catherine Merrill, *The Sol-*

dier of Indiana in the War for the Union, 2 vols. (Indianapolis: Merrill, 1866–69), 1:160; Stevenson, *Stone's River,* 110–11; Bickham, *Rosecrans' Campaign,* 270–72.

9. Bragg's report of Murfreesboro, Palmer Collection of Bragg Papers; *OR,* 20, pt. 1, 701, 783–84; Breckinridge to Bragg, 10:10 A. M., 31 December 1862, Palmer Collection of Bragg Papers; Buckner to Breckinridge, 20 May 1863, Breckinridge Papers, NYHS; Horn, *Army of Tennessee,* 202; Hardee's report of Murfreesboro, Hardee Papers; Grainger, *Four Years,* 13; Green, *Johnny Green,* 59.

10. *OR,* 20, pt. 1, 350, 366–67, 469, 493, 496, 545, 553–54, 556, 690, 793–95, 802, 838–39; Stormont, *Fifty-Eighth Indiana,* 116–18; Eby, *Illinois Boy,* 75; Kerwood, *Fifty-Seventh Indiana,* 163, 171; Kimberly, *Forty-First Ohio,* 41; Merrill, *Soldier of Indiana,* 1:160–62.

11. Breckinridge to Bragg, 5:00 P. M. (?), 31 December 1862, Palmer Collection of Bragg Papers; Buckner to Breckinridge, 20 May 1863, Breckinridge Papers, NYHS; William Preston to William Preston Johnston, 26 January 1863, Mrs. Mason Barret Collection of William Preston Johnston Papers, TU; *OR,* 20, pt. 1, 461, 477–78, 495, 545, 783–84, 805, 812–15, 819, 822, 836–37; Lindsley, *Military Annals of Tennessee,* 363, 391; Sheridan, *Memoirs* 1:234–35; John Lee Yaryan, "Stone River," *War Papers, Read before the Indiana Commandery, MOLLUS* (Indianapolis: By the Commandery, 1898), 169; Kerwood, *Fifty-Seventh Indiana,* 172; Wheeler, "Battle of Murfreesboro," Wheeler Papers.

CHAPTER THIRTEEN / WE LAID TO REST POOR BOYS GONE

1. Eby, *Illinois Boy,* 76; Henry Perry, *History of the Thirty-Eighth Indiana Volunteer Infantry, One of the Three Hundred Fighting Regiments of the Union Army in the War of the Rebellion, 1861–1865* (Palo Alto, Calif.: F. A. Stuart, 1906), 61–62; Will J. Carson to his parents, 7 January 1863, CWTI Coll.; Payne, *Thirty-Fourth Illinois,* 57; Womack, *Diary,* 78; Hannaford, "In the Ranks," 814–15; Cope, *Fifteenth Ohio,* 247.

2. Magee diary, 31 December 1862; *OR,* 20, pt. 1, 554; Erb, *Valley of Death,* 24–26; Perry, *Thirty-Eighth Indiana,* 62; Phisterer, *Regular Brigade,* 13.

3. Newlin, *Seventy-Third Illinois,* 143–44; Maxwell, *Autobiography,* 170–71; Marks, "Experiences at Stone River," 395–96; Bromfield Ridley, "Echoes from the Battles at Murfreesboro," *CV* 11, no. 2 (February 1903): 67; Hannaford, "In Hospital after Stone River," *Harper's Magazine* 28 (1863–64): 260; Charles Doolittle to Mollie Post, 6 February 1863, Post Papers; Ira S. Owen, *Greene County in the War, Being a History of the Seventy-Fourth Regiment, with Sketches of the Twelfth, Ninety-Fourth, One Hundred and Tenth, Forty-Fourth, and One Hundred and Fifty-Fourth Regiments, and the Tenth Ohio Battery, Embracing Anecdotes, Incidents and Narratives of the Camp, March and Battlefield, and the Author's Experience while in the Army* (Xenia, Ohio: Torchlight Job

Rooms, 1872), 34–35; William Preston to William Preston Johnston, 26 January 1863, Barret Collection of Johnston Papers; Dodge, *Seventy-Fifth Illinois*, 69.

4. Owen, *Greene County in the War*, 35; Isaac Longenecker to his father, 13 January 1863, CWTI Coll.; Wilbur F. Hinman, *The Story of the Sherman Brigade. The Camp, the March, the Bivouac, the Battle; and How the Boys Lived and Died during Four Years of Active Field Service* (Alliance, Ohio: By the Author, 1897), 357; Howe, *Civil War Times*, 117; James H. Wiswell to his father, 8 January 1863, Wiswell Papers, CWTI Coll.; James Nourse diary, 31 December 1862.

5. Wheeler to Bragg, 4:00, 30 December 1862, and 1:30 P. M., 1 January 1863, Wharton to Leonidas Polk, 6:00 P. M., 1 January 1863, Bragg's report of Murfreesboro, all in Palmer Collection of Bragg Papers; *OR*, 20, pt. 1, 958, 960; Fitch, *Echoes of the Civil War*, 91–94; Holmes, *Soldier of the Cumberland*, 134.

6. Scribner, *How Soldiers Were Made*, 81; Yaryan, "Stone River," 170; Crittenden, "Union Left at Stone's River," 643–44; Sheridan, *Memoirs* 1:236–37.

7. Wheeler, "Battle of Murfreesboro," Wheeler Papers; Urquhart, "Bragg's Advance and Retreat," 3:607; Buckner to Breckinridge, 20 May 1863, Breckinridge Papers, NYHS; *OR*, 20, pt. 1, 450, 471, 575–76, 598, 608, 691, 707; Bickham, *Rosecrans' Campaign*, 297–99.

8. Liddell, *Liddell's Record*, 113; Thompson, *Orphan Brigade*, 175–76; Urquhart, "Bragg's Advance and Retreat," 3:607; Charles T. De Velling, *History of the Seventeenth Regiment, First Brigade, Third Division, Fourteenth Corps, Army of the Cumberland, War of the Rebellion* (Zanesville, Ohio: E. R. Sullivan, 1889), 71; Perry, *Thirty-Eighth Indiana*, 63; Thruston, *Battle in the Rear*, 14; Beatty, *Citizen Soldier*, 206; Fitch, *Echoes of the Civil War*, 109; Nourse diary, 31 December 1862.

9. Beatty, *Citizen Soldier*, 206; *OR*, 20, pt. 1, 691; Cope, *Fifteenth Ohio*, 288–89.

CHAPTER FOURTEEN / THUNDER ON THE LEFT

1. Brent journal, 2 January 1863, Palmer Collection of Bragg Papers; *OR*, 20, pt. 1, 609, 759, 785–86, 958–61; Thompson, *Orphan Brigade*, 177; Green, *Johnny Green*, 67; Young, *Reminiscences*, 47; Pickett, "Reminiscences of Murfreesboro," 452; Buckner to Breckinridge, 20 May 1863, Breckinridge Papers, NYHS; Stevenson, *Stone's River*, 128–30.

2. Thompson, *Orphan Brigade*, 177; *OR*, 20, pt. 1, 561–62, 576, 587, 598–99, 609–11; Stevenson, *Stone's River*, 130–31; Canfield, *Twenty-First Ohio*, 74–75.

3. Nourse diary, 2 January 1863; *OR*, 20 pt. 1, 471, 476; Stormont, *Fifty-Eighth Indiana*, 123; Beatty, *Citizen Soldier*, 207; Hinman, *Sherman Brigade*, 354–55.

4. Thompson, *Orphan Brigade*, 178; Brent to Pegram, 1:00 P. M., 1 January 1863, Palmer Collection of Bragg Papers; H. B. Clay, "On the Right at Murfreesboro," *CV* 21, no. 12 (December 1913): 588–89; William Preston to William Preston Johnston, Barret Collection of Johnston Papers; *OR*, 20, pt. 1, 754–60, 798, 853.

5. Thompson, *Orphan Brigade*, 179–80, 200; *OR*, 20, pt. 1, 576–77, 587, 598–99, 610–11, 615, 853; Clay, "On the Right," 589; Post diary, 2 January 1863; Erb, *Valley of Death*, 28–29; Grainger, *Four Years*, 14; Pickett, "Reminiscences of Murfreesboro," 453–54.

6. Major Rice E. Graves, "Charges and Specifications of Charges Against Brigadier General Gideon J. Pillow," Breckinridge Papers, CHS; *OR*, 20, pt. 1, 577, 599, 601, 604, 806, 810, 815; William McMurray, *History of the Twentieth Tennessee Regiment Volunteer Infantry, C. S. A.* (Nashville: The Publication Committee, 1904), 238–39.

7. Grainger, *Four Years*, 15–16; *OR*, 20, pt. 1, 798–99, 827, 833; Thompson, *Orphan Brigade*, 180.

8. *OR*, 20, pt. 1, 593, 595; Grainger, *Four Years*, 16.

9. *OR*, 20, pt. 1, 573, 599, 601; Simmons, *84th Ill.*, 34–35; Heg, *Civil War Letters*, 167.

10. Thompson, *Orphan Brigade*, 181–82; *OR*, 20, pt. 1, 451, 455–56; Buckner to Breckinridge, 20 May 1863, Breckinridge Papers, NYHS; *History of the Services of the Third Battery Wisconsin Light Artillery in the Civil War of the United States, 1861–1865, Compiled from All Sources Possible, but Principally from Members Themselves* (Berlin, Wis.: Courant, 1902), 17; Eby, *Illinois Boy*, 80; Hinman, *Sherman Brigade*, 535; William Preston to William Preston Johnston, 26 January 1863, Barret Collection of Johnston Papers; Squire Helm Bush diary, 2 January 1863, Hardin County Historical Society; McMurray, *Twentieth Tennessee*, 239–40; Richmond *Examiner*, 11 January 1863, in Breckinridge Papers, NYHS.

11. Wilson Vance, "A Man and a Boy at Stones River," *B and G* 1 (1893): 357; *OR*, 20, pt. 1, 422, 427, 429, 434, 451, 518–19; Adams, *Diary*, 20; Joseph S. Johnston to his mother, 14 January 1863; Haynie, *Nineteenth Ohio*, 191; Gibson, *Seventy-Eighth Pennsylvania*, 62–63; Nourse diary, 2 January 1863; Grainger, *Four Years*, 15–16.

12. *OR*, 20, pt. 1, 588, 813, 817, 824, 834; Pickett, "Reminiscences of Murfreesboro," 454; William Preston to William Preston Johnston, 26 January 1863, Barret Collection of Johnston Papers; McMurray, *Twentieth Tennessee*, 240.

13. *OR*, 20, pt. 1, 422, 434–35, 548, 588, 759, 810; Thompson, *Orphan Brigade*, 200; Brent journal, 2 January 1863, Palmer Collection of Bragg Papers.

14. Thompson, *Orphan Brigade*, 183, 200; Young, *Reminiscences*, 51; *OR*, 20, pt. 1, 679, 826.

15. *OR*, 20, pt. 1, 825–26; Sykes, "Bragg's Campaigns," 472–74.

16. Beatty, *Citizen Soldier*, 207–8.

CHAPTER FIFTEEN / THIS ARMY SHOULD BE PROMPTLY
PUT IN RETREAT

1. Horn, *Army of Tennessee,* 209–10; Cheatham and Withers to Bragg,
12:15 A. M., 3 January 1863, Cheatham Papers, TSLA; Polk's endorsement
to Cheatham and Withers's letter to Bragg, 1:30 A. M., 3 January 1863,
Polk Papers; *OR,* 20, pt. 1, 683, 701.

2. Horn, *Army of Tennessee,* 210; Cheatham's draft report of the Battle
of Murfreesboro, Cheatham Papers; Hardee's report of Murfreesboro,
Hardee Papers, ADAH; Liddell to his wife, 12 January 1863, Liddell Papers; Bragg's report of Murfreesboro and Brent journal, 3 January 1863,
both in Palmer Collection of Bragg Papers.

3. B. F. Carter to his wife, 6 January 1863, Pope-Carter Family Papers,
DU; *OR,* 20, pt. 2, 449; Bush diary, 3 January 1863; Bragg's report of Murfreesboro and Brent journal, 4–9 January 1863, both in Palmer Collection
of Bragg Papers; Grainger, *Four Years,* 16–17; Green, *Johnny Green,* 69;
S. W. Steele to Leonidas Polk, 5 January 1863, Polk Papers; Mills Lane, ed.,
*Dear Mother: Don't Grieve About Me . . . Letters from Georgia Soldiers in
the Civil War* (Savannah: Beehive Press, 1977), 212.

4. Wheeler to Bragg, 4 January 1863, Palmer Collection of Bragg Papers;
Edwin Bearss, "Cavalry Operations in the Battle of Stones River (Concluded)," *THQ* 19 (1960): 140–42.

5. Beatty, *Citizen Soldier,* 210–12; Payne, *Thirty-Fourth Illinois,* 57;
Wagner reminiscences, CWTI Coll.; Hinman, *Sherman Brigade,* 357; John
Russell to his sister, 14 January 1863, CWTI Coll.; Adams, *Diary,* 21; Eli-
sha Peterson to his family, 10 January 1863, Peterson Papers, DU; T. F.
Dornblaser, *Sabre Strokes of the Pennsylvania Dragoons, in the War of
1861–1865. Interspersed with Personal Reminiscences* (Philadelphia:
Lutheran Publication Society, 1884), 107; Hannaford, "In the Hospital,"
262–63.

6. Abraham Lincoln, *The Collected Works of Abraham Lincoln,* ed. Roy
P. Basler, 8 vols. (New Brunswick, N. J.: Rutgers University Press, 1953),
6:424, Chicago *Tribune,* 6 January 1863; Bickham, *Rosecrans' Campaign,*
330; *OR,* 20, pt. 1, 186–88; Nevins, *War for the Union,* 3:388–95.

CHAPTER SIXTEEN / BRAGG'S ARMY? HE'S GOT NONE

1. William Preston to William Preston Johnston, 26 January 1863, Barret Collection of Johnston Papers; Urquhart, "Bragg's Advance and
Retreat," 608; Connelly, *Autumn of Glory,* 73–74.

2. Bragg to Davis, 17 January 1863, Dalton Collection of Jefferson Davis
Papers, DU; Connelly, *Autumn of Glory,* 74–75; Urquhart, "Bragg's Advance and Retreat," 608; *OR,* 20, pt. 1, 684; John K. Jackson to Bragg, 17
January 1863, Palmer Collection of Bragg Papers; Polk, *Polk,* 2:194–97;
Bragg to Polk, 11 January 1863, Hardee to Bragg and Breckinridge to Bragg,
12 January 1863, and Cleburne to Bragg, 15 January 1863, all in Breckinridge Papers, NYHS; Nathanial C. Hughes, Jr., *General William J. Hardee,*

Old Reliable (Baton Rouge: Louisiana State University Press, 1965).

3. Davis to Johnston, 22 January and 19 February 1863, and Johnston to Davis, 3 and 12 February and 2 March 1863, Johnston Papers, CWM; Polk, *Polk*, 2:194–97; Polk to Bragg and Bragg to Polk, 30 January 1863, Breckinridge Papers, NYHS; Connelly, *Autumn of Glory*, 84–87.

4. Preston to William Preston Johnston, 26 January 1863, Barret Collection of Johnston Papers; Polk, *Polk*, 2:372; Bragg's report of Murfreesboro and Bragg to Cooper, 9 April 1863, Palmer Collection of Bragg Papers; Howell and Elizabeth Purdue, *Pat Cleburne, Confederate General* (Tuscaloosa: Portals Press, 1978), 332; Liddell, *Liddell's Record*, 118–19.

5. Gideon Pillow to William Clare, 9 March, 1863, H. W. Walter to John P. McCown, 5 June 1863, and Bragg's Report of Murfreesboro, all in Palmer Collection of Bragg Papers; *OR*, 23, pt. 2, 653–54, 722; Knoxville *Register*, 2 May 1863, in Breckinridge Papers, NYHS.

6. Bragg's report of Murfreesboro, Palmer Collection of Bragg Papers; *OR*, 20, pt. 1, 758–61, 790–92; Bragg to Felix Robertson, 16 February 1863, Robertson to Breckinridge, 6 April 1863, Memorandum of Bragg, 26 May 1863, George Brent to Breckinridge, 2 and 4 April 1863, Memorandum of David Urquhart, 12 June 1863, Knoxville *Register*, 29 April 1863, and Richmond *Examiner*, 27 February 1863, all in Breckinridge Papers, NYHS; Davis, *Breckinridge*, 350–51.

7. Connelly, *Autumn of Glory*, 69, 201–3, 234–78; Thomas L. Connelly and Archer Jones, *The Politics of Command: Factions and Ideas in Confederate Strategy* (Baton Rouge: Louisiana State University Press, 1982), 67–72.

8. Urquhart, "Bragg's Advance and Retreat," 609.

BIBLIOGRAPHY

MANUSCRIPTS

Bender Family. Papers. U.S. Army Military History Institute, Carlisle Barracks, Pennsylvania.

Blakemore, George B. Letters. Ray D. Smith Civil War Collection, Henry M. Seymour Library, Knox College, Galesburg, Illinois.

Bragg, Braxton. Papers. William P. Palmer Collection. Western Reserve Historical Society, Cleveland, Ohio.

Breckinridge, John C. Papers. Chicago Historical Society.

———. Papers. Miscellaneous Microfilms, Reel 3. New-York Historical Society.

Breese, Sidney. Papers. Illinois State Historical Library, Springfield.

Bush, Squire Helm. Diary. Hardin County Historical Society, Elizabethtown, Kentucky.

Carson, Will. Letters. *Civil War Times Illustrated* Collection. U.S. Army Military History Institute, Carlisle Barracks, Pennsylvania.

Cheatham, Benjamin Franklin. Papers. Tennessee State Library and Archives, Nashville.

Cole, James M. Papers. Illinois State Historical Library, Springfield.

Cook, Ruth White. Confederate Scrapbook. Tennessee State Library and Archives, Nashville.

Davis, Jefferson. Papers. Dalton Collection. Manuscript Department, Duke University Library, Durham, North Carolina.

Elmore, Day. Letters. Chicago Historical Society.

Extracts of Special Orders Received by General Leonidas Polk's Command, 1862–1863 (Chapter II, Volume 53½). Record Group 109. War Department Collection of Confederate Records. National Archives.

Fox, David. Letters. Quincy and Adams County Historical Society, Quincy, Illinois.

Guthrie, John B. Papers. Manuscript Department, Duke University Library, Durham, North Carolina.

Hardee, William J. Papers. State of Alabama Department of Archives and History, Montgomery.

———. Papers. Chicago Historical Society.

Howlett, James C. Diaries. Illinois State Historical Library.

Johnson, Bushrod. Papers. Record Group 109. Entry 123. National Archives.

Johnston, Albert Sidney. Papers. Mrs. Mason Barret Collection. Howard-Tilton Memorial Library, Tulane University, New Orleans, Louisiana.

Johnston, Joseph E. Papers. Earl Gregg Swem Library, The College of William and Mary, Williamsburg, Virginia.

Johnston, Joseph S. Letters. Chicago Historical Society.

Johnston, William Preston. Papers. Mrs. Mason Barret Collection. Howard-Tilton Memorial Library, Tulane University, New Orleans, Louisiana.

Jordan, John Leland. Papers. Tennessee State Library and Archives, Nashville.

Letters Sent by General Leonidas Polk's Command (Chapter II, Volume 13). Record Group 109. National Archives.

Liddell, St. John R., and Family. Papers. Special Collections, Louisiana State University Libraries, Baton Rouge.

Longenecker, Isaac. Manuscript Reminiscences. *Civil War Times Illustrated* Collection. U.S. Army Military History Institute, Carlisle Barracks, Pennsylvania.

Magee, John. Diary. Manuscript Department, Duke University Library, Durham, North Carolina.

Maney, Lewis M. Papers. Manuscript Department, Duke University Library, Durham, North Carolina.

Marion, Frederick. Letters. Illinois State Historical Library, Springfield.

Mitchell, Robert. Letters. Chicago Historical Society.

Murray, Mongo. Letters. *Civil War Times Illustrated* Collection. U.S. Army Military History Institute, Carlisle Barracks, Pennsylvania.

Nourse, James. Diary. Manuscript Department, Duke University Library, Durham, North Carolina.

Palmer, John. Papers. Collection II. Illinois State Historical Library, Springfield.

Polk, Leonidas. Papers. Jessie Ball DuPont Library, The University of the South, Sewanee, Tennessee.

Pope-Carter Family. Papers. Manuscript Department, Duke University Library, Durham, North Carolina.

Post, P. Sidney. Papers. Henry M. Seymour Library, Knox College, Galesburg, Illinois.

Ross, Levi A. Papers. Illinois State Historical Library, Springfield.

Sackett, John H. and Edwin C. Papers. Illinois State Historical Library, Springfield.

Sherman, Francis T. Letters. Illinois State Historical Library, Springfield.

Smith, Dietrich C. Papers. Illinois State Historical Library, Springfield.
Timmons, John Wesley. Papers. Manuscript Department, Duke University Library, Durham, North Carolina.
Wagner, Levi. Manuscript Reminiscences. *Civil War Times Illustrated* Collection. U.S. Army Military History Institute, Carlisle Barracks, Pennsylvania.
Welshimer, Philip. Letters. Illinois State Historical Library, Springfield.
Wheeler, Joseph. Papers. Chicago Historical Society.
Wiswell, James H. Papers. Manuscript Department, Duke University Library, Durham, North Carolina.

NEWSPAPERS

Chattanooga *Daily Rebel.*
Chicago Tribune.
Cincinnati *Commercial.*
Knoxville *Register.*
Louisville *Journal.*
New York Times.

OFFICIAL DOCUMENTS

The War of the Rebellion: A Compilation of the Official Records of the Union and Confederate Armies. Washington, D.C.: U.S. Government Printing Office, 1880–1901.

AUTOBIOGRAPHIES, COLLECTED WORKS, DIARIES, LETTERS, MEMOIRS, AND PERSONAL NARRATIVES

Adams, Jacob. *Diary of Jacob Adams, Private in Company F, 21st O. V. I.* Columbus: F. J. Heer, 1930.
Beatty, John. *The Citizen Soldier; or, Memoirs of a Volunteer.* Cincinnati: Wilstach, Baldwin, 1879.
Berry, John M. "Reminiscences from Missouri." *Confederate Veteran* 8, no. 2 (February 1900): 73.
Bevens, W. E. *Reminiscences of a Private. Company "C" First Arkansas Regiment Infantry. May, 1861 to April, 1865.* N.p. [1912?].
Bickham, William. *Rosecrans' Campaign with the Fourteenth Army Corps, or the Army of the Cumberland: a Narrative of Personal Observations . . . with Official Reports of the Battle of Stone River.* Cincinnati: Moore, Wilstach, Keys, 1863.
Brown, A. H. "Reminiscences of a Private Soldier." *Confederate Veteran* 18, no. 10 (October 1910): 449.
Butler, Jay C. *Letters Home.* Binghamton, N.Y.: Privately printed, 1930.
Clay, H. B. "On the Right at Murfreesboro." *Confederate Veteran* 21, no. 12 (December 1913): 588–89.
Crippen, Edward W. "The Diary of Edward W. Crippen, Private 27th Illi-

nois Volunteers, War of the Rebellion, August 7, 1861 to September 19, 1863." *Publications of the Illinois State Historical Society* 14 (1909): 220–82.

Crittenden, Thomas L. "The Union Left at Stone's River." In *Battles and Leaders of the Civil War,* edited by Clarence Buell and Robert Johnson, vol. 3, 632–34. New York: Thomas Yoseloff, 1956.

Cummings, Kate. *A Journal of Hospital Life in the Confederate Army of Tennessee from the Battle of Shiloh to the End of the War.* Louisville: J. P. Morton, 1866.

Davis, Jefferson. *Jefferson Davis, Constitutionalist, His Letters, Papers, and Speeches.* Edited by Dunbar Rowland. Jackson: Printed for the Mississippi Department of Archives and History, 1923.

———. *The Rise and Fall of the Confederate Government.* 2 vols. New York: D. Appleton, 1881.

Dornblaser, T. F. *Sabre Strokes of the Pennsylvania Dragoons, in the War of 1861–1865. Interspersed with Personal Reminiscences.* Philadelphia: Lutheran Publication Society, 1884.

Eby, Henry. *Observations of an Illinois Boy in Battle, Camp and Prisons—1861–1865.* Mendota, Ill.: By the Author, 1910.

Erb, William. *The Valley of Death, the Battle of Stones River: Extract from the Battles of the Nineteenth Ohio.* Washington, D. C.: Judd and Detweiler, 1893.

Ferguson, Edward. "The Army of the Cumberland under Buell." *War Papers Read before the Commandery of the State of Wisconsin, Military Order of the Loyal Legion of the United States,* vol. 1, 424–32. Milwaukee: Burdick, Armitage and Allen, 1891.

Fisher, Horace Cecil. *The Personal Experiences of Colonel Horace Newton Fisher in the Civil War; a Staff Officer's Story.* Boston, N.p., 1960.

Fitch, Michael. *Echoes of the Civil War As I Hear Them.* New York: R. F. Fenno, 1905.

Freeman, Henry V. "Some Battle Recollections of Stone's River." In *Military Essays and Recollections; Papers Read before the Commandery of the State of Illinois, Military Order of the Loyal Legion of the United States,* vol. 3, 227–46. Chicago: The Dial Press, 1899.

Freemantle, Sir Arthur. *Three Months in the Southern States: April–June, 1863.* New York: J. Bradburn, 1864.

Gillaspie, Ira. *From Michigan to Murfreesboro: The Diary of Ira Gillaspie of the Eleventh Michigan Infantry.* Mount Pleasant: Central Michigan University Press, 1965.

Grainger, Gervis D. *Four Years with the Boys in Gray.* Dayton: Press of Morningside Bookshop, 1972.

Green, Johnny Williams. *Johnny Green of the Orphan Brigade: The Journal of a Confederate Soldier.* Edited by A. D. Kirwan. Lexington: University of Kentucky Press, 1956.

Griffin, Daniel. "A Hoosier Regiment at Stone's River," *The Filson Club History Quarterly* 37, no. 1 (January 1963): 24–28.

Hannaford, Ebenezer. "In Hospital after Stone River." *Harper's Magazine* 28 (1863–64): 260–65.

———. "In the Ranks at Stone River." *Harper's Magazine* 27 (1863): 809–15.

Hardee, William J. "Biographical Sketch of Major General Patrick R. Cleburne." *Southern Historical Society Papers* 31 (1903): 151–63.

Hazen, William B. *A Narrative of Military Service.* Boston: Ticknor, 1885.

Heg, Hans Christian. *The Civil War Letters of Colonel Hans Christian Heg.* Edited by Theodore C. Blegen. Northfield, Minn.: Norwegian-American Historical Association, 1936.

Heiner, A. H. "The Battle of Murfreesboro Again." *Confederate Veteran* 12, no. 3 (March 1904): 118.

Herr, George Washington. *Episodes of the Civil War, Nine Campaigns in Nine States; Fremont in Missouri—Curtis in Missouri and Arkansas—Halleck's Seige of Corinth—Buell in Kentucky—Rosecrans in Kentucky and Tennessee—Grant at the Battle of Chattanooga—Sherman from Chattanooga to Atlanta—Thomas in Tennessee and North Carolina—Stanley in Texas. In Which is Comprised the History of the Fifty-ninth Regiment Illinois Veteran Volunteer Infantry—Together with Special Mention of the Various Regiments with Which It Was Brigaded from 1861 to 1865.* San Francisco: Bancroft, 1890.

Hickman, F. G. "Events in the Battle of Murfreesboro." *Confederate Veteran* 3, no. 6 (June 1895): 162.

Holmes, Mead. *A Soldier of the Cumberland: Memoir of Mead Holmes Jr., Sergeant of Company K, 21st Regiment Wisconsin Volunteers.* Boston: American Tract Society, 1864.

Howe, Daniel W. *Civil War Times, 1861–1865.* Indianapolis: Bowen-Merrill, 1902.

Johnson, Richard W. *A Soldier's Reminiscences in Peace and War.* Philadelphia: J. R. Lippincott, 1886.

Johnston, Joseph. *Narrative of Military Operations, Directed during the Late War between the States.* New York: D. Appleton, 1874.

Keifer, J. Warren. *Slavery and Four Years of War, a Political History of Slavery in the United States, Together with a Narrative of the Campaigns and Battles of the Civil War in Which the Author Took Part, 1861–1865.* 2 vols. New York: G. P. Putnam, 1900.

Kendall, Henry M. "The Battle of Stone River." *Military Order of the Loyal Legion of the United States, D. C. Commandery, War Paper 49.* 4 November 1903.

Lane, Mills, ed. *Dear Mother: Don't Grieve About Me . . . Letters from Georgia Soldiers in the Civil War.* Savannah: Beehive Press, 1977.

Liddell, St. John Richardson. *Liddell's Record.* Edited by Nathaniel C. Hughes. Dayton, Ohio: Morningside, 1985.

Lincoln, Abraham. *The Collected Works of Abraham Lincoln.* Edited by Roy P. Basler. 8 vols. New Brunswick N. J.: Rutgers University Press, 1953.

McConnell, William. *Diary of William McConnell, Private Company I,*

15th O. V. V. I., lst Brigade, 3rd Div., 4th Army Corps, Army of the Cumberland, from September 16th, 1861 to August 2nd, 1865. Tiro, Ohio: Chas. McConnell, 1899.

McNeil, Samuel. *Personal Recollections of Service in the Army of the Cumberland and Sherman's Army, from August 17, 1861, to July 20, 1865, by S. A. McNeil, Company F., 31st Ohio.* N.p., n.d.

Manderson, Charles F. *The Twin Seven-Shooters.* New York: F. Tennyson Neely, 1902.

Marks, Solon. "Experiences at the Battle of Stones River." *War Papers Read before the Commandery of the State of Wisconsin, Military Order of the Loyal Legion of the United States,* vol. 2, 385–98. Milwaukee: Burdick, Armitage and Allen, 1896.

Maxwell, James Robert. *Autobiography of James Robert Maxwell of Tuscaloosa, Alabama.* New York: Greenberg, 1926.

Merrill, Catherine. *The Soldier of Indiana in the War for the Union.* 2 vols. Indianapolis: Merrill, 1866–69.

Military Historical Society of Massachusetts. *Papers of the Military Historical Society of Massachusetts.* Vol. 7, *Campaigns in Kentucky and Tennessee Including the Battle of Chickamauga, 1862–1864.* Boston: By the Society, 1908.

Palmer, John M. *Personal Recollections of John M. Palmer. The Story of an Earnest Life.* Cincinnati: R. Clarke, 1901.

Pickett, W. D. "Reminiscences of Murfreesboro." *Confederate Veteran* 16, no. 9 (September 1908): 449–54.

Powers, Elvira. *Hospital Pencillings: Being a Diary While in Jefferson General Hospital, Jeffersonville, Ind., and Others at Nashville, Tennessee, as Matron and Visitor.* Boston: E. L. Mitchell, 1866.

Richards, Henry. *Letters of Captain Henry Richards of the Ninety-third Ohio Infantry.* Cincinnati: Valley Press, 1893.

Ridley, Bromfield. "Echoes from the Battles at Murfreesboro." *Confederate Veteran* 11, no. 2 (February 1903): 65–68.

Roberts, Charles. "At Murfreesboro Just Before the Battle." *Confederate Veteran* 6, no. 12 (December 1908): 631–32.

Robuck, J. E. *My Own Personal Experience and Observation as a Soldier in the Confederate Army during the Civil War, 1861–1865; Also during the Period of Reconstruction.* Birmingham, Ala.: By the Author, 1911.

Scribner, Benjamin. *How Soldiers were Made; or, the War As I Saw It under Buell, Rosecrans, Thomas, Grant and Sherman.* Chicago: Donohue and Henneberry, 1887.

Shanks, William. *Personal Recollections of Distinguished Generals.* New York: Harper, 1866.

Sheridan, Philip Henry. *Personal Memoirs of P. H. Sheridan.* 2 vols. New York: Charles L. Webster, 1888.

Sorrel, Gilbert Moxley. *Recollections of a Confederate Staff Officer.* New York and Washington: Neale, 1905.

Stanley, David. *Personal Memoirs of Major-General David Sloane Stanley, U. S. A.* Cambridge: Harvard University Press, 1917.

Stewart, Robert. "The Battle of Stone River, As Seen by One Who Was There." *Blue and Gray* 5 (1895): 10–14.

Stout, L. H. *Reminiscences of General Braxton Bragg.* Hattiesburg, Miss.: The Book Farm, 1942.

Sykes, E. T. "A Cursory Sketch of General Bragg's Campaigns. Paper Number 2." *Southern Historical Society Papers* 11 (1883): 466–74.

Taylor, Richard. *Destruction and Reconstruction: Personal Experiences of the Late War.* New York: D. Appleton, 1879.

Thruston, Gates P. *Personal Recollections of the Battle in the Rear at Stone's River, Tennessee.* Nashville: n. d.

Urquhart, David. "Bragg's Advance and Retreat." In *Battles and Leaders of the Civil War,* edited by Clarence Buell and Robert Johnson, vol. 3, 600–609. New York: Thomas Yoseloff, 1956.

Vance, Wilson. "A Man and a Boy at Stones River." *Blue and Gray* 1 (1893): 347–60.

Walker, C. Irvine. "Visit to the Battlefield of Murfreesboro." *Confederate Veteran* 15, no. 6 (June 1907): 263.

Wheeler, Joseph. "Bragg's Invasion of Kentucky." In *Battles and Leaders of the Civil War,* edited by Clarence Buell and Robert Johnson, vol. 3, 1–25. New York: Thomas Yoseloff, 1956.

Williams, G. A. "Blow Your Horn, Jake." *Confederate Veteran* 5, no. 5 (May 1897): 226.

Wise, John S. *The End of an Era.* Boston and New York: Houghton, Mifflin, 1902.

Womack, J. J. *The Civil War Diary of Captain J. J. Womack, Company E, 16th Tennessee Volunteers.* McMinnville, Tenn.: Womack, 1961.

Woodward, James H. "General A. McD. McCook at Stone River." *A Paper Read before the California Commandery of the Military Order of the Loyal Legion of the United States at Los Angeles, Cal., Feb. 22, 1892.* Los Angeles: Times-Mirror, 1892.

Wright, Louise. *A Southern Girl in '61; the War-Time Memories of a Confederate Senator's Daughter.* New York: Doubleday, Page, 1905.

Yaryan, John Lee. "Stone River." *War Papers, Read before the Indiana Commandery, Military Order of the Loyal Legion of the United States,* vol. 1, 157–77. Indianapolis: By the Commandery, 1898.

Young, Lot D. *Reminiscences of a Soldier of the Orphan Brigade.* Louisville: Courier-Journal Job Printing Company, 1918.

Unit Histories

Aten, Henry J. *History of the Eighty-Fifth Regiment, Illinois Volunteer Infantry.* Hiawatha, Kans.: Comp. and Pub. under the Auspices of the Regimental Association, 1901.

Barnes, James A. *The Eighty-Sixth Regiment, Indiana Volunteer Infantry. A Narrative of Its Service in the Civil War of 1861–1865.* Crawfordsville, Ind.: The Journal Company, 1895.

Bennett, Charles. *Historical Sketches of the Ninth Michigan Infantry (General Thomas' Headquarters Guards) with an Account of the Battle of Murfreesboro, Tennessee, Sunday, July 13, 1862.* Coldwater, Mich.: Daily Courier, 1913.

Bennett, Lyman G., and William Haigh. *History of the Thirty-Sixth Regiment Illinois Volunteers, during the War of the Rebellion.* Aurora, Ill.: Knickerbocker and Hodder, 1876.

Briant, Charles. *History of the Sixth Regiment Indiana Volunteer Infantry. Of Both the Three Months' and Three Years' Services.* Indianapolis: W. B. Burford, 1891.

Canfield, Silas S. *History of the 21st Regiment Ohio Volunteer Infantry, in the War of the Rebellion.* Toledo: Vrooman, Anderson and Bateman, 1893.

Cist, Henry M. *The Army of the Cumberland.* New York: Scribner's, 1882.

Cope, Alexis. *The Fifteenth Ohio Volunteers and Its Campaigns, War of 1861–5.* Columbus: By the Author, 1916.

Crofts, Thomas. *History of the Service of the Third Ohio Veteran Volunteer Cavalry in the War of the Preservation of the Union from 1861–1865.* Toledo: Columbus, Stoneman Press, 1910.

Curry, William Leontes. *Four Years in the Saddle. History of the First Regiment, Ohio Volunteer Cavalry. War of the Rebellion, 1861–1865.* Columbus: Champlin, 1898.

Dacus, Robert. *Reminiscences of Company "H" First Arkansas Mounted Rifles.* Dayton: Press of Morningside Bookshop, 1972.

Day, Lewis W. *Story of the One Hundred and First Ohio Infantry. A Memorial Volume.* Cleveland: W. M. Bayne, 1894.

Demoret, Alfred. *A Brief History of the Ninety-Third Regiment, Ohio Volunteer Infantry. Recollections of a Private.* Ross, Ohio: Graphic Print, 1898.

De Velling, Charles T. *History of the Seventeenth Regiment, First Brigade, Third Division, Fourteenth Corps, Army of the Cumberland, War of the Rebellion.* Zanesville, Ohio: E. R. Sullivan, 1889.

Dobson, James. *Historical Sketch of Company K of the 79th Regiment Indiana Volunteers.* Plainfield, Ind.: Progress Print, 1894.

Dodge, William Sumner. *History of the Old Second Division, Army of the Cumberland.* Chicago: Church and Goodman, 1864.

———. *A Waif of the War; or, the History of the Seventy-Fifth Illinois Infantry.* Chicago: Church and Goodman, 1866.

Gammage, Washington Lafayette. *The Camp, the Bivouac, and the Battlefield; being a History of the Fourth Arkansas Regiment, from Its First Organization down to the Present Date: Its Campaigns and Its Battles, with an Occasional Reference to the Current Events of the Times, including Biographical Sketches of Its Field Officers and Others of the "Old Brigade." The Whole Interspersed Here and There with Descriptions of Scenery, Incidents of Camp Life, Etc.* Little Rock: Arkansas Southern Press, 1958.

Gibson, Joseph, *History of the Seventy-Eighth Pennsylvania Volunteer Infantry*. Pittsburgh: Pittsburgh Print. Co., 1905.

Giles, Leonidas B. *Terry's Texas Rangers*. Austin, Tex.: Von Boeckmann-Jones, 1911.

Green, Charles Ransley. *Volunteer Service in Army of Cumberland. Part First. History of the Volunteers from Clarksfield, Huron Co., Ohio, in the 101st O. V. I. . . . Part Second. List of the Volunteers from Wakeman, O., the Whole War. And their History Since . . . Part Third. Sergeant Benj. T. Strong's Biography, and History of the Chickamauga Campaign . . . Part Fourth. Descendants of Justus Minor, Who Moved from Conn. in 1821 to Wakeman, O*. Olathe, Kans.: By the Author, 1913–14.

Grose, William. *The Story of the Marches, Battles and Incidents of the 36th Regiment Indiana Volunteer Infantry*. New Castle, Ind.: The Courier Company Press, 1891.

Hannaford, Ebenezer. *The Story of a Regiment: a History of the Campaigns, and Associations in the Field, of the Sixth Regiment Ohio Volunteer Infantry*. Cincinnati: By the Author, 1868.

Harden, Henry O. *History of the 90th Ohio Volunteer Infantry in the War of the Great Rebellion in the United States, 1861 to 1865*. Stoutsville, Ohio: Press of Fairfield-Pickaway News, 1902.

Hartpence, William Ross. *History of the Fifty-First Indiana Veteran Volunteer Infantry. A Narrative of Its Organization, Marches, Battles and Other Experiences in Camp and Prison; from 1861 to 1866. With Revised Roster*. Harrison, Ohio: By the Author, 1894.

Haynie, James Henry. *The Nineteenth Illinois; a Memoir of a Regiment of Volunteer Infantry Famous in the Civil War of Fifty Years Ago for Its Drill, Bravery, and Distinguished Services*. Chicago: M. A. Donohue, 1912.

Hinman, Wilbur F. *The Story of the Sherman Brigade. The Camp, the March, the Bivouac, the Battle; and How the Boys Lived and Died during Four Years of Active Field Service*. Alliance, Ohio: By the Author, 1897.

History of Battery A, First Regiment Ohio Vol. Light Artillery. Milwaukee: Daily Wisconsin Printing House, 1865.

History of the Services of the Third Battery Wisconsin Light Artillery in the Civil War of the United States, 1861–1865, Compiled from All Sources Possible, but Principally from Members Themselves. Berlin, Wis.: Courant Press, 1902.

History of the Seventy-Ninth Regiment Indiana Volunteer Infantry in the Civil War of Eighteen Sixty-One in the United States. Indianapolis: Hollenbeck Press, 1899.

Horn, Stanley. *The Army of Tennessee*. Norman: University of Oklahoma Press, 1941.

Horrall, Spillard F. *History of the Forty-Second Indiana Volunteer Infantry*. Chicago: Donohue and Henneberry, 1892.

Hunter, Alfred. *History of the Eighty-Second Indiana Volunteer Infantry, Its Organization, Campaigns and Battles.* Indianapolis: W. B. Burford, 1893.

Kerwood, Asbury L. *Annals of the Fifty-Seventh Regiment Indiana Volunteers. Marches, Battles, and Incidents of Army Life, by a Member of the Regiment.* Dayton, Ohio: W. J. Shuey, 1868.

Kimberly, Robert L. *The Forty-First Ohio Veteran Volunteer Infantry in the War of the Rebellion. 1861–1865.* Cleveland: W. R. Smellie, 1897.

Lathrop, David. *The History of the Fifty-Ninth Regiment Illinois Volunteers, or a Three Years' Campaign through Missouri, Arkansas, Mississippi, Tennessee and Kentucky, with a Description of the Country, Towns, Skirmishes and Battles . . . Embellished with Twenty-four Lithographed Portraits of the Officers of the Regiment.* Indianapolis: Hall and Hutchinson, 1865.

Lavender, John W. *The War Memoirs of Captain John W. Lavender, C. S. A. They Never Came Back; the Story of Co. F. Fourth Arks. Infantry, C. S. A., Orginally Known as the Montgomery Hunters, as Told by Their Commanding Officer.* Edited by Ted. R. Worley. Pine Bluff, Ark.: W. M. Hackett and D. R. Perdue, 1956.

Lindsley, John. *The Military Annals of Tennessee. Confederate. First Series: Embracing a Review of Military Operations, with Regimental Histories and Memorial Rolls.* Nashville: J. M. Lindsley, 1886.

Little, George, and James Maxwell. *A History of Lumsden's Battery, C. S. A.* Tuscaloosa, Ala.: R. E. Rhodes Chapter, United Daughters of the Confederacy, n.d.

McMurray, William. *History of the Twentieth Tennessee Regiment Volunteer Infantry, C. S. A.* Nashville: The Publication Committee, 1904.

Mitchell, John. *In Memoriam: Twenty-Fourth Wisconsin Infantry.* Milwaukee, N.p.: 1906.

Morris, George W. *History of the Eighty-First Regiment of Indiana Volunteer Infantry in the Great War of the Rebellion, 1861–1865, Telling of Its Origin and Organization, a Description of the Material of Which It Was Composed, Its Rapid and Severe Marches, Hard Service and Fierce Conflicts on Many Bloody Fields. Pathetic Scenes, Amusing Incidents and Thrilling Episodes. A Regimental Roster. Prison Life, Adventures, Etc.* Louisville: Franklin, 1901.

Newlin, William H. *A History of the Seventy-Third Regiment of Illinois Infantry Volunteers, Its Services and Experiences in Camp, on the March, on the Picket and Skirmish Lines, and in Many Battles of the War, 1861–1865.* Springfield, Ill.: The Regimental Reunion Association, 1890.

Owens, Ira S. *Greene County in the War, Being a History of the Seventy-Fourth Regiment, with Sketches of the Twelfth, Ninety-Fourth, One Hundred and Tenth, Forty-Fourth, and One Hundred and Fifty-Fourth Regiments, and the Tenth Ohio Battery, Embracing Anecdotes, Incidents and Narratives of the Camp, March and Battlefield, and the Author's Experience while in the Army.* Xenia, Ohio: Torchlight Job Rooms, 1872.

Payne, Edwin W. *History of the Thirty-Fourth Regiment of Illinois Infantry, September 7, 1861–July 12, 1865.* Clinton, Iowa: Allen, 1902.

Perry, Henry. *History of the Thirty-Eighth Regiment Indiana Volunteer Infantry, One of the Three Hundred Fighting Regiments of the Union Army in the War of the Rebellion, 1861–1865.* Palo Alto, Calif.: F. A. Stuart, 1906.

Phisterer, Frederick. *The Regular Brigade of the Fourteenth Army Corps, the Army of the Cumberland, in the Battle of Stone River, or Murfreesboro, Tennessee.* N.p., n.d.

Puntenney, George. *History of the Thirty-Seventh Regiment of Indiana Infantry Volunteers, Its Organization, Campaigns, and Battles, Sept. '61–Oct. '64.* Rushville, Ind.: Jacksonian Book and Job Dept., 1896.

Record of the Ninety-Fourth Regiment Ohio Volunteer Infantry in the War of the Rebellion. Cincinnati: Valley Press, 189-.

Rerick, John. *The Forty-fourth Indiana Volunteer Infantry, History of Its Services in the War of the Rebellion and a Personal Record of Its Members.* Lagrange, Ind.: By the Author, 1880.

Simmons, Louis A. *The History of the 84th Reg't Ill. Vols.* Macomb, Ill.: Hampton Brothers, 1866.

Smith John, *A History of the Thirty-First Regiment of Indiana Volunteer Infantry in the War of the Rebellion.* Cincinnati: Western Methodist Book Concern, 1900.

Society of the Seventy-Fourth Illinois Volunteer Infantry. Reunion Proceedings and History of the Regiment. Rockford, Ill.: W. P. Lamb, 1903.

Stormont, Gilbert. *History of the Fifty-Eighth Regiment of Indiana Volunteer Infantry, Its Organization, Campaigns and Battles, from 1861 to 1865.* Princeton, Ind.: Press of Clarion, 1895.

Thompson, Edwin Porter. *History of the Orphan Brigade.* Louisville: L. N. Thompson, 1898.

Thompson, J. N. "The Gallant Old Forty-Fourth Mississippi." *Confederate Veteran* 28, no. 10 (November 1920): 406–7.

Vale, Joseph G. *Minty and the Cavalry. A History of Cavalry Campaigns in the Western Armies.* Harrisburg, Pa.: E. K. Meyers, 1886.

Van Horne, Thomas B. *History of the Army of the Cumberland; Its Organization, Campaigns, and Battles.* 2 vols. Cincinnati: R. Clarke, 1875.

Watkins, Samuel R. *"Co. Aytch," Maury Grays, First Tennessee Regiment; or, a Side Show of the Big Show.* Chattanooga: Times Printing Company, 1900.

Worsham, William. *Old Nineteenth Tennessee Regiment, C. S. A. June, 1861. April, 1865.* Knoxville, Tenn.: Press of Paragon Printing Company, 1902.

Wright, Thomas. *History of the Eighth Regiment Kentucky Vol. Inf., during Its Three Years Campaigns, Embracing Organizations, Marches,*

Skirmishes, and Battles of the Command, with Much of the History of the Old Reliable Third Brigade, Commanded by Hon. Stanley Matthews, and Containing Many Interesting and Amusing Incidents of Army Life. St. Joseph, Mo.: St. Joseph Steam and Printing Co., 1880.

SECONDARY SOURCES

Bearss, Edwin C. "Cavalry Operations in the Battle of Stones River. Part 1: Cavalry Operations during the Union Approach." *Tennessee Historical Quarterly* 19 (1960): 23–53.

———. "Cavalry Operations in the Battle of Stones River (Continued)." *Tennessee Historical Quarterly* 19 (1960): 110–48.

Cleaves, Freeman. *Rock of Chickamauga: The Life of General George Thomas.* Norman: University of Oklahoma Press, 1948.

Connelly, Thomas Lawrence. *Autumn of Glory: The Army of Tennessee, 1862–1865.* Baton Rouge: Louisiana State University Press, 1971.

Connelly, Thomas Lawrence, and Archer Jones. *The Politics of Command: Factions and Ideas in Confederate Strategy.* Baton Rouge: Louisiana State University Press, 1982.

Davis, William C. *Breckinridge: Statesman, Soldier, Symbol.* Baton Rouge: Louisiana State University Press, 1973.

Dubose, John. *General Joseph Wheeler and the Army of Tennessee.* New York: Neale, 1912.

Dyer, Frederick H. *A Compendium of the War of the Rebellion, Comp. and Arranged from Official Records of the Federal and Confederate Armies, Reports of the Adjutant Generals of the Several States, the Army Registers, and Other Reliable Documents and Sources.* Des Moines: Dyer Publishing Company, 1908. Reprint (3 vols.) New York: Thomas Yoseloff, 1959.

Eddy, Thomas M. *The Patriotism of Illinois. A Record of the Civil and Military History of the Campaigns in Which Illinois Soldiers Have Been Conspicuous, Sketches of Distinguished Officers, the Roll of the Illustrious Dead, Movements of the Sanitary and Christian Commissions.* 2 vols. Chicago: Clarke, 1865–66.

Evans, Clement, ed. *Confederate Military History: A Library of Confederate States History.* Vol. 3, *Tennessee.* Atlanta: Confederate Publishing Company, 1899.

Fertig, James. *The Secession and Reconstruction of Tennessee. A Dissertation Submitted to the Faculties of the Graduate Schools of Arts, Literature, and Science, in Candidacy for the Degree of Doctor of Philosophy.* Chicago: University of Chicago Press, 1898.

Fry, James. *Operations of the Army under Buell from June 10th to October 30th, 1862, and the "Buell Commission."* New York: D. Van Nostrand, 1884.

"General Patton Anderson." *Confederate Veteran* 9, no. 8 (August 1901): 340–41.

Hattaway, Herman, and Archer Jones. *How the North Won: A Military History of the Civil War.* Urbana: University of Illinois Press, 1983.

Henderson, C. C. *The Story of Murfreesboro*. Murfreesboro, Tenn., N.p.: 1929.

Hughes, Nathaniel C., Jr. *General William J. Hardee, Old Reliable*. Baton Rouge: Louisiana State University Press, 1965.

Johnson, Richard W. *Memoir of Maj.-Gen. George H. Thomas*. Philadelphia: J. B. Lippincott, 1881.

Lamers, William M. *The Edge of Glory: A Biography of General William S. Rosecrans, U.S.A.* New York: Harcourt, Brace and World, 1961.

McKinney, Francis. *Education in Violence: The Life of George H. Thomas and the History of the Army of the Cumberland*. Detroit: Wayne State University Press, 1961.

McWhiney, Grady. *Braxton Bragg and Confederate Defeat. Volume I. Field Command*. New York: Columbia University Press, 1969.

McWhiney, Grady, and Perry D. Jamieson. *Attack and Die: Civil War Military Tactics and the Southern Heritage*. University, Ala.: University of Alabama Press, 1982.

Nevins, Allan. *The War for the Union*. 4 vols. New York: Scribner's, 1959–71.

Paris, Louis Philippe Albert d'Orleans. *History of the Civil War in America*. 4 vols. Philadelphia: Porter and Coates, 1875–88.

Parks, Joseph H. *General Edmund Kirby Smith, C. S. A.* Baton Rouge: Louisiana State University Press, 1954.

———. *General Leonidas Polk, C. S. A.: The Fighting Bishop*. Baton Rouge: Louisiana State University Press, 1962.

Polk, William. *Leonidas Polk, Bishop and General*. 2 vols. New York: Longmans, Green, 1893.

Purdue, Howell and Elizabeth. *Pat Cleburne: Confederate General*. Tuscaloosa: Portals Press, 1978.

Reid, Whitelaw. *Ohio in the War: Her Statesmen, Her Generals, and Soldiers*. 2 vols. Cincinnati: Moore, Wilstach and Baldwin, 1868.

Seitz, Don C. *Braxton Bragg, General of the Confederacy*. Columbia, S.C.: The State Company, 1924.

Stevenson, Alexander. *The Battle of Stone's River near Murfreesboro', Tenn., December 30, 1862, to January 3, 1863*. Boston: J. R. Osgood, 1884.

Van Horne, Thomas. *History of the Army of the Cumberland, Its Organization, Campaigns, and Battles*. 2 vols. Cincinnati: Robert Clarke, 1875.

———. *The Life of General George H. Thomas*. New York: Charles Scribner's Sons, 1882.

Warner, Ezra. *Generals in Blue: Lives of the Union Commanders*. Baton Rouge: Louisiana State University Press, 1964.

———. *Generals in Gray: Lives of the Confederate Commanders*. Baton Rouge: Louisiana State University Press, 1959.

Wilson, James. *Biographical Sketches of Illinois Officers Engaged in the War against the Rebellion of 1861*. Chicago: James Barnet, 1862.

Subject Index

Fighting units of both Confederate and Union armies have been indexed in the following manner: Entire armies are indexed under their full name at the time of the events related. Corps, wings, and divisions have been indexed as entries following the main entry for each army, but only when some action was taken by the entire unit. Where brigades are identified in the text, they have been indexed as subentries of their divisions. Individual regiments (listed in the appendix) are indexed alphabetically and identified parenthetically as to army by the abbreviations AC for Army of the Cumberland and AT for Army of Tennessee.

INDEX OF PERSONAL NAMES

A NOTE ON THE AUTHOR

Peter Cozzens is a foreign service officer with the U.S. Department of State. He graduated summa cum laude from Knox College with a degree in international relations. He also attended the Chinese University of Hong Kong and is a member of Phi Beta Kappa. Cozzens served as a military intelligence officer with the rank of captain before joining the Foreign Service. He has contributed articles to the *Illinois Historical Journal* and has written historical introductions to modern editions of Thomas Van Horne's *History of the Army of the Cumberland* and Henry Cist's *Army of the Cumberland*.